Street by Street

BRIGH'
WORTHING
HOVE, LEWES, NEWHAVEN

Ferring, Lancing, Peacehaven, Portslade-by-Sea, Rottingdean, Seaford, Shoreham-by-Sea, Sompting, Southwick, Steyning, Upper Beeding, Woodingdean

2nd edition November 2002

© Automobile Association Developments Limited 2002

Ordnance Survey® This product includes map data licensed from Ordnance Survey® with the permission of the Controller of Her Majesty's Stationery Office. © Crown copyright 2002. All rights reserved. Licence No: 399221.

Published by AA Publishing (a trading name of Automobile Association Developments Limited, whose registered office is Millstream, Maidenhead Road, Windsor, Berkshire SL4 5GD. Registered number 1878835).

The Post Office is a registered trademark of Post Office Ltd. in the UK and other countries.

Schools address data provided by Education Direct.

One-way street data provided by:

Tele Atlas   © Tele Atlas N.V.

Mapping produced by the Cartographic Department of The Automobile Association. A01569

A CIP Catalogue record for this book is available from the British Library.

Printed by GRAFIASA S.A., Porto, Portugal

Ref: ML018z

Key to map pages	ii-iii
Key to map symbols	iv-1
Enlarged scale pages	2-5
Street by Street	6-73
Index – towns & villages	74
Index – streets	75-89
Index – featured places	89-91

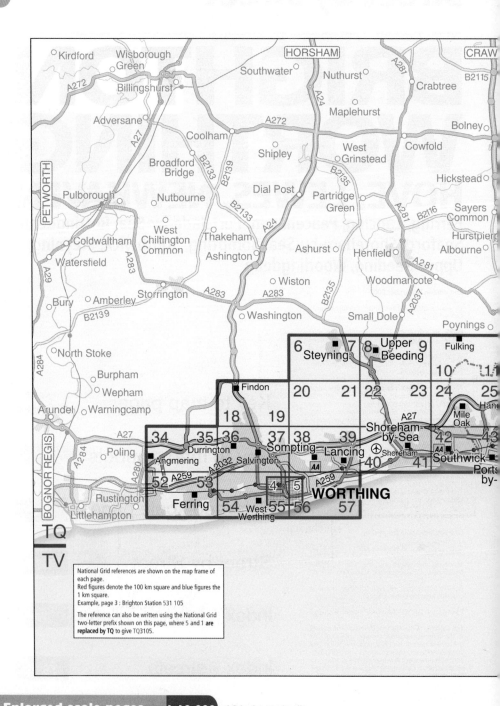

National Grid references are shown on the map frame of each page.
Red figures denote the 100 km square and blue figures the 1 km square.
Example, page 3 : Brighton Station 531 105

The reference can also be written using the National Grid two-letter prefix shown on this page, where 5 and 1 **are replaced by TQ** to give TQ3105.

Enlarged scale pages   **1:10,000**   6.3 inches to 1 mile

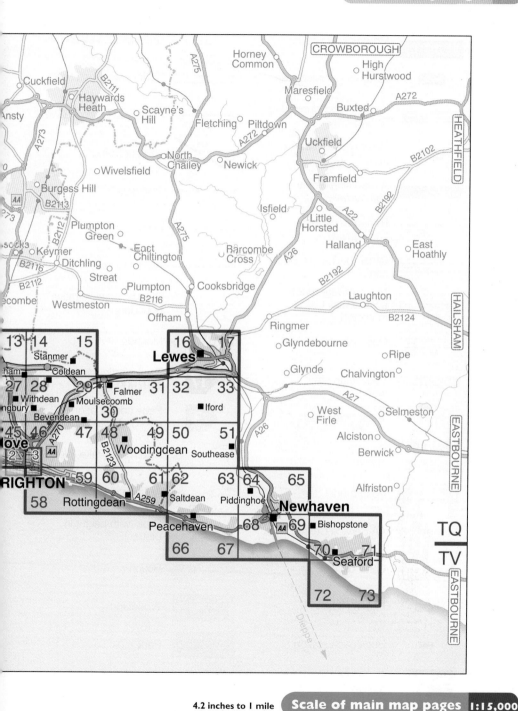

CROWBOROUGH

Cuckfield · Horney Common · High Hurstwood · Maresfield · Buxted · A272 · HEATHFIELD

Haywards Heath · Scayne's Hill · Fletching · Piltdown · Uckfield · B2102

Ansty · A273 · North Chailey · Newick · Framfield

Wivelsfield · Isfield · Little Horsted · A22 · B2192 · HAILSHAM

Burgess Hill · B2113 · Halland · East Hoathly

Plumpton Green · East Chiltington · Barcombe Cross · A26 · B2192 · Laughton · B2124

Keymer · Ditchling · Streat · Plumpton · B2116 · Cooksbridge · Offham · Ringmer · Glyndebourne · Ripe

Westmeston · Lewes · Glynde · Chalvington · Selmeston

13 14 15 · Stanmer · Goldean · **16 17** · **Lewes** · West Firle · Alciston · Berwick · EASTBOURNE

27 28 29 · Falmer · **31 32 33** · Iford · A27

30 · Moulsecoomb · Bevendean

45 46 47 48 49 50 51 · Woodingdean · Southease · Alfriston

2 3 · **58 59 60 61 62 63 64 65** · Rottingdean · Saltdean · Piddinghoe · **Newhaven** · Bishopstone

BRIGHTON · Peacehaven · **68 69** · **66 67** · **70 71** · Seaford · **72 73**

A259 · A2123 · A270 · A275 · A2111 · A2112 · A2113 · A2116

TQ / TV

EASTBOURNE

4.2 inches to 1 mile

Scale of main map pages 1:15,000

0 · 1/4 · miles · 1/2 · 3/4 · 1
0 · 1/4 · 1/2 · kilometres 3/4 · 1 · 1 1/4 · 1 1/2

iv

Junction 9	Motorway & junction	⊖	Underground station
Services	Motorway service area	⊖	Light railway & station
	Primary road single/dual carriageway	++++++++	Preserved private railway
Services	Primary road service area	_LC_	Level crossing
	A road single/dual carriageway	●—●—●—●	Tramway
	B road single/dual carriageway	- - - - - - -	Ferry route
	Other road single/dual carriageway	....	Airport runway
	Minor/private road, access may be restricted	- · - · - · -	County, administrative boundary
← ←	One-way street	▾▾▾▾▾▾▾▾	Mounds
	Pedestrian area	**17**	Page continuation 1:15,000
- - - - - - -	Track or footpath	**3**	Page continuation to enlarged scale 1:10,000
▮▮▮▮▮▮▮	Road under construction		River/canal, lake, pier
⌐ - - - ⌐	Road tunnel		Aqueduct, lock, weir
AA	AA Service Centre	465 ▲ Winter Hill	Peak (with height in metres)
P	Parking		Beach
P+🚌	Park & Ride		Woodland
🚌	Bus/coach station		Park
	Railway & main railway station	✝	Cemetery
	Railway & minor railway station		Built-up area

Featured building		Abbey, cathedral or priory
City wall		Castle
A&E	Hospital with 24-hour A&E department		Historic house or building
PO	Post Office	Wakehurst Place NT	National Trust property
	Public library	M	Museum or art gallery
i	Tourist Information Centre		Roman antiquity
	Petrol station Major suppliers only		Ancient site, battlefield or monument
†	Church/chapel		Industrial interest
	Public toilets		Garden
	Toilet with disabled facilities		Arboretum
PH	Public house AA recommended		Farm or animal centre
	Restaurant AA inspected		Zoological or wildlife collection
	Theatre or performing arts centre		Bird collection
	Cinema		Nature reserve
	Golf course	V	Visitor or heritage centre
▲	Camping AA inspected		Country park
	Caravan Site AA inspected		Cave
	Camping & caravan site AA inspected		Windmill
	Theme park		Distillery, brewery or vineyard

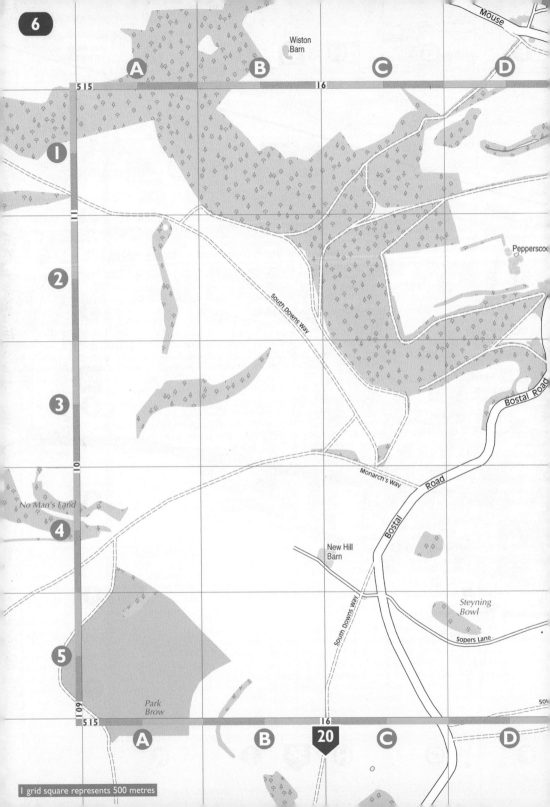

6

A   B   C   D

Mouse

Wiston
Barn

515   16

1

2

Peppersco

South Downs Way

3

Bostal Road

Monarch's Way

No Man's Land

Road

4

Bostal

New Hill
Barn

Steyning
Bowl

5

South Downs Way

Sopers Lane

Park
Brow

So

509

515   16

A   B   **20**   C   D

1 grid square represents 500 metres

Steyning Sports Centre

Steyning Grammar School

Coxham Lane

E

Penns Ct

Sir George's

Mill Road

Breach Close

Tanyard Lane

Steyning Health Centre

Charlton Street

High Street

Steyning Athletic Club

F

Shooting Field

Steyning Town

Church Lane

Museum

Elm Lane

PO

Church Street

Grammar School

School Lane

Sheep Pen La

Dog Lane

Wykeham School

Bank passage

Jarvis

Pied Piper

Bowmans Cl

Canons Way

Abbey Rd

Church Rd

BY-PASS

Market Fd

Station Rd

St Ter

Vicarage La

Kng Alf Cl

G

Kings Barn Farm

Saltwor

H

19

Rosemary Close

King's Barn Vis

Rosemary Av

De Braose Way

Road

Roman

Castle Lane

Castle La

Holland Rd

Clivedale Gdns

STEYNING

Peas La

Chandlers Way

Ingram

Goastalls La

Perrots La

Penfold Way

Bramber Rd

College Hill

The Crescent

Goring

Andrew Cl

Bramber Way

Saxon Road

King's Stone Avenue

Castle Way

Bramber Castle

Bramber

I

chrch

Priory Saltwor

Cruttens Wood

2

Hills

Lainies Road

Portway

Penlands Rise

The Furlongs

Penlands Way

Penlands Cl

Crossacres

Little Brove

Clays

Hill

The Hotel

Street

PO

Coombe Rd

Penlands

Combe Drive

Maudlyn Close

Maudlyn Park

Monarchs Way

UPPER BEED

A283

STEYNING BY-P

3

Bostal Road

The Ridings

Maudlyn Park

Maudlin

Sopers Lane

Maudlyn Parkway

Kingsmead Close

Annington Road

8

010

4

Upper Maudlin Farm

Annington

Downs

Link

Annington Farm

Sopers Lane

South Downs Way

Botolphs

5

Annington Road

E

F

21

G

H

18

19

609

Annington Mill Barn

HENFIELD

Tottington Manor Farm

Manor Farm

Edburt

E

F

G

H

I

2

213
Truleigh Hill

South Downs Way

Tottington Barn

Freshcombe Farm

3

10

4

The Warren

Bushy Bottom

5

Monarchs Way

22

23

E

F

23

G

H

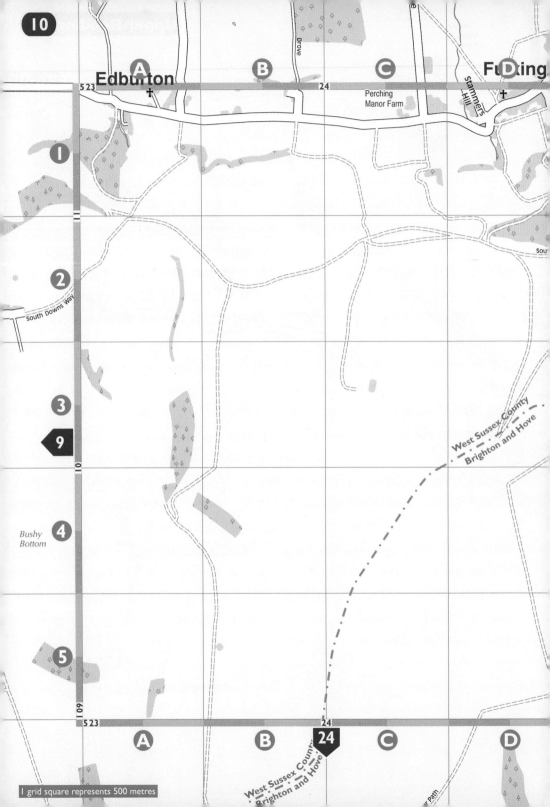

10

Edburton
A · B · C · Fu**D**ing

5 23 · 24

Drove

Perching
Manor Farm

Stammers
Hill

I

Sou

2

South Downs Way

3

9

West Sussex County
Brighton and Hove

4

Bushy
Bottom

1 10

5

1 09

5 23 · 24

A · B · 24 · C · D

West Sussex County
Brighton and Hove

Path

Wickhurst
Barns

E   F   G   H

26   27

S

I

Devil's
Dyke

Devil's Dyke Road

South Downs Way

2

Dyke Golf Club

Golf Course

3

Devil's

Dyke

12

Devil's
Dyke Farm

Road

Border Path

4

5

Skeleton
Hovel

Brighton &
Hove Golf Club

E   F   25   G   H

26   27

Monarchs Way

12

A B C

West Sussex County
Brighton and Hove

5 27 28

Saddlescombe

I

2

Sussex Border Path

3

II

011

4

Brighton and Hove
West Sussex County

Sussex Border Path

Golf Course

5

Skeleton
Hovel

Brighton &
Hove Golf Club

601

5 27 28

A B 26 C D

Waterhall
Golf Club

Devil's Dyke Road

Brighton
RFC

1 grid square represents 500 metres

Pangdean Farm

E   F   G   H

30   31

West Sussex County
Brighton and Hove

I

South
Hill Farm

Sussex Border Path

2

3

14

Sussex Border Path

4

A23

LONDON ROAD

Braypool Lane

A27

Avenue

Braeside

Kenmure Av
Bengairn Av
Thornhill Av
Plainfields Av

5

Paranscraig Av

Heston Av 601

Sanvhils Av

Solway Av

Craignair Avenue

Barrhill Av

Mackie Av 3 Lue

Waterhall

London Road

Court
Close

Vale

Church Hill

The Village Barn

Ashley Cl

Highview Av North

Avenue

Dharma
School

Ladies' Mile Road

Singleton
Road

Hayw
R

Waterhall Road

Hill Road

E   F   27   G   H

30   LONDON ROAD

PATCHAM B

PO

Highvw Rd
Highview
Way

Wrmd Av

Mile
Ladies

Cl

Warndene

Sunnyvale
Close

Sunnyvale Ave

Carden

Brangwyn

Patcham

Bn Cl

Ove

Ladies' Mile Road

Winfie

Cr C

Patcham
Junior
School

Stoneleigh
Close

Stoneleigh Av

14

Lower
Standean
B
C
D

531 32

1

New
Barn

2

3

13

4

Ditchling Road

Ditchling Road

Coldean Lane

A2

Mackie Avenue

Avenue
Bengairn Av
Kenmure Av
Glenfalls Av
Thornhill Av
Baranscraig Av
Heston Av601531
East Wick Cl
Lomond
Eskbank
Plainfields Av
The Deeside

BN1

Carden Avenue
Crowhurst Road

Hollingbury
Industrial
Estate

Superstore

Hollingbury
Industrial
Estate

Saunders Hill

Beatty Av
Kenwa

Solway Av
Sanyhils Av
Braeside
Craignair
Ladies
Mile Cl

Mackie Aven531

Clovers
End
Old Boat
CWk
Buttercup

A

Dharma
School

Ladies' Mile

Singleton
Road
Portfield Av
Sunnyd
Haywards
Close
Morecambe Rd
Midhurst Rd
Tangmere
Rd
Windmill
Vw

Petworth Road

B

32

28

C

Orchid Vw
Bramble
Wy
Elsted
wood

D

Crawley
Road

Beatty Av
Hawkhurst
Waldron
T Chtll

PO

Road

Stoneleigh
Close
Stoneleigh

Cuckmere
Way
Cs Field
Elsted
Cres

Avenue

1 grid square represents 500 metres

E High F Farm
F
G
H
34
35

I

St Mary's Farm
2

East Sussex County
Brighton and Hove
3

Stanmer Down

Stanmer Park
Ridge Rd
Ridge Road
Sussex County
nton & Hove

Stanmer

4

Ridge

Road
University of Sussex

PO

Gardner Arts Centre Cinema
Falmer House Road
5
Park Street
Mill Stre

Great Wood

chool
34
35
29
E
F
G
H
M

rnean Lane
Kingston Clo
Chalvin gton
Selsey Cl
Badger Way

University of Sussex Sports Centre
University of Sussex

Falmer Station

Framfield Close
LEWES ROAD
Falmer Station

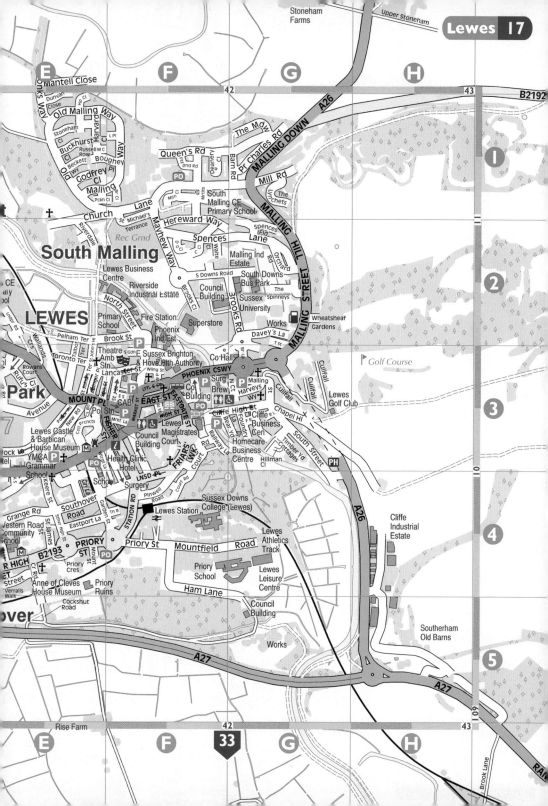

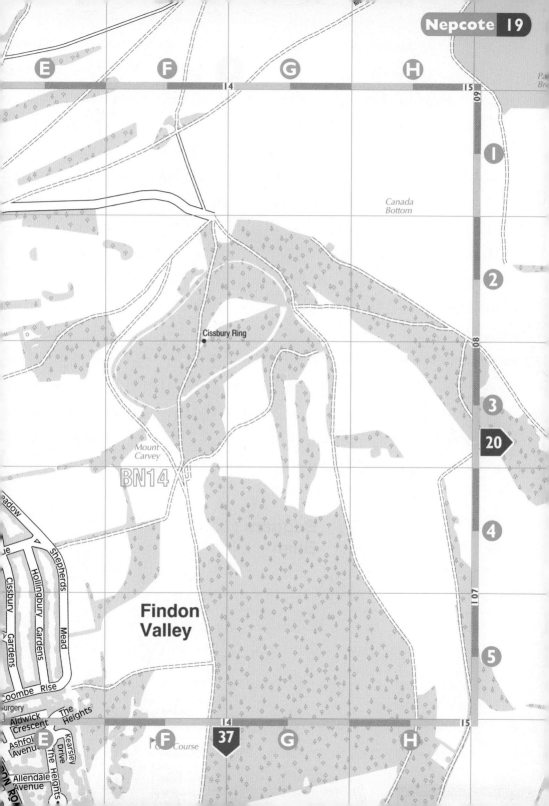

E F G H

14 15

09

I

Canada
Bottom

2

08

Cissbury Ring

3

20

4

Mount
Carvey

BN14

07

**Findon
Valley**

5

Cissbury Gardens

Hollingbury Gardens

Shepherds Mead

Coombe Rise

Surgery

The Heights

Aidwick Crescent

Ashfol
Avenue

E

Kearsley Drive

The Heights

Allendale
Avenue

14 15

F 37 G H

Course

Sopers Lane

A ark Brow   B   6   C   D   Sout

515   16

60

1

ada
om

2

08

3

Lychpole Farm

19

4

107

Beggars Bush

Titch Hill

St
D

5

515   16   Titch Hill Farm

A   B   38   C   D

Dankton

Lambleys
Barn

1 grid square represents 500 metres

E F **7** G H

I

18 19 60

Annington
Hill Barn

I

Coombes

2

†

3

22

Valley
Barn

4

107

5

18 19

E F **39** G H

Honey

Annington

Coombes Road

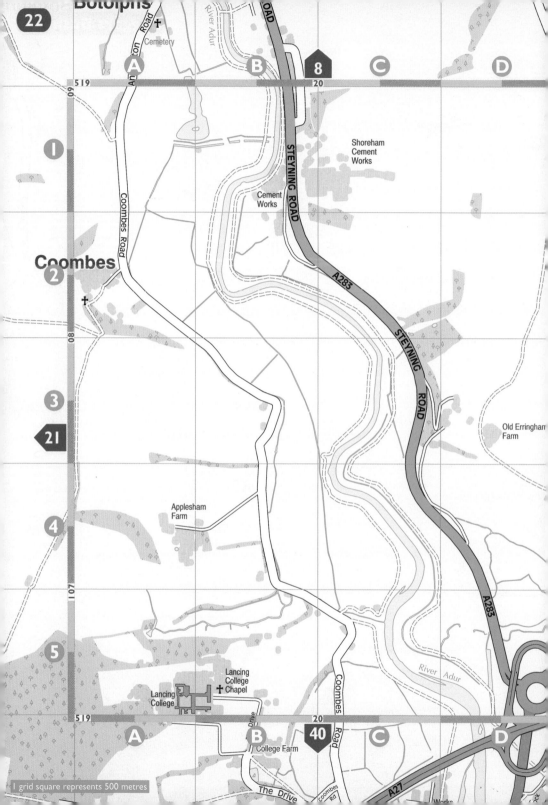

22

A **B** **8** **C** **D**

Botolphs

Cemetery

Anyton Road

River Adur

519

60

OAD

STEYNING ROAD

I

Shoreham Cement Works

Cement Works

Coombes

Coombes Road

2

✝

80

A283

3

21

STEYNING ROAD

Old Erringham Farm

107

4

Applesham Farm

5

A283

River Adur

Lancing College Chapel

519

Lancing College

✝ Chapel

20

Drive

Coombes Road

A **B** **40** **C** **D**

College Farm

The Drive

Coombes Rd

A27

Works

Monarchs Way

E   F   **9**   G   H

22   23

09

I

New Erringham
Farm

2

08

BN43

3

24

4

107

Mill Hill

Buckingham
Barn

Slonk Hill
Farm

5

Chanctonbury Drive   Saxons   Slonk   Hill   Road

Old
Shoreham

E   F   **41**   G Downside   H

22   23

Ravensbourne Av

Greenways
Crescent

Rosemary Drive

Shoreham

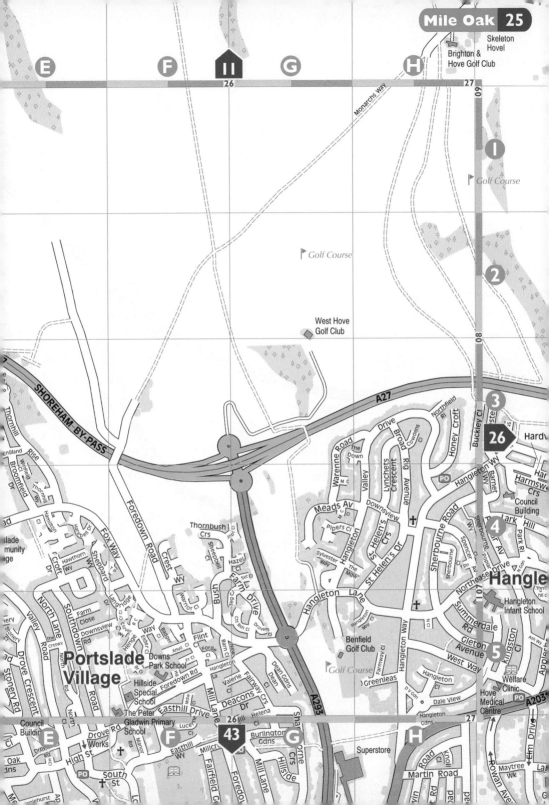

Skeleton Hovel

Brighton & Hove Golf Club

E F II 26 G 27 H 60

Monarchs Way

I

Golf Course

2

08

Golf Course

West Hove Golf Club

A27

Northfield Rd

3

Buckley Cl

26

Hard

Honey Croft

PO

Hangleton Wy

Barnet

Harmsw

Crs

Council Building

Warenne Road

The Down

Broad Rig Avenue

Cowders Cl

Drive

Valley

Lynchets Crescent

Sherbourne Road

Lark Hill

Park Rd

4

Meads Av

Downsview Cl

Pipers Cl

St. Helen's Crs

Sherbourne

Spencer Av

Poplar

Northease Drive

HANGLE

Thornbush Crs

Steepbell Cl

Hazel Cl

Sylvester Way

The Mdw

Hangleton

St. Helen's Dr

Hangleton Lane

Hangleton Way

Hangleton Infant School

SHOREHAM BY-PASS

Thornhill

England Rise

Winfield

Broomfield

Thornhill Way

Hamilton

Hawthorn Wy

Sheppard

FOX WAY

Foredown Road

Crest Wy

Bush Farm Drive

Warnol Cl

Drovers

Summerdale Rd

5

Gleton Avenue

Kingston

Appledo

Benfield Golf Club

West Way

Hangleton Wy

Hove Medical Centre

PO

A203

Portslade Community Village

North Lane

Southdown

Farm Close

Downsview Rd

Henge Way

Elder Cl

Anvil Cl

Flint Cl

Forge

Barn Cl

Downs Park School

Hillside Special School

Foredown Rd

Valerie Cl

Fairway Crs

Dean Gdns

Dean Cl

Farmway Cl

Greenleas

Dale View

Hangleton Gdns

Valley Road

Drove Crescent

Stonery Rd

The Peter Gladwin Primary School

Easthill Drive

Mill Lane

Deacons Dr

Helena Cl

Lucern

Fairfield

Burlington Gdns

Shaftesbury Crs

Hillside

Superstore

Martin Road

Council Buildin

E

Drove Rd

High St

PO

South St

F

Easthill Wy

Millcroft

26 43 G 27 H

Foredown

Mill Lane

Rowan Av

Elm Drive

Maytree Wk

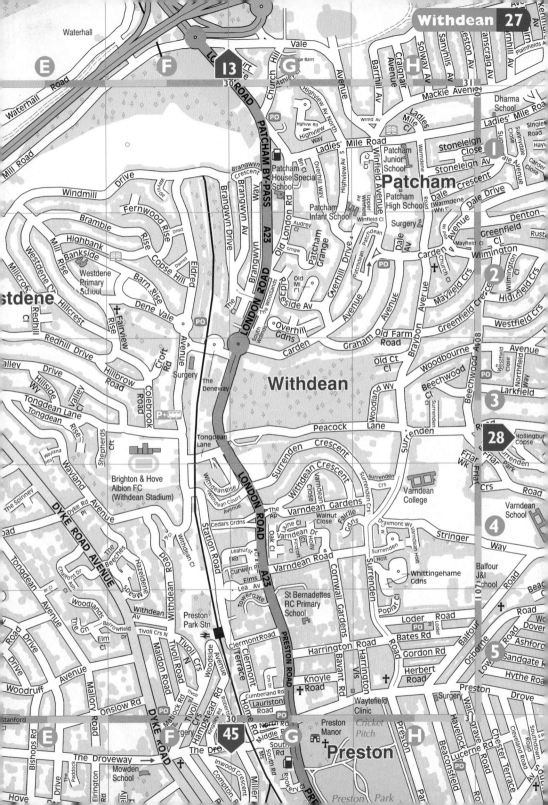

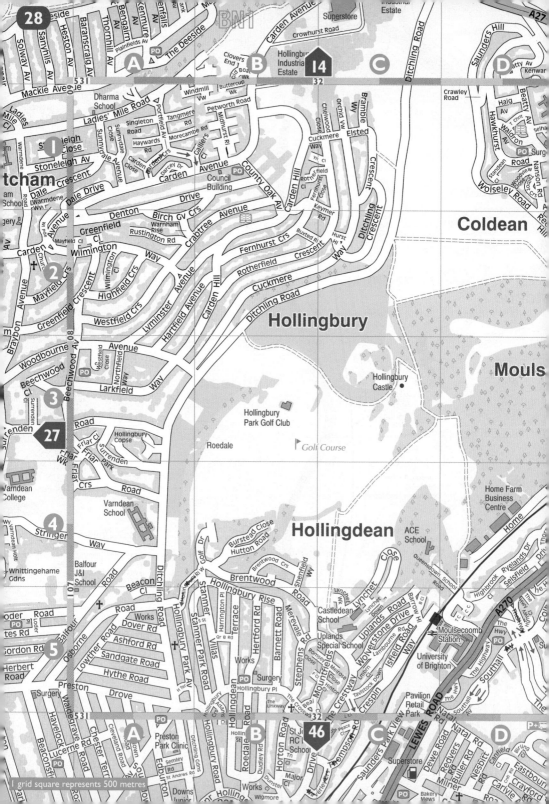

Great Wood

Gardner Arts Centre Cinema

E   F   15   G   H

University of Sussex Sports Centre

University of Sussex

LEWES ROAD

Falmer Station

University of Brighton

University of Brighton

Egginton Close

Lucraft Road

Egginton Road

Ashurst Road

Barcombe Rd

Ringmer Rd

Challey Road

Halland Road

Bolney Rd

Stonecross Rd

Shortgate Rd

Sullington Cl

Appledore Rd

Ersron

Fairway Trading Estate

Superstore

Westergate Rd

Ee Rd

Moulsecoomb

Council Building

Moulsecoomb Primary School

Moulsecoomb Health Clinic

East Moulsecoomb

Goodwood Wy

Birdham Rd

Wheatfield Wy

Selba Dr

Stapefield Drive

Hodshrove Road

Beech Gv

Hillside

Moulsecoomb

Nyetimber Hill

Medmerry Hill

Bevendean Crs

Bevendean Widdicombe Way

Hillside

Bevendean

Kenilworth Close

Norwich

Hogs Edge

Norwich Drive

Bamford Close

Heath Hill Avenue

Bodiam Avenue

Bodiam Close

Knepp Cl

Bevendean

Leybourne Road

Durham Cl

Ludlow Rd

Walmer Crs

Upr Bevendean Av

Lower Bevendean Av

Manton Rd

Surgery

Plymouth Av

Fitch Drive

Dartmouth Close

Taunton

Hornby Rd

Auckland Drive

E   F   47   G   H

Upper Bevendean

Great Wood

School

Framfield Close

Arl Crs

Rushlake Rd

Middleton

Coldean Lane

Park Road

Park Close

LEWES ROAD

A27

A270

Barcombe Rd

Newick Rd

PO

PO

Kingsta Cl

Chalvington Cl

Badger Way

Sevec Cl

The Byway

Forest Road

Rushlake

Woburn Pl

Ringmer Cl

Village Way

Station App

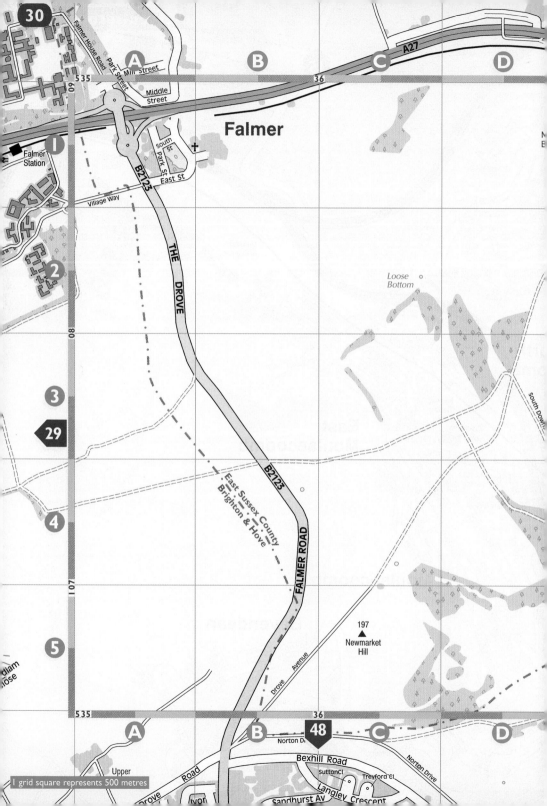

30

A Mill Street

Park Street

Falmer House Road

B

C A27

36

D

535

60

Middle Street

Falmer

B2123

South St

Park St

East St

✝

1 Falmer Station

Village Way

THE DROVE

Loose Bottom

2

80

3

29

East Sussex County
Brighton & Hove

B2123

4

1 07

FALMER ROAD

197
▲
Newmarket Hill

South Down

5

Drove Avenue

dlam
ose

535

A

B

48

Norton Dr

Bexhill Road

C

36

Norton Drive

D

Upper

Drove Road

Ivor

SuttonCl

Treyford Cl

Langley Crescent

Sandhurst Av

1 grid square represents 500 metres

A27

E F G H

38 39

South Downs Way

Ashcombe Hollow 60

Kingston Hollow

I

Kingston Ridge

Ridgway Paddock

Ashcombe La

The Avenue

Lockitt Way

Church La

Cordons

St Pancras

Moncton Way

Bramley

The Flints

Ashcomb

Hyde

Ba Cl

Stre

Church Lane

2

K

n

The

08

South Downs Way

3

32

South Downs Way

4

Dencher

107

Wildfowl Reserve

5

38 39

E F **49** G H

32

A   B   **16**   C   D

539
60 Hollow

Works

Juggs

Cranedown

Kingston Road

Lewes Sports Club

Kingston Hollow

1

Kingston Ridge
Ridgway Paddock
Ashcombe Lane

The Avenue
Lockitt Way
The Flints
Monkton Way
Bramleys
Mushroom
Hyde
St Pancras Gn
Flds

2

Church La
Cordons
Church Lane
PH
Barn Cl Street
Kent Flds

Iford & Kingston
CE Primary School
Snednore

Wellgreen   Lane

The Holdings

The

Kingston
near Lewes

80

3

31

Swanborough Hollow

4

South Downs Way

Dencher   Road

Swanborough   Drove

†

5

07

539   40

A   South   B   **50**   C   D

Downs

Way

White   Way

I grid square represents 500 metres

Works

A27

E   F   **17**   G   H

Rise Farm

I

Brook Lane

2

Rise Barn

River Ouse

The Brooks

3

rd

4

07

5

Northease Manor School

E   F   **51**   G   H

Northease Farm

Rodmell CE Primary School

A   B   C   D   The Pa

507   08

90

I

Norfolk
House

Swillage Lane

Selden Lane

Selden
Farm

Coldhart

France Lane

Selden

Ham②erpot
PH

Arundel Road

B2225

ARUNDEL

ARUNDEL

WATER LANE   A280

3
St Margarets
Primary School

Furzefield   pine Trees Cl
Cl   Garden   Cl
Chantryfie   Road
Woodlands
Cl

Dapper's Lane

Beech View

Brm Cl

Ecclesden
Farm

ROAD

Lloyd
Goring
Close

Shardeloes Rd

Meadowside

Fr Wk

Crescent

WATER LANE   A280

4
Lansdown   Way
Ashleigh Cl

Elmhurst
Cl

Greenacres Ring

Mertyrfiel

Weavers Hill

Lansdowne Road   Lnsd Cl

Cumberland Rd   Hg Cl
Hillside Crs

The Avenals

HIGH STREET
B2225

5
The
ottrells

Honey La   PO   Weavers Ring

Mill   Road

Mill Road

Avenue

Old Darlington
Mushroom Farm
Industrial Estate

507   08

A   B   **52**   C   D

Foxdale   Drive
Dell Drive
Briar Cl   Birch
Cl

Worthing
RFC

Roundstone Lane

Singleton Lane

Drive

1 grid square represents 500 metres

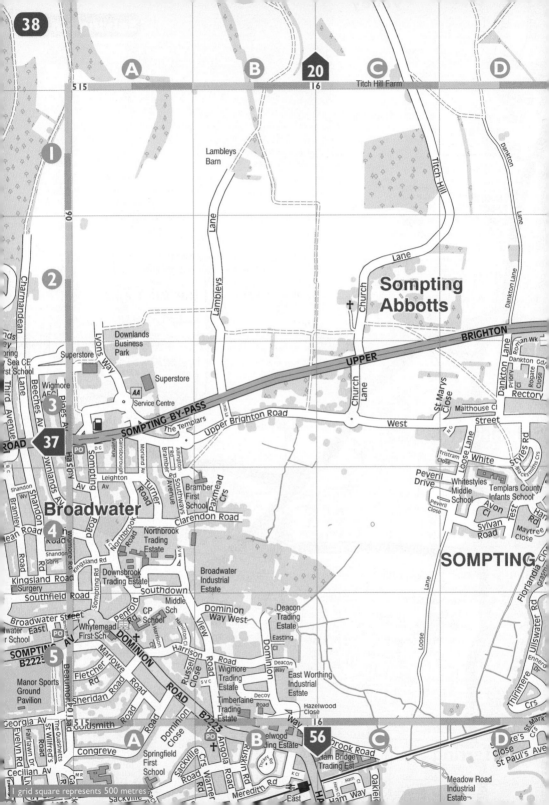

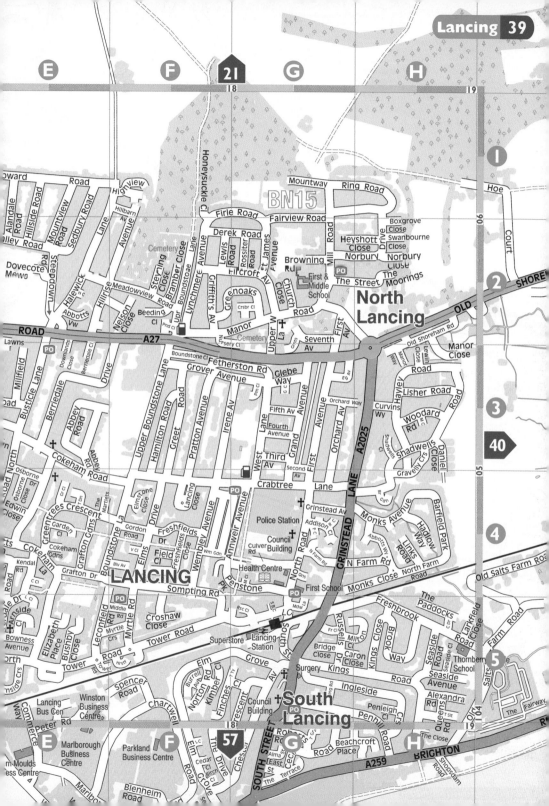

E F **21** G H

I

2

3

40

4

5

BN15

Mountway Ring Road
Boxgrove
Close
Firle Road Heyshott Swanbourne
Derek Road Fairview Road Close Close
Lewis St James Avenue Norbury Norbury
Road Rossiter Close Close
Hilcroft Av Browning The Moorings
Greenoaks Close Rd First & The Street
Manor Middle **North**
School **Lancing**
Cemetery
Seventh
Av Old Shoreham Rd Manor
Close
ROAD A27
Lisher Road
Boundstone Cl Fetherston Rd Glebe Hayley Woodard
Grover Avenue Way Curvins Rd
Wy Road
Fifth Av Orchard Way Shadwells
Irene Av Fourth Shadwells
Avenue Grand First Shadwells Crs Daniel
West Third Avenue Avenue Orchard Av Gravelly Close
Av Second Lane Barfield Park
Crabtree Av Lane Monks Avenue Hadlow
Grinstead Av Way
Lancing Addison Links
Police Station Road
Freshfields Council N Farm Rd Abbotts Wy
Gordon Building Monks Close North Farm
Road Culver N Farm Rd Road Old Salts Farm Rd
Field Rd First School The
LANCING Health Centre Paddocks
Sompting Rd Grinstead Lane
Penstone Freshbrook
South Road Russells Freshbrook
Croshaw Kings Brook The
Close Mill Caron Way Larkfield
Tower Road Bridge Close Seaside Road
Superstore Lancing Close Kings Road Thornbury
Station Surgery Seaside School
Elm Kings Road Avenue
Spencer Grove Ingleside Alexandra
Road Av Rd The Fairway
Chartwell Council Penleigh The Close
Lancing Building **South** Crs
Bus Cen Winston **Lancing** Penhill Rd
Business Beachcroft BRIGHTON
E Marlborough Centre F **57** G Place H
Business Parkland A259
Centre Business Centre

OLD SHOREHAM

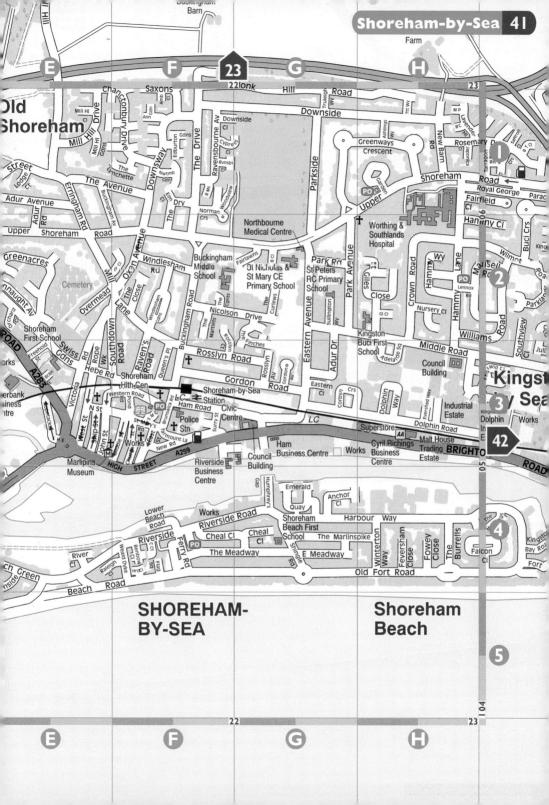

Buckingham Barn

Farm

E   F   **23**   G   H

22 lonk

Old Shoreham

Saxons

Mill Hill Drive
Chanctonbury Drive

Downside   Hill   Road

Downside

Truleigh Road

Ravensbourne Av
Parkside

Greenways Crescent

Shoreham   Road

New Barn Rd

Rosemary Dr

Lavender Dr

I

Royal George

Fairfield Cl

Hanbury Cl

Buci Crs

Street

Adur Avenue

Upper Shoreham

The Avenue
The Drive

Downsway

The Tynchette

The Dry

Adur Rd
Erringham Rd
Buckingham Av

Norman Crs

Upper Shoreham Road

Northbourne Medical Centre

Worthing & Southlands Hospital

Mansell Rd

Wilmot

2

Greenacres

Windlesham

Buckingham Middle School

Fairlawns

St Nicholas & St Mary CE Primary School

Park Rd

St Peters RC Primary School

Park Avenue

Crown Road

Hammy Wy

Hammy Lane

Southview

Cemetery

Overmead

Connaught Av

Windlesham Gdns

The Close

Nicolson Drive

The Curlews

Giles Close

Nursery Cl

Lennox Rd

Parkland

Shoreham First School

Swiss Gdns

Southdown Road

Raven's Road

Buckingham Road

Rosslyn Road

Adur Dr

Eastern Avenue

Kingston Buci First School

Adelaide Sq

Middle Road

Williams

3

Kingst by Sea

A283

Hebe Rd

Victoria

Gordon   Road

Rosslyn Av

Shoreham-by-Sea Station

Eastern Ct

Cortbyn Crs

Dolphin Way

Council Building

Industrial Estate

Dolphin In E

Works

Shoreham Hlth Cen

Western Road

PO

Ham Road

Civic Centre

LC

Dolphin Road

Malt House Trading Estate

42

BRIGHTO

Police Stn

New Rd

Surry St

Ham Business Centre

Works

Superstore

AA

Cyril Richings Business Centre

ROAD

Marlipins Museum

HIGH   STREET

A259

Riverside Business Centre

Council Building

05

Lower Beach Road

Works

Humphreys

Emerald Quay

Anchor Cl

Shoreham Harbour   Way

Riverside Road

Cheal Cl

Cheal Cl

Shoreham Beach First School

The Marlinspike

Winterton Way

Feversham Close

Fowey Close

The Burrells

Falcon Cl

4

Kingston Bay Rd

River

Riverside

Ferry Rd

PO

The Meadway

Shingle Rd

E Meadway

Old Fort Road

Fort

Beach   Road

Raleigh

Weald Dyke

Flag

SHOREHAM-BY-SEA

Shoreham Beach

5

104

22   23

E   F   G   H

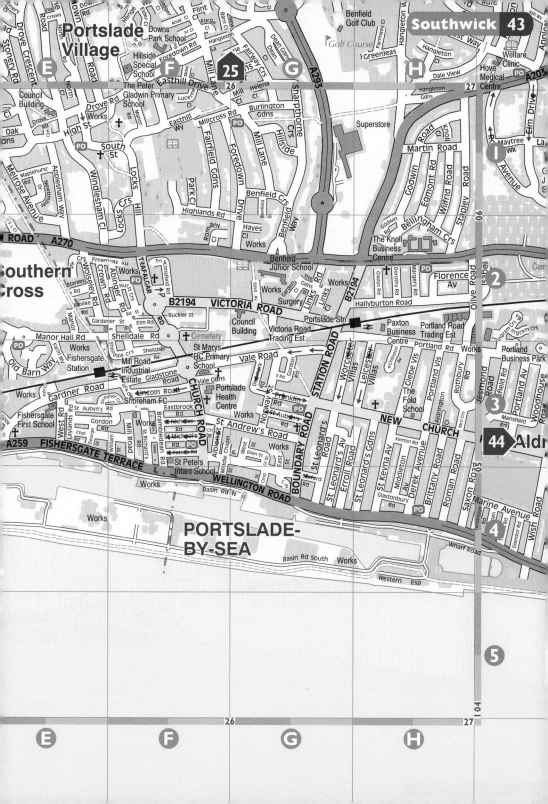

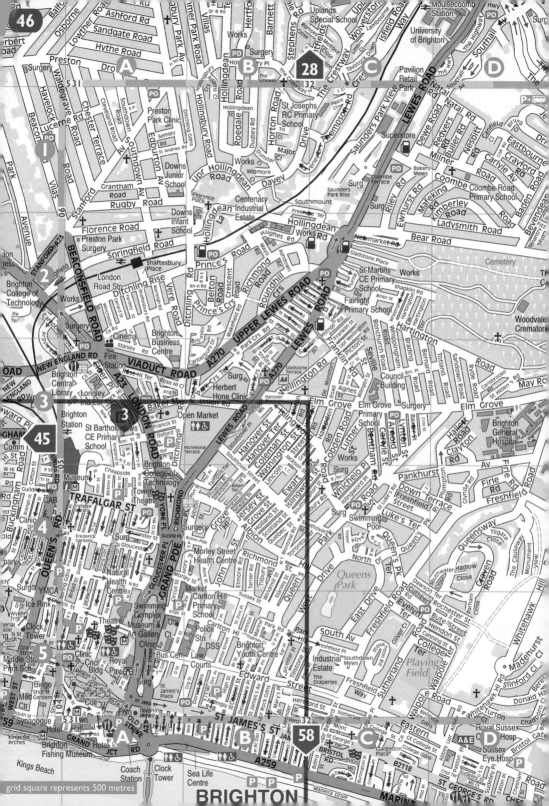

BRIGHTON

E F 29 G H

Kenilworth Close
Hogs Edge
Norwich
Norwich Close
Bamford Close
Bodiam Cinse
Knep
Norwich Drive
Leybourne Road
Geath Hill Avenue
Bodiam Avenue

I Upper Bevendea

Bevendean Wd
Med
Hill
Bevendean Crs
Bevendean C

PO

E

Upr Bevendean Av
Lower Bevendean Av
Heath Hi Av
Surgery
Bevendean Primary School
Bevendean Av

Leybourne Road
Durham Avenue
Bodiam Avenue

PO

Plymouth Av
Taunton
Hornby
Auckland
Ludlow
Road
Drive
Walmer Crs

Baywood Gdns & Roseber Avenue
Downsview Avenue
Warren Av

Fitch Drive
Dartmouth Cr
Dartmouth Close

Downland
Road
Midway Road
Seaview Rd
Warren
Warren Road

Meadowview
Dawlish Cl
Torcross
Chyliside

Drove
Channel View Rd
Channel Rd
Warren Edge
Hillview
Holtview
Warren C
Hollyview

2
H
Sussex Nuffield Hospital

Cemetery
Robin Davis

Bear Road
Tenantry Down Road

Warren Road

Warren Road

The Hyde Business Park
The Hyde

Wo

Lodsworth Cl
Alpourne
Swanborough Road
Twineham Rd
Swnb
Seasaw
Vines Cross Rd

3

48

Brighton Racecourse
Haybourne Road
Way
Limney Rd
Ninfield Pl
Coolham Dr
St Cuthmans
Whitehawk
Wiston
Platstow Cl
Ackfield Cl
Colgate Cl
Aldrich Cl

Wilson Avenue
Wiston Road
Downsm Pl

Wick Bottom
4

B

Whitehawk Primary School
Coolsbridge Close
Cruttmans
Crossbush
Pittdown Rd
Plechill
Nuthurst Pl
Sadler Wy
Desmond Wy

Whitehawk

Sheepcote Valley

Golf Course

Maresfield Road
Cowfold Road
Whitehawk Hill
Whitehawk Close
Whitehawk Rd
Chawington Crs
Iden
Beckley Cl
Council Building
Hellingly Cl
Whitehawk Clinic
The Meadway
Pennant Pl
Alan Way
Ticehurst Rd
Danehill
Findon Road

Wilson Avenue

5

Manor
Manor Crescent
Manor Way
Mnr Grn
P+
Playden Cl
Manor Pl
Surgery
Peel Road
Hamsey Cl
Bede
Fl Cl
Reading
Whitehawk Road
Wadhurst Rise

Stanley Deason Leisure Centre

Marks CE Primary School

E F 59 G H

Duck
Manor
Princes Rd
Regent's St
Bristol
Bennett Rd
Rugby Pl
Marlow Road
Henley Rd
Brighton Steiner School
St Faith Clinic
B2118
PO
BRISTOL

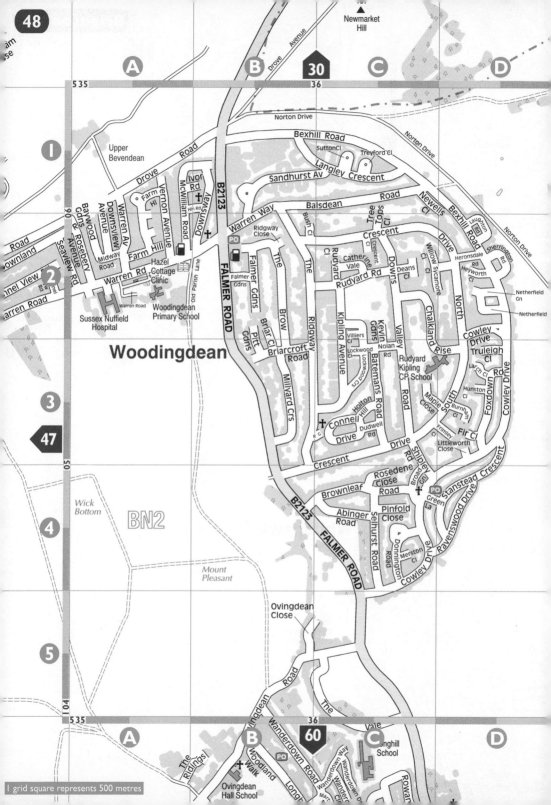

48

A   B   **30**   C   D

535   36

① Upper Bevendean

Drove Road

Norton Drive

Bexhill Road
Sutton Cl   Trevford Cl
Langley Crescent

Sandhurst Av   Road

Newells Cl

Bexhill Road

Norton Drive

Warren Av
Downsview Avenue
Baywood Gdns & Roseberry
Vernon Avenue
Ivor Rd
Downsway
B2123

Midway Road
Farm Hill
Warren Rd
Seaview Avenue
Downland Road
nnel View Rd

② Warren Road

Warren Way
Ridgway Close
PO
Balsdean   Road
Warren Road
Hazel Cottage Clinic
Old Parish Lane
FALMER ROAD
Falmer Gdns
The Brow
Falmer Gdns
Pitt Gdns
Briar Cl
Bush Cl
Crescent
Rudyard Cl
Catherine Vale
Rudyard Rd
Downs
Deans Cl
Willow
Sycamore
Chalkland Rise
Heronsdale Rd
Heyworth Cl
Sherrington Rd
Laughton
Netherfield Gn
Netherfield

Sussex Nuffield Hospital

Woodingdean Primary School

Woodingdean

Briarcroft Road
Millyard Crs
Ridgway Crescent
Kipling Avenue
Villiers
Lockwood
Kevin Gdns
Batemans Road
Nolan Rd
Valley Road
Rudyard Kipling CP School
North
Cowley Drive
Truleigh Cl
Larch Rd
Hunston Cl
Burnham Cl
Foxdown Rd
Cowley Drive

③

◀ 47

Conner Hill Drive
Holton Hill
R G
Dudwell Rd
Crescent
Drive
Maple Close
South
Shipley Rd
Fir Cl
Frimley Cl
Littleworth Close
Broad Green La

④ Wick Bottom

BN2

Brownleaf Road
Rosedene Close Road
Pinfold Close
Abinger Road
Selhurst Road
Donnington Road
Merston Cl
PO
Green
Cowley Drive
Ravenswood Drive
Stanstead Crescent

B2123   FALMER ROAD

Mount Pleasant

Ovingdean Close

Wangdean Road

⑤

535   36

A   **B**   **60**   C   D

PO
The Ridings
Woodland Walk
Wanderdown Road
Longhill School
Longhill Road
The Vale
Rowan
Wanderdown Way
Ovingdean Hall School

1 grid square represents 500 metres

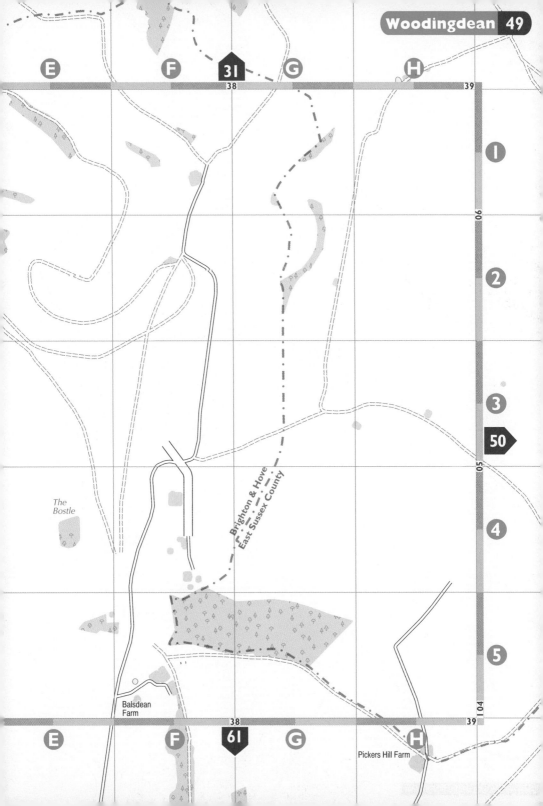

E F **31** G **H**

38 39

I

90

2

3

50

05

The
Bostle

Brighton & Hove
East Sussex County

4

5

104

Balsdean
Farm

E F **61** G **H**

38 39

Pickers Hill Farm

A B **32** C D

539 40

I

06

2

Whiteway
Bottom

3

49

05

4

5

104

539 40

A B **62** C D

South Downs Way

South Downs Way

White Way

Breaky
Bottom

1 grid square represents 500 metres

E F **33** G H
42 43

Northease
Manor
School

Northease Farm

I
06

Rodmell
CE Primary
School

2

Itford F

Rodmell

The
Dicklands

LC

Southease
Station

Badgers
Dene

3

The
Paddocks

Mill
Lane

Southease

River Ouse

05

4

5

104

Durham Farm

E F **63** G H
42 43

Dean's Farm

Money Burgh

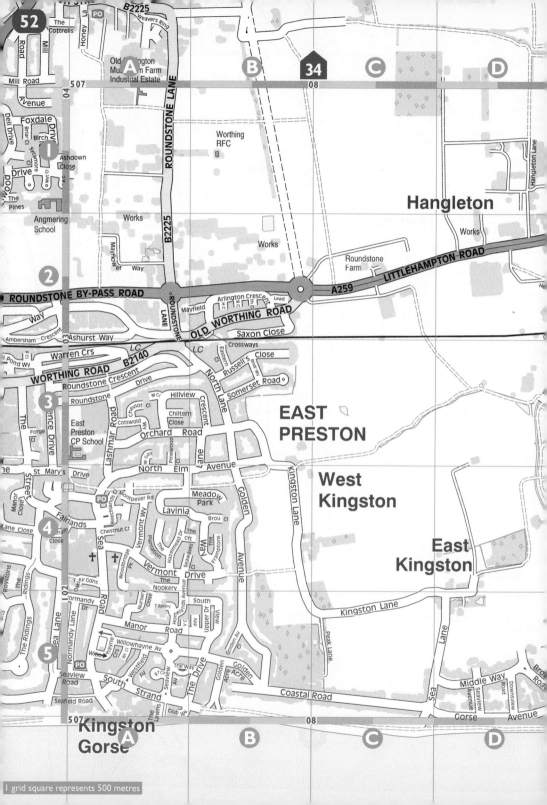

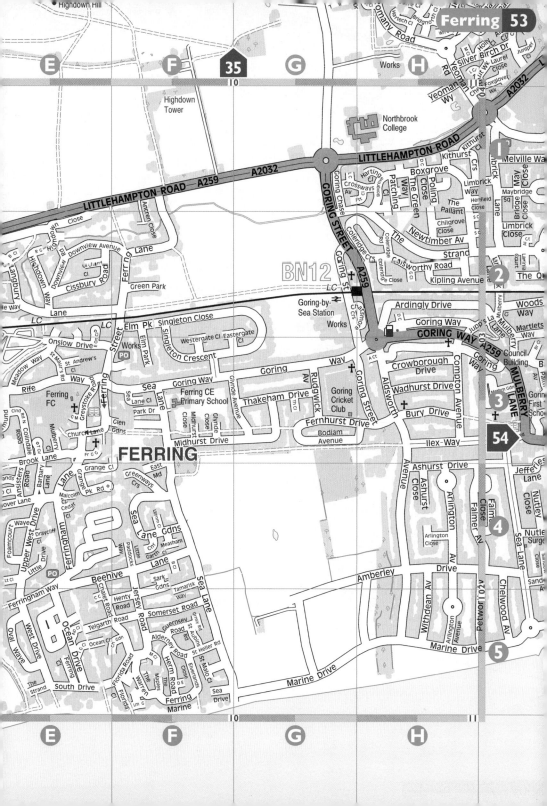

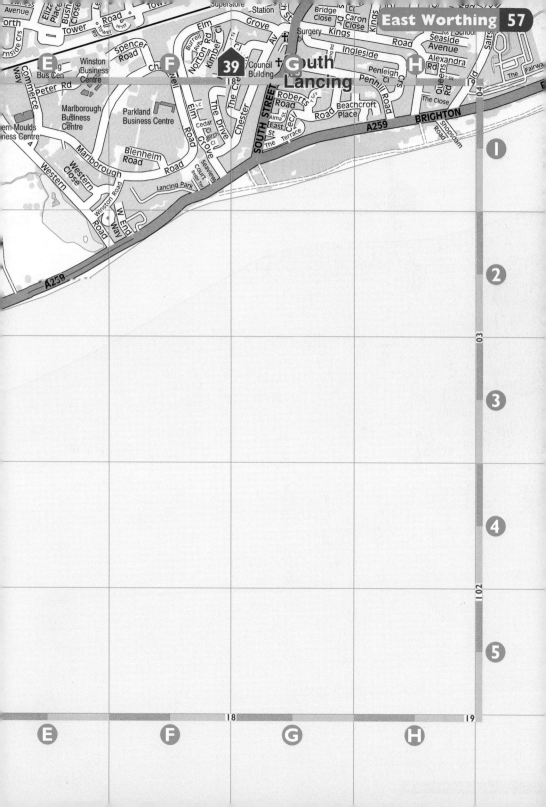

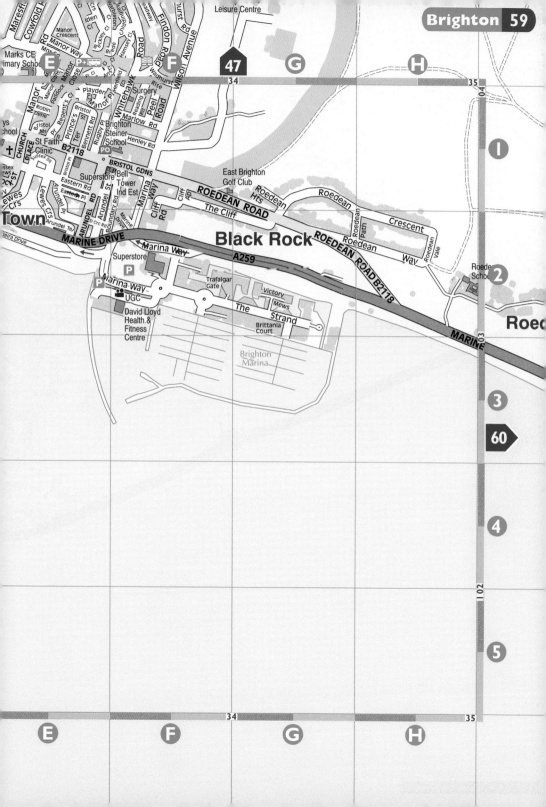

A   B   **48**   C   D

5 35

04

Ovingdean Road

36

Vale

Longhill School

The Ridings

Woodland Walk

PO

Wanderdown Road

Wanderdown Way

Wanderdown Drive

Wanderdown Close

Rowan Way

Eley

B2123

Ovingdean Hall School

Longhill

Martyn's

Elvin Crescent

Eley

Greenways

Ainsworth Close

Dower Close

Longhill Road

Rowan Wy

New Barn Road

Court Farm Rd

FALMER ROAD

Ainsworth Avenue

Eley Crs

Drive

Court Ord Rd

QW Cl

Meadow Vale Surgery

I

2 Roedean School

Roedean Vale

Beacon Hill

Ovingdean

Meadow Vale

Wilkinson Close

Rottingdean FC

Roedean

MARINE

03

DRIVE

A259

Greenways

The Rotyngs

Challoners Ms

THE GREEN

The Grn

3

59

Olde Pl

HIGH

Sheepcote Wk

M5

Nevill Road

Nevill Road

MARINE

Park Crs

Park Rd

West

4

I 02

5

5 35

36

A   B   C   D

I grid square represents 500 metres

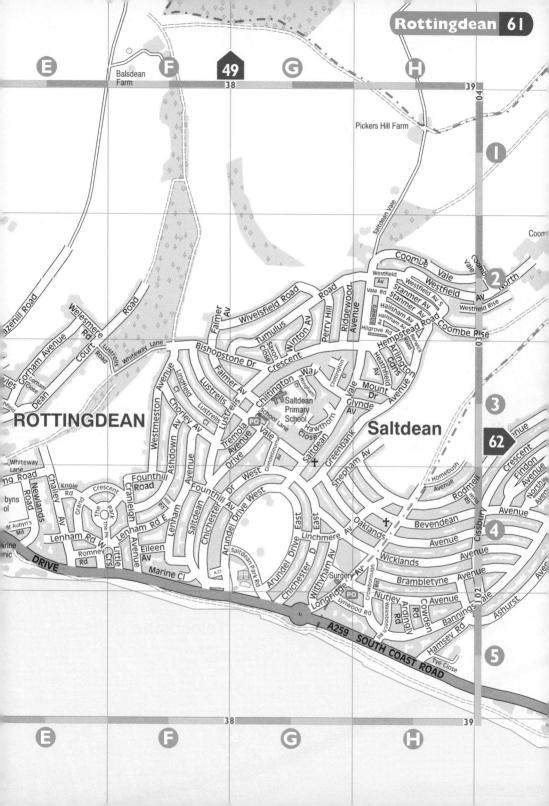

E F **49** G H

38 39

Balsdean Farm

Pickers Hill Farm

I

Coom

Coombe Vale

Westfield Av
Westfield Av S
Stanmer Av
Stanmer Av
Vale Rd
Westfield Rise

2

Coombe Rise

Hazehill Road
Welesmere Rd
Road
Lustrells Road
Whiteway Lane

Falmer Av
Wivelsfield Road
Road
Perry Hill
Ridgeword
Avenue
Hempstead Road
Hailsham Av
Hailsham Av
Berwick
Hilgrove Rd

Gorham Avenue
Gorham Close
Court Road
Dean
Tumulus
Winton Av
Saxon Close
Crescent
Bishopstone Dr
Falmer Av

Chiltington
Chiltington Cl
Arlington Gdns
Heathfield Av
Mount Dr

ROTTINGDEAN

Westmeston Avenue
Chorley Av
Ashdown Av
Lindfield Cl
Lustrells Cl
Lustrells
Lustrells
Tremola Avenue
Chiltington Way
Effingham
Saltdean Primary School
School Lane
Hawthorn
Saltdean
Glynde Av
Vale

Saltdean

Whiteway Lane
Whiteway Lane
Road

St Aubyn's Md
Chailey Av
Knole Rd
Grand Crescent
The Pk
Park
Cranleigh Avenue
Founthill Road
Founthill Av
Chichester Cl
Saltdean
Lenham
Arundel Dr
Saltdean Park Rd
Glyndebourne Av
West
Greenbank
Shepham Av
Homebush Avenue
Rodmell
Hythe Rd
Cissbury
Findon Avenue
Northw Aven

3

62

Avenue
Crescent
Oaklands
Bevedean Avenue

4

ng Road
Newlands Road
Lenham Rd W
Little Crs
Romney Rd
Marine Cl
Eileen Av
Arundel Drive East
Chichester D
Linchmere Av
Withynham Av
Oaklands
Wicklands Avenue
Brambletyne Avenue
Cowden Rd
Ashurst
Hamsey Rd
Bannings Rd
Ardingly Rd
Nutley Avenue
Crowborough
Wallesdene
Lynwood Rd
Longridge
Surgery Av
Tye Close

Marine
nic
DRIVE

A259 SOUTH COAST ROAD

5

38 39

E F G H

A B **50** C D
40

I

539
04

Coombe Farm

Brighton & Hove
East Sussex County

Telscom

Homebush Av

†

2

Coombe Va
Coombe

Westfield

North

Westfield Av S

Av

mer Av

mer Av

Westfield Rise

Coombe Rise

Road

Berwick

Upper Bannings Road

3

Rye Cl

Pedlersburgh

61

Avenue

Ifield Close

Homebush
Avenue

Crescent

Findon

Lewes

Avenue

Northwood

Bannings Vale

Avenue

Chailey

The Ridings

Barley Cl

Rustic Rd

Rogmell

Avenue

Crs

Cl

Rustic Close

Shannon

Way

Drive

Stanley Rd

Bevendean

Cissbury

Avenue

Chesworth Av

Ambleside Av

Heathy

4

Avenue

Nrthct La

Manor

Cavendish Cl

Avenue

Warren Way

Cliffs

Kirby

Bridle

Dr

Tollgate

Avenue

Telscombe

Way

C
Cht Pk

mbletyne

Bannings Vale

Ashurst

Avenue

Park

Lea Rd

Avenue

Avenue

Rowe Avenue

Cowden

Avenue

Telscombe Cliffs

Balcombe

ds

Rd

Springfield

Av

Grassmere

Telscombe Cliffs
Primary School

Avenue

Avenue

Roa

Hamsey Rd

Highview
Road

Av

Clifton
Way

Avenue

Hoddern County
Junior School

5

Tye Close

Gorham Way

Highview Rd

Tyedean Road

Broomfield Avenue

Cliff Gardens

St Peter's Av

Chatsworth Cl

Avenue

Arundel Rd

Cairo Rd

Phyllis

Hoddern Av

Lake
Dr

AST ROAD

539

A259

A SOUTH COAST ROAD B

Fairlight Avenue

†

66

C

Lincoln Rd

Malines

West

Avenue

Sutton

D

Amhurst Rd

Central

Ambleside

PO

S COAST RD

Surgery

The Esplanade

Police

Surgery

E F **51** G H

Durham Farm

42 04 43

Dean's Farm

I

Money Burgh

Bullock Down

The Lookout

2

Roderick Avenue North

Valley Road Halcombe Farm

Gold Lane

Avenue

Johns Cl

Grnh Wy

Heathdown Close

Wendale Drive

Highsted Park

Greenacres

Telscombe Road

Piddin

3

03

64

Nore
Down

combe Road

Oval

Bretts Field

Mnt Cbrn Crs

Ashmore

Coney Furlong

Morestead

skyline
Vw

Meridian
CP School

4

Hoddern Farm

Tor Road

Roderick

Anzac Cl

Badgers Field

Cripps Avenue

Swln

Swln Cl

Rise

Road

Glynn

Abbey Cl

Trnfgt

Sycm

Road

Clingwd

02

Hairpin Croft

Avenue

Turnpike Cl

Rosemary Close

Pelham Rise

Cinquefoil

The Bricky

5

Roderick Road

North

Edith Av N

Horsham Av N

Dorothy Av

Bramber Av N

View
Road

Bee
Raod
Road

BN10

southview

Dorothy
Avenue
North

Br Cl

Surgery

School

Council
Building

Meridian
Leisure
Centre

PEACEHAVEN

42 43

PO

E The Meridian
Industrial Estate F **67** G H

Newton Rd

Hovie
Road

Greenwich
Way

Jason Cl

School

Danford

Ryfrd Cl

Arundel Avenue

Peacehaven
Sports
Centre

Cliff Pk
Close

Avenue

E F G H

46

47

04

I

2

03

3

Poverty
Bottom

**South
Heighton**

Harfield
Close

Leonard's Road

Cantercrow
Hill

Wellington Road

The Close

Thompson Road

Cantercrow
Hill

Cantercrow Cl

PO

Heighton Road

Rookery
Way

Rx Cl

Lewis Road

St Leonards Cl

Port
VW

Denton Rise

Rectory

Vicra Cl

O M

Park
Drive

St Leonards
Close

Acacia Road

The Crove

The Road

Denton Rd

Hill Rise

Hill Road

Denton

Denton County
Primary
School

Denton Drive

Denton

The
Crescent

Fairholme Road

Crest
Road

Palmerston Rd

3

King's Avenue

Seaview Road

Palmerston-
Road

**Mount
Pleasant**

Beresford

Arundel Road

Claremont Road

Howel
Close

Holmdale Road

4

Avis Close

Station Road

Mount Road

Palace
Road

102

Rich
Industrial
Est

PO

Avis Rd

ROAD

Way

Mount

Mount Close

Bishopstone Road

AA

THE DROVE

A259

5

Avis
Way

No

E RD

A259

Works

E F G H

B

46

47

SEAFORD

69

Stud Farm

Brightwell

stbridge Rd

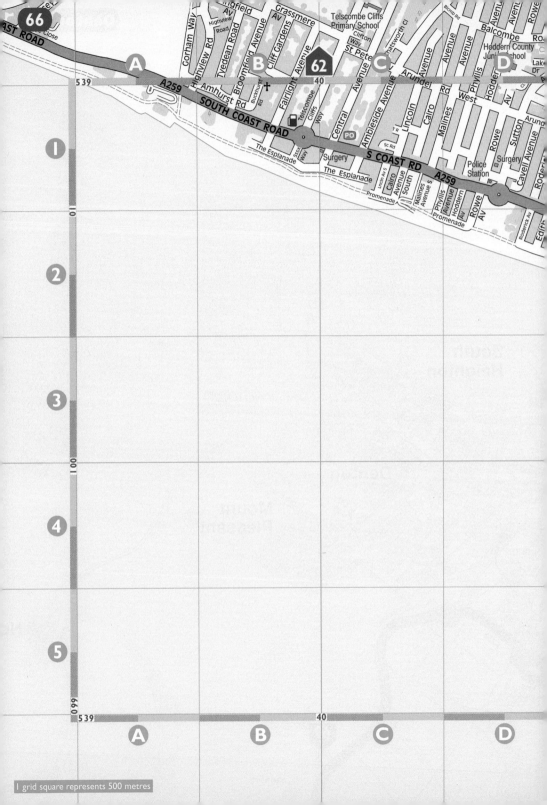

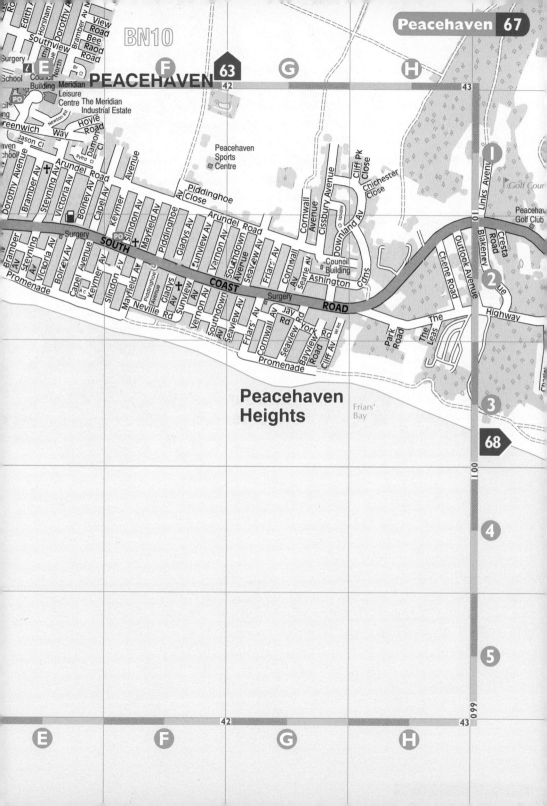

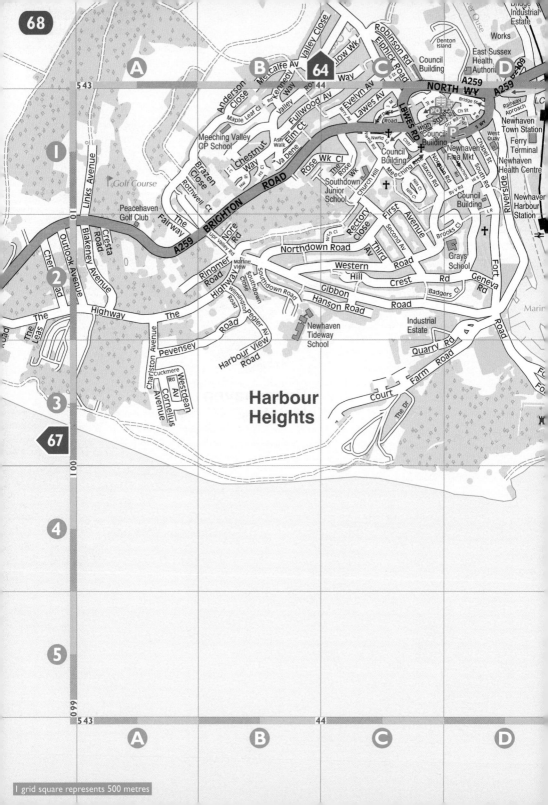

A **B** **64 44** **C** **D**

I

2

67

3

4

5

Harbour
Heights

Golf Course

Peacehaven
Golf Club

Links Avenue

Cher ad

Outlook Avenue

Blakeney Avenue

Cresta Road

The Fairway

Rothwell Ct

Brazen Close

Chestnut Way

Meeching Valley CP School

Anderson Close

Maple Leaf Cl

Metcalfe Av

Kennedy Way

Valley Way

llow Wk

Valley Close

Fullwood Av

Elm Ct

Ash Walk

Va Dene

BRIGHTON ROAD

A259

The Fairway

Upr Valley Rd

Nore Rd

Ringmer Road

Highway

Southdown Close

Willington Rd

Pegler Av

Southdown Road

Marine View

Rose Wk Cl

The Rose

Rose Wk

Southdown Junior School

Church Hill

First Avenue

Rectory Close

Second Av

Northdown Road

Third AV

Western Hill

Gibbon Road

Hanson Road

Crest Rd

Road

Geneva Rd

Brooks Cl

Badgers Cl

Grays School

Newhaven Tideway School

Industrial Estate

Harbour View Road

Charlston Avenue

Pevensey Road

The

Highway

The Leas

The Leas

Cuckmere Rd

Westdean AV

Cornelius Avenue

Court

The Dr

Quarry Rd

Farm Road

Robinson Rd

Elphick Road

Denton Island

East Sussex Health Authori

Works

Council Building

NORTH WY

A259

A259

Bridge St

Evelyn Av

Lawes Av

LEWES RD

High Street

PO

Ch St

Council Building

Meeching Rd

Saxon Rd

Norman Rd

Council Building

Newhaven Flea Mkt

Railway Approach

Newhaven Town Station

West Quay

Newhaven Health Centre

Newhaven Harbour Station

Fort Road

Marin

r Ouse

Bridge Industrial Estate

Ferry Terminal

Riverside

I grid square represents 500 metres

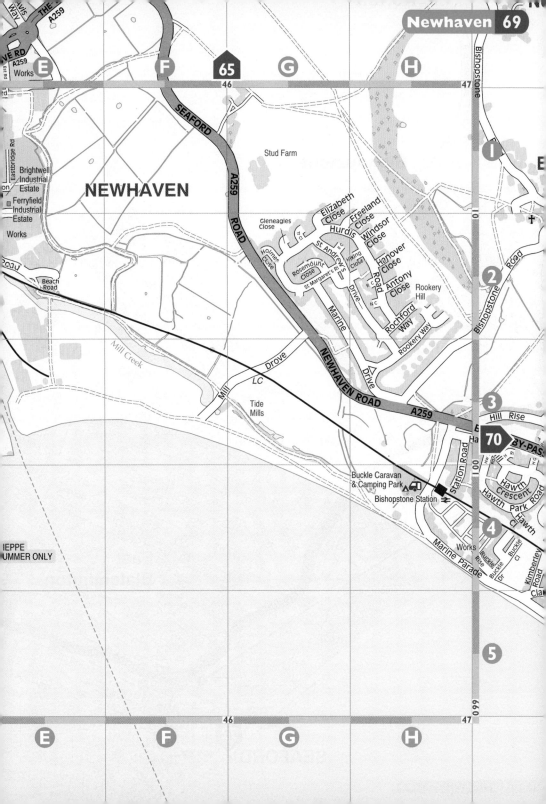

E

F

65 46

G

H

Bishopstone

NEWHAVEN

Stud Farm

SEAFORD ROAD

A259

Brightwell Industrial Estate

Ferryfield Industrial Estate

Works

I

E

†

Elizabeth Close

Freeland Close

Windsor Close

Hurdis Close

Gleneagles Close

Holmes Close

St Andrew's

Rosemount Close

St Margaret's Rd

Viking Close

Hanover Close

Antony Close

Marine Road

Rochford Way

Rookery Hill

Rookery Way

2

Bishopstone Road

Beach Road

Mill Creek

Mill Drive

LC

Tide Mills

NEWHAVEN ROAD

A259

Drive

3

Hill Rise

Ha

70 BY-PASS

Hawth Crescent

Hawth Park Road

Hawth Cl

Station Road

Buckle Caravan & Camping Park

Bishopstone Station

Works

Marine Parade

Buckle Rise

Buckle Dr

Buckle Cl

4

Kimberley Road

Cla

IEPPE UMMER ONLY

5

46

47

E

F

G

H

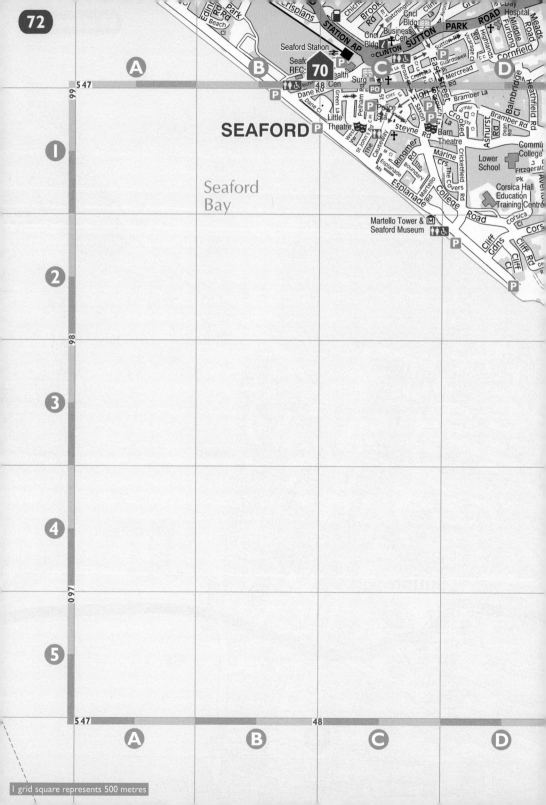

SEAFORD

Seaford
Bay

Martello Tower &
Seaford Museum

1 grid square represents 500 metres

Chesterton Drive
Special-School

artfield
Road

Headlan
Avenue

wnsview Road

Manor
Cl

Manor
Rd

Badgers Copse

Willow Drive

Jumper
Close

Ash Drive

E

nnecy RC
imary
chool

Links Rd

Arundel Rd

Hazeldene

St Wilfred's

Oakwall
Dr

Kingston
Gn

Kingston
Cl

F

King
Way

May

Field
Cl

50

Barcombe
Avenue

G

Chyngton
Lane

H

51

99

Seaford Head
Community
College

Sutton

Bracken
Road

Green
Wk

Steyning
Road

Lindfield Avenue

Hamsey
Lane

Chyngton
Farm

I

Rother Road

Cuckmere

Road

Rodmell Rd

Pvnn Cl

Pvnn Cl

98

Vanguard Way

Chyngton Rd

Chyngton Pl

Fairways Road

PO

Chyngton Road

Lullington Cl

Chyngton Way

South Way

Golf Course

Southdown

Seaford Head
Golf Club

Hill Fort

South
Hill

2

Vanguard Way

3

Nature Rese

Seaford
Head

Vanguard Way

4

090

5

Aldrington	44 A3	Findon Valley	19 F5	North Moulsecoomb	28 D3	South Heighton	65 E
Beggars Bush	20 B4	Fishersgate	42 D3	Old Shoreham	41 E1	South Lancing	39 C
Bevendean	29 G5	Goring-by-Sea	54 B2	Ovingdean	60 C2	South Malling	17 E
Bishopstone	70 A1	Hangleton	26 A4	Patcham	27 H1	Southover	16 D
Black Rock	59 F2	Hangleton	52 C1	Peacehaven	63 E5	Southwick	42 C
Botolphs	7 H5	Harbour Heights	68 B3	Peacehaven Heights	67 G3	Stanmer	15 E
Bramber	7 H2	High Salvington	36 A1	Piddinghoe	64 A3	Steyning	7 F
Brighton	3 C6	Hollingbury	28 B2	Portslade-by-Sea	43 F4	Sutton	71 E
Broadwater	37 H4	Hollingdean	28 B4	Portslade Village	25 E5	Tarring Neville	64 D
Castle Town	8 C3	Hove	44 D5	Preston	45 G1	Telscombe	62 D
Clapham	35 F1	Iford	32 D4	Rodmell	51 F2	Telscombe Cliffs	62 C
Coldean	28 D2	Kemp Town	58 D2	Roedean	60 A2	Upper Beeding	7 H
Coombes	21 H2	Kingston by Sea	42 A3	Rottingdean	61 E3	Wallands Park	16 D
Cote	36 A2	Kingston near Lewes	32 A2	Saddlescombe	12 A1	West Blatchington	44 B3
Denton	65 F4	Lancing	39 F4	Saltdean	61 H3	Westdene	26 D
Durrington	36 B3	Landport	16 D1	Salvington	37 E3	West Kingston	52 C
East Blatchington	70 C4	Lewes	17 E2	Seaford	72 B1	West Tarring	55 E
East Kingston	52 C4	Mile Oak	24 D5	Shoreham Beach	41 H5	West Worthing	54 D
East Moulsecoomb	29 F3	Moulsecoomb	29 F4	Shoreham-by-Sea	41 F5	Whitehawk	47 F
East Preston	52 B3	Mount Pleasant	65 G4	Sompting	38 D4	Withdean	27 C
East Worthing	56 D2	Nepcote	18 D2	Sompting Abbotts	38 C2	Woodingdean	48 A
Falmer	30 B1	Newhaven	69 E1	Southease	51 G3	Worthing	4 D
Ferring	53 F5	North Lancing	39 H2	Southern Cross	43 E2		

USING THE STREET INDEX

Street names are listed alphabetically. Each street name is followed by its postal town or area locality, the Postcode District, the page number, and the reference to the square in which the name is found.

Standard index entries are shown as follows:

Abbey Cl *LAN/SOMP* BN15 ....**40** B4

Street names and selected addresses not shown on the map due to scale restrictions are shown in the index with an asterisk:

Adur Valley Ct *STEY/UB* * BN44 ....**8** B2

GENERAL ABBREVIATIONS

ACC	ACCESS	E	EAST	LDG	LODGE	R	RIVER
ALY	ALLEY	EMB	EMBANKMENT	LGT	LIGHT	RBT	ROUNDABOUT
AP	APPROACH	EMBY	EMBASSY	LK	LOCK	RD	ROAD
AR	ARCADE	ESP	ESPLANADE	LKS	LAKES	RDG	RIDGE
ASS	ASSOCIATION	EST	ESTATE	LNDG	LANDING	REP	REPUBLIC
AV	AVENUE	EX	EXCHANGE	LTL	LITTLE	RES	RESERVOIR
BCH	BEACH	EXPY	EXPRESSWAY	LWR	LOWER	RFC	RUGBY FOOTBALL CLUB
BLDS	BUILDINGS	EXT	EXTENSION	MAG	MAGISTRATE	RI	RISE
BND	BEND	F/O	FLYOVER	MAN	MANSIONS	RP	RAMP
BNK	BANK	FC	FOOTBALL CLUB	MD	MEAD	RW	ROW
BR	BRIDGE	FK	FORK	MDW	MEADOWS	S	SOUTH
BRK	BROOK	FLD	FIELD	MEM	MEMORIAL	SCH	SCHOOL
BTM	BOTTOM	FLDS	FIELDS	MKT	MARKET	SE	SOUTH EAST
BUS	BUSINESS	FLS	FALLS	MKTS	MARKETS	SER	SERVICE AREA
BVD	BOULEVARD	FLS	FLATS	ML	MALL	SH	SHORE
BY	BYPASS	FM	FARM	ML	MILL	SHOP	SHOPPING
CATH	CATHEDRAL	FT	FORT	MNR	MANOR	SKWY	SKYWAY
CEM	CEMETERY	FWY	FREEWAY	MS	MEWS	SMT	SUMMIT
CEN	CENTRE	FY	FERRY	MSN	MISSION	SOC	SOCIETY
CFT	CROFT	GA	GATE	MT	MOUNT	SP	SPUR
CH	CHURCH	GAL	GALLERY	MTN	MOUNTAIN	SPR	SPRING
CHA	CHASE	GDN	GARDEN	MTS	MOUNTAINS	SQ	SQUARE
CHYD	CHURCHYARD	GDNS	GARDENS	MUS	MUSEUM	ST	STREET
CIR	CIRCLE	GLD	GLADE	MWY	MOTORWAY	STN	STATION
CIRC	CIRCUS	GLN	GLEN	N	NORTH	STR	STREAM
CL	CLOSE	GN	GREEN	NE	NORTH EAST	STRD	STRAND
CLFS	CLIFFS	GND	GROUND	NW	NORTH WEST	SW	SOUTH WEST
CMP	CAMP	GRA	GRANGE	O/P	OVERPASS	TDG	TRADING
CNR	CORNER	GRG	GARAGE	OFF	OFFICE	TER	TERRACE
CO	COUNTY	GT	GREAT	ORCH	ORCHARD	THWY	THROUGHWAY
COLL	COLLEGE	GTWY	GATEWAY	OV	OVAL	TNL	TUNNEL
COM	COMMON	GV	GROVE	PAL	PALACE	TOLL	TOLLWAY
COMM	COMMISSION	HGR	HIGHER	PAS	PASSAGE	TPK	TURNPIKE
CON	CONVENT	HL	HILL	PAV	PAVILION	TR	TRACK
COT	COTTAGE	HLS	HILLS	PDE	PARADE	TRL	TRAIL
COTS	COTTAGES	HO	HOUSE	PH	PUBLIC HOUSE	TWR	TOWER
CP	CAPE	HOL	HOLLOW	PK	PARK	U/P	UNDERPASS
CPS	COPSE	HOSP	HOSPITAL	PKWY	PARKWAY	UNI	UNIVERSITY
CR	CREEK	HRB	HARBOUR	PL	PLACE	UPR	UPPER
CREM	CREMATORIUM	HTH	HEATH	PLN	PLAIN	V	VALE
CRS	CRESCENT	HTS	HEIGHTS	PLNS	PLAINS	VA	VALLEY
CSWY	CAUSEWAY	HVN	HAVEN	PLZ	PLAZA	VIAD	VIADUCT
CT	COURT	HWY	HIGHWAY	POL	POLICE STATION	VIL	VILLA
CTRL	CENTRAL	IMP	IMPERIAL	PR	PRINCE	VIS	VISTA
CTS	COURTS	IN	INLET	PREC	PRECINCT	VLG	VILLAGE
CTYD	COURTYARD	IND EST	INDUSTRIAL ESTATE	PREP	PREPARATORY	VLS	VILLAS
CUTT	CUTTINGS	INF	INFIRMARY	PRIM	PRIMARY	VW	VIEW
CV	COVE	INFO	INFORMATION	PROM	PROMENADE	W	WEST
CYN	CANYON	INT	INTERCHANGE	PRS	PRINCESS	WD	WOOD
DEPT	DEPARTMENT	IS	ISLAND	PRT	PORT	WHF	WHARF
DL	DALE	JCT	JUNCTION	PT	POINT	WK	WALK
DM	DAM	JTY	JETTY	PTH	PATH	WKS	WALKS
DR	DRIVE	KG	KING	PZ	PIAZZA	WLS	WELLS
DRO	DROVE	KNL	KNOLL	QD	QUADRANT	WY	WAY
DRY	DRIVEWAY	L	LAKE	QU	QUEEN	YD	YARD
DWGS	DWELLINGS	LA	LANE	QY	QUAY	YHA	YOUTH HOSTEL

POSTCODE TOWNS AND AREA ABBREVIATIONS

ANG/EP ....Angmering/East Preston
BRI ....Brighton
FERR ....Ferring
FIN/BW ....Findon/Broadwater
HFD ....Henfield

HOVE...Hove
LAN/SOMP ....Lancing/Sompting
LEW ....Lewes
NEWHV ....Newhaven
PEAHV ....Peacehaven

POY/PYE ....Poynings/Pyecombe
PTSD ....Portslade
RING/NEW ....Ringmer/Newick
ROTT ....Rottingdean
SALV ....Salvington

SEAF ....Seaford
SHOR ....Shoreham
STEY/UB ....Steyning/Upper Beeding
STHW ....Southwick
WTHG ....Worthing

A

Abbey Cl LAN/SOMP BN15 ....40 B4
PEAHV BN10 ....63 E4
Abbey Rd LAN/SOMP BN15 ....39 E3
ROTT BN2 ....58 D1
WTHG BN11 ....4 B7
Abbotsbury Cl ROTT BN2 ....61 F4
Abbotts Cl WTHG BN11 ....4 D4
Abbotts Vw LAN/SOMP BN15 ....39 E4
Abbotts Wy LAN/SOMP BN15 ....39 H4
Aberdeen Rd ROTT BN2 ....48 B2
Abergavenny Rd LEWES BN7 ....16 D3
Abinger Pl LEWES BN7 ....17 E3
Abinger Rd PTSD BN41 ....43 F2
ROTT BN2 ....48 C4
Acacia Av HOVE BN3 ....44 B1
SALV BN13 ....36 D3
Acacia Rd NEWHV BN9 ....65 E3
Acre Cl WTHG BN11 ....4 A5
Adams Cl BRI BN1 ....28 B5
Addison Cl LAN/SOMP BN15...........39 E4
Addison Rd HOVE BN3 ....2 C1
Adelaide Cl SALV BN13 ....36 A4
SEAF BN25 ....70 C3
Adelaide Crs HOVE BN3 ....45 E5
Adelaide Man HOVE BN3 ....45 E5
Adelaide Sq SHOR BN43 ....41 H3
Adur Av SALV BN13 ....36 A2
SHOR BN43 ....41 E1
Adur Cl LAN/SOMP BN15 ....40 C5
Adur Dr SHOR BN43 ....41 E2
Adur Rd SHOR BN43 ....41 E2
Adur Valley Ct STEY/UB * BN44.......8 B2
Adur Vw STEY/UB * BN44 ....8 A2
Adversane Rd FIN/BW BN14 ....37 F5
Aglaia Rd WTHG BN11 ....54 D4
Agnes St ROTT BN2 ....46 C3
Ainsdale Cl SALV BN13 ....36 B4
Ainsdale Rd SALV BN13 ....36 B4
Ainsworth Av ROTT BN2 ....60 B2
Ainsworth Cl ROTT BN2 ....60 B1
Air St BRI * BN1 ....3 F4
Alandale Rd LAN/SOMP BN15 ....39 E2
Alan Wy ROTT BN2 ....47 F4
Albany Cl WTHG BN11 ....55 F5
Albany Ms HOVE BN3 ....44 D4
Albany Rd SEAF BN25 ....70 A5
Albany Vls HOVE BN3 ....44 D5
Albemarle ROTT * BN2 ....3 H6
Alberta Rd SALV BN13 ....36 B4
Albert Man HOVE * BN3 ....45 E4
Albert Ms HOVE BN3 ....44 D4
Albert Rd BRI BN1 ....2 E2
STHW BN42 ....42 B3
Albion Hl ROTT BN2 ....3 K3
Albion St LEWES BN7 ....17 E4
PTSD BN41 ....42 B4
PTSD BN41 ....43 F3
ROTT BN2 ....3 J2
Albourne Cl ROTT BN2 ....47 E3
Alder Cl SALV BN13 ....36 A5
Alderney Rd FERR BN12 ....53 F2
Aldrich Cl ROTT BN2 ....47 F4
Aldrington Av HOVE BN3 ....44 C2
Aldrington Cl HOVE BN3 ....43 H3
Aldsworth Av FERR BN12 ....53 H3
Aldsworth Ct FERR BN12 ....53 H3
Aldsworth Pde FERR * BN12 ....53 H3
Aldwick Crs FIN/BW BN14 ....5 K1
Alexander Ter WTHG * BN11 ....5 F5
Alexandra Cl SEAF BN25 ....70 C3
Alexandra Ct FERR BN12 ....54 A2
Alexandra Rd LAN/SOMP BN15 ......39 H4
WTHG BN11 ....5 K4
Alexandra Vls BRI BN1 ....2 E2
Alford Cl FIN/BW BN14 ....37 E3
Alfred Pl WTHG BN11 ....5 H5
Alfred Rd BRI BN1 ....2 E1
Alfriston Cl FIN/BW BN14 ....37 F5
ROTT BN2 ....47 F4
Alfriston Pk SEAF BN25 ....71 G3

Alfriston Rd FIN/BW BN14 ....37 F5
SEAF BN25 ....71 E4
Alice St HOVE BN3 ....2 A4
Alinora Av FERR BN12 ....54 B3
Alinora Cl FERR BN12 ....54 B3
Alinora Crs FERR BN12 ....54 A5
Alinora Dr FERR BN12 ....54 A4
Allendale Av FIN/BW BN14 ....37 E1
Allington Rd FIN/BW BN14 ....38 A3
Alma St LAN/SOMP BN15 ....57 G1
Almond Av SHOR BN43 ....40 C2
Alpine Rd HOVE BN3 ....44 B2
Alverstone Rd WTHG BN11 ....5 J2
Amberley Cl SHOR BN43 ....41 F1
Amberley Dr FERR BN12 ....53 H4
HOVE BN3 ....26 A4
Ambleside Av PEAHV BN10 ....66 C1
Ambleside Rd LAN/SOMP BN15 ......39 E5
Ambrose Pl WTHG BN11 ....4 D4
Amelia Rd WTHG BN11 ....4 D4
Amesbury Crs HOVE BN3 ....44 A3
Amherst Crs HOVE BN3 ....44 B2
Amhurst Rd PEAHV BN10 ....66 B1
Anchor Cl SHOR BN43 ....41 G4
Anchor Ct FERR * BN12 ....54 A1
Ancren Ct BRI BN12 ....53 F1
Anderson Cl NEWHV BN9 ....68 B3
Andrew Cl STEY/UB BN44 ....7 F2
Anglesea St WTHG BN11 ....4 D4
Angola Rd FIN/BW BN14 ....56 B1
Angus Rd FERR BN12 ....54 C3
Annington Gdns SHOR BN43 ....41 F1
Annington Rd LAN/SOMP BN15 .....22 A1
STEY/UB BN44 ....7 G3
Ann St BRI BN1 ....3 G1
WTHG BN11 ....5 F5
Annwear Rd LAN/SOMP BN15 ....39 G4
Anscombe Cl WTHG BN11 ....54 D4
Anscombe Rd WTHG BN11 ....54 D4
Ansisters Rd FERR BN12 ....53 E4
Anson Ct FERR * BN12 ....54 A1
Anson Rd FERR BN12 ....54 A1
Ansty Cl ROTT BN2 ....47 E5
Antioch St LEWES BN7 ....17 E4
Antony Cl SEAF BN25 ....69 H2
Anvil Cl PTSD BN41 ....25 F5
Anzac Cl PEAHV BN10 ....63 E4
Appledore Rd ROTT BN2 ....29 F3
Applesham Av HOVE BN3 ....26 A5
Applesham Wy PTSD BN41 ....43 E1
Appletrees ANG/EP BN16 ....52 B5
The Approach BRI BN1 ....27 G4
April Cl FERR BN12 ....53 E5
Apsley Wy SALV BN13 ....35 G5
Aquarius Cl PEAHV BN10 ....67 E2
Aquila Pk SEAF BN25 ....71 E5
Arcade Buildings WTHG * BN11 ....5 F6
Archibald Rd WTHG BN11 ....56 C2
Ardale Cl WTHG BN11 ....54 D3
Ardingly Ct ROTT * BN2 ....3 J5
Ardingly Dr FERR BN12 ....53 H2
Ardingly Rd ROTT BN2 ....61 H5
Ardingly St ROTT BN2 ....3 J5
Ardsheal Cl FIN/BW BN14 ....37 G5
Ardsheal Rd FIN/BW BN14 ....37 G4
Argent Cl SEAF BN25 ....71 G1
Argyle Rd BRI BN1 ....45 H2
Ariadne Rd WTHG BN11 ....4 A7
Arlington Av FERR BN12 ....53 H5
Arlington Cl FERR BN12 ....53 H4
Arlington Crs ANG/EP BN16 ....52 B2
BRI BN1 ....29 E2
Arlington Gdns ROTT BN2 ....61 H3
Arnold St ROTT BN2 ....46 C3
Arnside Cl LAN/SOMP BN15 ....39 E5
Arthur St HOVE BN3 ....44 C1
Arun Cl LAN/SOMP BN15 ....39 E3
SALV BN13 ....36 A3
Arun Crs SALV BN13 ....36 A3
Arundel Cl SHOR BN43 ....42 A2
Arundel Dr East ROTT BN2 ....61 G4
Arundel Dr West ROTT BN2 ....61 F4
Arundel Gn LEWES BN7 ....16 D2
Arundel Ms ROTT * BN2 ....59 E1

Arundel Pl ROTT BN2 ....59 E1
Arundel Rd ANG/EP BN16 ....34 C2
NEWHV BN9 ....65 E4
PEAHV BN10 ....67 E1
ROTT BN2 ....59 E2
SALV BN13 ....35 H2
SEAF BN25 ....71 E5
Arundel Rd Central
PEAHV BN10 ....66 D1
Arundel Rd West PEAHV BN10 ....62 C5
Arundel St ROTT BN2 ....59 E2
Arundel Ter ROTT BN2 ....59 E2
Ashacre La SALV BN13 ....36 D3
Ashacre Ms SALV BN13 ....36 D3
Ashacre Wy SALV BN13 ....36 D3
Ashburnham Cl BRI BN1 ....29 E2
SALV BN13 ....35 H5
Ashburnham Dr BRI BN1 ....28 D1
Ash Cl FIN/BW BN14 ....18 C1
HOVE BN3 ....26 A4
Ashcombe La LEWES BN7...............32 A1
Ashcroft Cl SHOR BN43 ....42 A3
Ashdown Av ROTT BN2 ....61 F4
Ashdown Rd ROTT BN2 ....46 B2
WTHG BN11 ....5 F2
Ash Dr SEAF BN25 ....71 G5
Ashfold Av FIN/BW BN14 ....37 E1
Ashford Rd BRI BN1 ....28 A5
Ash Gv WTHG BN11 ....5 G4
Ashington Gdns PEAHV BN10 ....67 G2
Ashley Cl BRI BN1 ....13 G5
Ashlings Wy HOVE BN3 ....26 A5
SHOR BN43 ....41 H1
Ashmore Cl PEAHV BN10 ....63 F3
Ashton Ri ROTT BN2 ....3 J3
Ashurst Av ROTT BN2 ....62 A5
Ashurst Cl FERR BN12 ....53 H4
Ashurst Dr FERR BN12 ....53 H4
Ashurst Rd ROTT BN2 ....29 H5
SEAF BN25 ....72 D1
Ash Wk NEWHV BN9 ....68 B1
Ashwood Cl WTHG BN11 ....5 K1
Aspen Ct LAN/SOMP * BN15 ....57 E1
Athelstan Rd SALV BN13 ....55 F1
Atlingworth St ROTT BN2 ....3 K6
Attree Dr ROTT BN2 ....46 C4
Auckland Dr ROTT BN2 ....47 F1
Audrey Cl BRI BN1 ....27 G2
SEAF BN25 ....70 B3
Augusta Pl WTHG BN11 ....4 E6
Avalon Wy SALV BN13 ....36 B4
The Avenals ANG/EP BN16 ....34 A1
The Avenue FERR BN12 ....54 A1
LEWES BN7 ....16 D3
LEWES BN7 ....31 H2
ROTT BN2 ....61 D5
SHOR BN43 ....41 E1
Avery Cl PTSD BN41 ....24 D3
Avis Cl NEWHV BN9 ....65 E4
Avis Rd NEWHV BN9 ....64 D4
Avis Wy NEWHV BN9 ....65 E5
Avon Cl LAN/SOMP BN15 ....38 D4
Avondale Cl FERR BN12 ....54 B2
Avondale Rd HOVE BN3 ....45 F3
SEAF BN25 ....70 D5
Aymer Rd HOVE BN3 ....44 C4

B

Baden Rd ROTT BN2 ....46 D2
Badger Cl PTSD BN41 ....25 F5
Badgers Cl NEWHV BN9 ....68 C2
Badgers Copse SEAF BN25 ....70 B3
Badgers Dene LEWES BN7 ....51 F2
Badgers Fld PEAHV BN10 ....63 E4
Badger Wy BRI BN1 ....29 E1
Bainbridge Cl SEAF BN25 ....72 D1
Baker St BRI BN1 ....3 H1
Bakery Ms ROTT BN2 ....46 C1
Balcombe Av FIN/BW BN14 ....37 G2
Balcombe Rd PEAHV BN10 ....62 D5
Balfour Rd BRI BN1 ....27 H5
Balmoral Cl SEAF BN25 ....71 E2

Balsdean Rd ROTT BN2 ....48 B1
Bamford Cl ROTT BN2 ....29 G5
Bampfield St PTSD BN41 ....43 F2
Bank Pas STEY/UB BN44 ....7 F1
Bankside BRI BN1 ....27 E2
Bankside Ct BRI * BN1 ....27 E2
Bannings V ROTT BN2 ....61 H5
Banstead Cl FERR BN12 ....54 A4
Baranscraig Av BRI BN1 ....14 A5
Barbary La FERR BN12 ....53 E4
Barcombe Av SEAF BN25 ....71 G5
Barcombe Cl SEAF BN25 ....71 G5
Barcombe Rd BRI BN1 ....29 E3
Barfield Pk LAN/SOMP BN15 ....39 H4
Barley Cl PEAHV DN10 ....00 D3
Barn Cl LEWES BN7 ....32 A2
SALV BN13 ....36 D3
SEAF BN25 ....71 E2
Barnes Rd PTSD BN41 ....43 F2
Barnett Rd BRI BN1 ....28 B5
Barnet Wy HOVE BN3 ....26 A4
Barn Field Gdns ROTT BN2 ....46 C4
Barn Hatch Cl LEWES BN7 ....16 C4
Barn Ri BRI BN1 ....27 F2
SEAF BN25 ....71 E3
Barn Rd LEWES BN7 ....17 C1
Barons Cl SEAF BN25 ....70 A3
Barons Down Rd LEWES BN7 ....16 C4
Barons Wk LEWES BN7 ....16 C4
Barrhill Av BRI BN1 ....13 H5
Barrington Cl FERR BN12 ....54 A3
Barrington Rd FERR BN12 ....54 B3
Barrow Cl BRI BN1 ....28 C5
Barrowfield Cl HOVE BN3 ....27 E5
Barrowfield Dr HOVE BN3 ....27 E5
Barrow Hl BRI BN1 ....28 C5
Barry Wk ROTT BN2 ....46 C4
Bartholomews BRI BN1 ....3 G5
Bartholomew Sq BRI * BN1 ....3 F5
Barton Cl SALV BN13 ....37 E5
Bashfords La FIN/BW BN14 ....5 F1
Basin Rd North PTSD BN41 ....43 H4
Basin Rd South PTSD BN41 ....42 D4
Batemans Cl SALV BN13 ....35 H5
Batemans Rd ROTT BN2 ....48 C3
Bates Rd BRI BN1 ....27 H5
Bath Pl WTHG BN11 ....5 F6
Bath Rd WTHG BN11 ....4 A7
Bath St BRI BN1 ....2 E1
Battle Cl SEAF BN25 ....71 G3
Bavant Rd BRI BN1 ....27 G5
Baxter Rd LEWES BN7 ....16 D2
Baxter St ROTT BN2 ....46 C3
Bay Tree Cl SHOR BN43 ....42 A1
Bayview Rd PEAHV BN10 ....67 G3
Bay Vue Rd NEWHV BN9 ....68 D1
Baywood Gdns ROTT BN2 ....48 A1
Bazehill Rd ROTT BN2 ....61 E2
Beach Cl SEAF BN25 ....70 B5
Beachcroft Pl LAN/SOMP BN15 ......57 G1
Beach Gn SHOR BN43 ....40 D4
Beach Pde WTHG BN11 ....5 H5
Beach Rd NEWHV BN9 ....69 E2
SHOR BN43 ....41 E5
Beachside Cl FERR BN12 ....54 C4
Beacon Cl BRI BN1 ....28 A5
SEAF BN25 ....70 B3
Beacon Dr SEAF BN25 ....70 C3
Beacon Hl ROTT BN2 ....60 C2
Beacon Rd SEAF BN25 ....70 B4
Beaconsfield Pde BRI * BN1 ....46 A2
Beaconsfield Rd BRI BN1 ....46 A2
PTSD BN41 ....43 F2
Beaconsfield Vls BRI BN1 ....45 H1
Beal Crs BRI BN1 ....28 B5
Bear Rd ROTT BN2 ....46 C2
Bear Yd LEWES BN7 ....17 F3
Beatty Av BRI BN1 ....14 C3
Beaufort Ter ROTT BN2 ....46 C4
Beaumont Rd FIN/BW BN14 ....37 H5
Beccles Rd WTHG BN11 ....4 B4
Becket Rd FIN/BW BN14 ....55 E2
Beckett Wy LEWES BN7 ....17 E1
Beckley Cl ROTT BN2 ....47 E5
Beckworth Cl SALV BN13 ....35 H5

Bedford Pl *BRI* BN1 ......2 C4
Bedford Rw *WTHG* BN11 ......5 C5
Bedford Sq *BRI* BN1 ......2 C5
BedforThed St *ROTT* BN2 ......58 C1
Beech La *PTSD* BN41 ......24 D4
Beechers Rd *PTSD* BN41 ......24 D4
The Beeches *BRI* BN1 ......27 F4
Beeches Av *FIN/BW* BN14 ......37 H3
Beech Gv *LAN/SOMP* * BN15 ......39 H4
ROTT BN2 ......29 E4
Beechlands Cl *ANG/EP* BN16 ......52 A4
Beech Rd *FIN/BW* BN14 ......18 C1
Beech Vw *ANG/EP* BN16 ......34 A3
Beechwood Av *BRI* BN1 ......27 H3
SALV BN13 ......36 D3
Beechwood Cl *BRI* BN1 ......27 H3
Beeding Av *HOVE* BN3 ......26 B4
Beeding Cl *LAN/SOMP* BN15 ......39 F2
Beehive Cl *FERR* BN12 ......53 F4
Beehive La *FERR* BN12 ......53 E4
Bee Rd *PEAHV* BN10 ......63 E5
Belfast St *HOVE* BN3 ......44 D5
Belgrave Crs *SEAF* BN25 ......70 D3
Belgrave Pl *ROTT* BN2 ......58 D1
Belgrave Rd *SEAF* BN25 ......70 B4
Belgrave St *ROTT* BN2 ......3 J2
Belle Vue *WTHG* * BN11 ......4 E4
Bellevue Gdns *ROTT* BN2 ......46 C5
Bellingham Crs *HOVE* BN3 ......43 H2
Bell La *LEWES* BN7 ......16 D4
Bell Md *HOVE* * BN3 ......2 A1
Bellview Rd *SALV* BN13 ......37 E5
Belmont *BRI* BN1 ......45 E3
Belmont Ct *BRI* * BN1 ......45 G3
Belmont St *BRI* BN1 ......3 H1
Belsize Cl *WTHG* BN11 ......4 A3
Belsize Rd *WTHG* BN11 ......4 A3
Belton Rd *ROTT* BN2 ......46 B2
Belvedere Av *LAN/SOMP* BN15 ......39 F4
Belvedere Gdns *SEAF* BN25 ......71 E3
Belvedere Ter *HOVE* BN3 ......2 C3
Bembridge St *ROTT* BN2 ......46 C2
Benbow Cl *SHOR* BN43 ......41 F4
Benedict Cl *WTHG* BN11 ......56 D2
Benedict Dr *WTHG* BN11 ......56 C2
Benenden Cl *SEAF* BN25 ......71 E4
Benett Av *HOVE* BN3 ......26 D5
Benett Dr *HOVE* BN3 ......26 D5
Benfield Cl *PTSD* BN41 ......43 G2
Benfield Crs *PTSD* BN41 ......43 G1
Benfield Wy *PTSD* BN41 ......43 G1
Bengairn Av *BRI* BN1 ......14 A5
Bennett Rd *ROTT* BN2 ......59 E1
Bentham Rd *ROTT* BN2 ......46 C3
Berberis Ct *SHOR* BN43 ......41 F4
Beresford Rd *NEWHV* BN9 ......65 E4
ROTT BN2 ......46 D5
Bergamot Crs *SHOR* BN43 ......42 A1
Berkeley Rw *LEWES* BN7 ......16 C4
Berkeley Sq *WTHG* BN11 ......55 E3
Berkshire Ct *FERR* * BN12 ......53 H2
Bernard Pl *ROTT* BN2 ......46 C3
Bernard Rd *ROTT* BN2 ......46 C3
WTHG BN11 ......54 D1
Berriedale Av *HOVE* BN3 ......44 A4
Berriedale Cl *LAN/SOMP* BN15 ......39 E3
Berriedale Dr *LAN/SOMP* BN15 ......39 E3
Berry Cl *PEAHV* BN10 ......62 C4
Berwick Cl *SEAF* BN25 ......70 B4
Berwick Rd *ROTT* BN2 ......61 H2
Bessborough Ter
LAN/SOMP BN15 ......57 F1
Bevendean Av *ROTT* BN2 ......61 H4
Bevendean Crs *ROTT* BN2 ......29 E5
Bevendean Rd *ROTT* BN2 ......46 D2
Bexhill Rd *ROTT* BN2 ......48 B1
Bigwood Av *HOVE* BN3 ......45 F3
Billam Ter *ROTT* * BN2 ......3 J2
Birch Cl *LAN/SOMP* BN15 ......57 F1
Birches Cl *SALV* BN13 ......36 A5
Birch Grove Crs *BRI* BN1 ......28 A2
Birdham Pl *ROTT* * BN2 ......29 E4
Birdham Rd *ROTT* BN2 ......29 E4
Birkdale Cl *SALV* BN13 ......36 B4
Birkdale Rd *SALV* BN13 ......36 B4
Birling Cl *ROTT* BN2 ......46 D1
SEAF BN25 ......70 A4
Bishops Cl *SALV* BN13 ......55 E1
SEAF BN25 ......70 A4
Bishops Dr *LEWES* BN7 ......16 C4
Bishops Rd *HOVE* BN3 ......45 E1
Bishopstone Dr *ROTT* BN2 ......61 F3
Bishopstone Rd *SEAF* BN25 ......70 A2
Blackdown Rd *SALV* BN13 ......36 D3
Black Lion St *BRI* BN1 ......3 C6
Blackman St *BRI* BN1 ......3 G2
Blacksmiths Crs
LAN/SOMP BN15 ......38 D4

Blackthorn Cl *BRI* BN1 ......27 F4
PTSD BN41 ......25 F5
Blakeney Av *NEWHV* BN9 ......68 A2
Blaker St *ROTT* BN2 ......3 J5
Blatchington Cl *SEAF* BN25 ......70 D4
Blatchington Hl *SEAF* BN25 ......70 C4
Blatchington Rd *HOVE* BN3 ......44 C3
SEAF BN25 ......70 C5
Blenheim Ms *SALV* BN13 ......36 C4
Blenheim Pl *BRI* BN1 ......3 H3
Blenheim Rd *LAN/SOMP* BN15 ......57 F1
Blois Rd *LEWES* BN7 ......16 C1
Bloomsbury Pl *ROTT* BN2 ......58 C1
Bloomsbury St *ROTT* BN2 ......58 C1
Blue Haze Av *SEAF* BN25 ......71 F4
Bodiam Av *FERR* BN12 ......53 C3
ROTT BN2 ......47 H1
Bodiam Cl *ROTT* BN2 ......29 H5
SEAF BN25 ......71 C4
Bodmin Cl *SALV* BN13 ......36 B2
Bodmin Rd *SALV* BN13 ......36 B2
Bolney Av *PEAHV* BN10 ......67 E2
Bolney Rd *ROTT* BN2 ......29 F3
Bolsover Rd *HOVE* BN3 ......44 A3
SALV BN13 ......54 C2
Bonchurch Rd *ROTT* BN2 ......46 C2
Bond St *BRI* BN1 ......3 G4
Borough St *BRI* BN1 ......2 C4
Borrow King Cl *ROTT* BN2 ......46 D2
Bostal Rd *STEY/UB* BN44 ......6 C4
The Bostal *STEY/UB* BN44 ......8 C3
Bost Hl *FIN/BW* BN14 ......18 C4
Boston St *BRI* BN1 ......46 A3
Boughey Pl *LEWES* BN7 ......17 E1
The Boulevard *FERR* BN12 ......54 C1
SALV BN13 ......36 B5
The Boundary *SEAF* BN25 ......72 C1
Boundary Cl *WTHG* BN11 ......4 A6
Boundary Rd *LAN/SOMP* BN15 ......40 B5
ROTT BN2 ......59 E2
WTHG BN11 ......55 E4
Boundary & Station Roads
PTSD BN41 ......43 G4
Boundary Wy *ANG/EP* BN16 ......52 B3
Boundstone Cl
LAN/SOMP BN15 ......39 F3
Boundstone La
LAN/SOMP BN15 ......39 E4
Bourne Cl *SALV* BN13 ......35 H4
Bowden Ri *SEAF* BN25 ......70 C2
Bowness Av *LAN/SOMP* BN15 ......39 E5
Bowring Wy *ROTT* BN2 ......58 D1
Boxgrove *FERR* BN12 ......53 H1
Boxgrove Cl *LAN/SOMP* BN15 ......39 H2
Boyce's St *BRI* BN1 ......3 F5
Brackenbury Cl *PTSD* BN41 ......25 F5
Bracken Rd *SEAF* BN25 ......73 E1
Bradford Rd *LEWES* BN7 ......16 D3
Brading Rd *ROTT* BN2 ......46 C2
Braemore Rd *HOVE* BN3 ......44 A4
Braeside Av *BRI* BN1 ......13 H5
Bramber Av *HOVE* BN3 ......26 B4
PEAHV BN10 ......67 E2
Bramber Av North
PEAHV BN10 ......63 E5
Bramber Cl *LAN/SOMP* BN15 ......39 F2
PEAHV BN10 ......63 E5
SEAF BN25 ......72 D1
Bramber La *SEAF* BN25 ......72 D1
Bramber Rd *FIN/BW* BN14 ......38 A3
SEAF BN25 ......72 D1
STEY/UB BN44 ......7 F2
Bramble Cl *SALV* BN13 ......36 B3
Bramble Crs *SALV* BN13 ......36 B2
Brambledean Rd *PTSD* BN41 ......43 F3
Bramble La *SALV* BN13 ......36 B3
Bramble Ri *BRI* BN1 ......27 E2
Brambletyne Av *ROTT* BN2 ......61 H4
Brambletyne Cl *ANG/EP* BN16 ......34 A4
Bramble Wy *BRI* BN1 ......28 C1
Bramley Cl *FIN/BW* BN14 ......37 H3
Bramley Rd *FIN/BW* BN14 ......37 H4
Bramleys *LEWES* BN7 ......32 A2
Brands Cl *NEWHV* BN9 ......64 D5
Brangwyn Av *BRI* BN1 ......27 G1
Brangwyn Crs *BRI* BN1 ......27 G1
Brangwyn Dr *BRI* BN1 ......27 F1
Brangwyn Wy *BRI* BN1 ......27 G2
Brasslands Dr *PTSD* BN41 ......42 D1
Braybon Av *BRI* BN1 ......27 H3
Braypool La *BRI* BN1 ......13 F4
Brazen Cl *NEWHV* BN9 ......68 A1
Breach Cl *STEY/UB* BN44 ......7 F1
Bread St *BRI* BN1 ......3 G4
Brecon Cl *SALV* BN13 ......36 D3
Brede Cl *ROTT* BN2 ......47 E5
Brendon Rd *SALV* BN13 ......36 C2
Brentwood Crs *BRI* BN1 ......28 B4

Brentwood Rd *BRI* BN1 ......28 B4
Bretts Fld *PEAHV* BN10 ......63 E3
Brewer St *ROTT* BN2 ......46 B3
Briar Cl *ROTT* BN2 ......48 B2
Briarcroft Rd *ROTT* BN2 ......48 B3
The Bricky *PEAHV* BN10 ......63 F5
Bridge Cl *FERR* BN12 ......54 A2
LAN/SOMP BN15 ......39 G5
Bridge Rd *FIN/BW* BN14 ......4 B2
Bridge St *NEWHV* BN9 ......68 D1
Bridgewick Cl *LEWES* BN7 ......17 F1
Bridgnorth Cl *SALV* BN13 ......35 H5
Bridle Cl *STEY/UB* BN44 ......8 B2
Bridle Wy *PEAHV* BN10 ......62 C4
Brierley Gdns *LAN/SOMP* BN15 ......39 H4
Brigden St *BRI* BN1 ......45 H3
Brighton Pl *BRI* BN1 ......3 C5
Brighton Rd *LEWES* BN7 ......16 A5
NEWHV BN9 ......68 B2
SHOR BN43 ......40 D4
WTHG BN11 ......5 C5
Brighton Sq *BRI* * BN1 ......3 G5
Brills La *BRI* BN1 ......3 G6
Brisbane Cl *SALV* BN13 ......35 H4
Bristol Av *LAN/SOMP* BN15 ......40 B5
Bristol Gdns *ROTT* BN2 ......59 E1
Bristol Ga *ROTT* BN2 ......58 D1
Bristol Ms *ROTT* BN2 ......59 E1
Bristol Pl *ROTT* BN2 ......59 E1
Bristol Rd *ROTT* BN2 ......59 E1
Bristol St *ROTT* BN2 ......59 E1
Brittania Cl *ROTT* BN2 ......59 C2
Brittany Rd *FIN/BW* BN14 ......55 C1
HOVE BN3 ......43 H4
Broadfields *ROTT* BN2 ......29 E4
Broadfields Rd *ROTT* BN2 ......29 E4
Broad Gn *ROTT* BN2 ......48 C4
Broad Rig Av *HOVE* BN3 ......25 H3
Broad St *ROTT* BN2 ......3 H6
SEAF BN25 ......70 C5
Broadview Gdns *SALV* BN13 ......36 C2
Broadwater Bvd
FIN/BW BN14 ......37 G5
Broadwater Hall
FIN/BW * BN14 ......4 C1
Broadwater Ms
FIN/BW * BN14 ......37 H5
Broadwater Rd
FIN/BW BN14 ......37 H5
Broadwater St East
FIN/BW BN14 ......37 H5
Broadwater St West
FIN/BW BN14 ......37 G4
Broadwater Wy
FIN/BW BN14 ......37 H4
The Broadway
LAN/SOMP BN15 ......40 B5
Brock Ct *SEAF* * BN25 ......71 C5
Brockley Cl *FIN/BW* BN14 ......4 C1
Bromley Rd *ROTT* BN2 ......46 B3
SEAF BN25 ......71 F4
Brompton Cl *BRI* BN1 ......27 C1
Brook Barn Wy *FERR* BN12 ......54 C4
Brook Cl *WTHG* BN11 ......56 C1
Brookdean Rd *WTHG* BN11 ......56 D2
Brooker Pl *HOVE* BN3 ......44 C3
Brooker St *HOVE* BN3 ......44 C3
Brook La *FERR* BN12 ......53 E4
Brooklyn Av *WTHG* BN11 ......54 D3
Brooklyn Chambers
WTHG * BN11 ......54 D3
Brooklyn Rd *SEAF* BN25 ......70 C5
Brooks Cl *LEWES* BN7 ......17 F2
NEWHV BN9 ......68 C2
Brookside *NEWHV* BN9 ......64 B3
Brookside Cl *FERR* BN12 ......53 E2
Brookside Rd *ANG/EP* BN16 ......52 D5
Brooks La *LEWES* BN7 ......17 F2
Brooks Rd *LEWES* BN7 ......17 F2
Brook St *LEWES* BN7 ......17 E2
Brook Wy *LAN/SOMP* BN15 ......39 H5
Broomfield Av *FIN/BW* BN14 ......37 H5
PEAHV BN10 ......66 B1
Broomfield Dr *PTSD* BN41 ......25 E3
Brou Cl *ANG/EP* BN16 ......52 B4
Brougham Rd *WTHG* BN11 ......56 C2
The Brow *ROTT* BN2 ......48 B2
Browning Rd *LAN/SOMP* BN15 ......39 G2
WTHG BN11 ......4 B3
Brownleaf Rd *ROTT* BN2 ......48 C4
Bruce Av *WTHG* BN11 ......54 D3
Bruce Vls *WTHG* * BN11 ......54 D2
Bruce Wy *WTHG* BN11 ......54 D2
Brunswick Ms *HOVE* BN3 ......2 A4
Brunswick Pl *HOVE* BN3 ......2 A3
Brunswick Rd *HOVE* BN3 ......2 B3
SHOR BN43 ......41 F3
WTHG BN11 ......4 C7

Brunswick Sq *HOVE* BN3 ......2 A4
Brunswick St East *HOVE* BN3 ......2 A3
Brunswick St West *HOVE* BN3 ......2 A3
Brunswick Ter *HOVE* BN3 ......2 A4
Buci Crs *SHOR* BN43 ......42 A4
Buckhurst Cl *LEWES* BN7 ......17 E1
Buckhurst Rd *PEAHV* BN10 ......66 B1
Buckingham Av *SHOR* BN43 ......41 H3
Buckingham Cl *BRI* * BN1 ......2 D3
SEAF BN25 ......70 C3
SHOR BN43 ......41 H3
Buckingham Ms *SHOR* BN43 ......41 H3
Buckingham Pl *BRI* BN1 ......2 D2
Buckingham Rd *BRI* BN1 ......3 F3
SHOR BN43 ......41 H3
WTHG BN11 ......4 E3
Buckingham St *SHOR* BN43 ......41 H3
Buckland Rd *SEAF* BN25 ......70 C3
Buckle By-Pass *SEAF* BN25 ......70 A4
Buckle Cl *SEAF* BN25 ......70 A4
Buckle Dr *SEAF* BN25 ......70 A4
Buckle Ri *SEAF* BN25 ......70 A4
Buckler St *PTSD* BN41 ......43 F3
Buckley Cl *HOVE* BN3 ......26 A4
Buckthorn Cl *SEAF* BN25 ......71 C4
Buckwell Ct *LEWES* BN7 ......16 C4
Bulkington Av *FIN/BW* BN14 ......4 A1
Buller Rd *ROTT* BN2 ......46 C2
The Burchens *FIN/BW* * BN14 ......37 C2
Burford Cl *SALV* BN13 ......37 E3
Burley Cl *LAN/SOMP* * BN15 ......39 C1
Burlington Gdns *PTSD* BN41 ......43 C2
Burlington Rd *FERR* BN12 ......54 A2
Burlington St *ROTT* BN2 ......58 C1
Burlow Cl *ROTT* BN2 ......47 E5
Burnham Cl *ROTT* BN2 ......48 C2
Burnham Rd *SALV* BN13 ......36 C1
Burnside Crs *LAN/SOMP* BN15 ......39 E3
Burrell Av *LAN/SOMP* BN15 ......39 F3
Burrell Buildings
LAN/SOMP * BN15 ......39 F3
The Burrells *SHOR* BN43 ......41 H3
Burstead Cl *BRI* BN1 ......28 B3
Burton Vls *HOVE* BN3 ......45 F1
Burwash Cl *ANG/EP* BN16 ......52 B4
Burwash Rd *HOVE* BN3 ......26 B5
Bury Dr *FERR* BN12 ......53 H2
Bushby Cl *LAN/SOMP* BN15 ......39 E1
Bush Cl *PEAHV* BN10 ......62 C4
ROTT BN2 ......48 B2
Bush Farm Dr *PTSD* BN41 ......25 F3
Bush Rd *NEWHV* BN9 ......64 B4
Busticle La *LAN/SOMP* BN15 ......39 E3
Butchers La *NEWHV* * BN9 ......68 C2
Bute St *ROTT* BN2 ......46 D2
Butler Ct *SALV* BN13 ......36 C2
Buttercup Wk *BRI* BN1 ......28 C1
Button Ct *ROTT* * BN2 ......46 D2
Butts Rd *STHW* BN42 ......42 C2
Buxted Ri *BRI* BN1 ......28 B3
Buxton Rd *BRI* BN1 ......45 C2
Bydown *SEAF* BN25 ......71 E4
The Byeways *SEAF* BN25 ......70 C5
Byron Rd *WTHG* BN11 ......4 E2
Byron St *HOVE* BN3 ......44 C4
The Byway *BRI* BN1 ......29 E2
Byworth Cl *ROTT* BN2 ......47 E5

C

Caburn Crs *LEWES* BN7 ......16 D3
Caburn Rd *HOVE* BN3 ......45 E1
Cairo Av *PEAHV* BN10 ......66 C4
Cairo Av South *PEAHV* BN10 ......66 C5
Caister's Cl *HOVE* BN3 ......45 E3
Caledonian Pl *WTHG* * BN11 ......4 E4
Caledonian Rd *ROTT* BN2 ......46 B3
Callon Cl *SALV* * BN13 ......35 H4
Cambridge Gv *HOVE* BN3 ......45 E3
Cambridge Rd *HOVE* BN3 ......2 B4
WTHG BN11 ......4 D3
Camden St *PTSD* BN41 ......43 G3
Camelford St *ROTT* BN2 ......3 J5
Campbell Ct *FERR* * BN12 ......53 H2
Campbell Rd *BRI* BN1 ......45 H1
Canada Cl *PEAHV* BN10 ......62 D4
Canberra Rd *SALV* BN13 ......36 A4
Canfield Cl *ROTT* BN2 ......46 D3
Canfield Rd *ROTT* BN2 ......46 D3
Canning St *ROTT* BN2 ......46 C3
Cannon Pl *BRI* BN1 ......3 E5
Canterbury Ct *SALV* BN13 ......54 C1
Canterbury Dr *ROTT* BN2 ......46 D4
Canterbury Rd *SALV* BN13 ......54 C1
Cantercrow Hl *NEWHV* BN9 ......65 E5
Capel Av *PEAHV* BN10 ......67 E2

arden Av *BRI* BN1 ....27 G3
arden Cl *BRI* BN1 ....28 A1
arden Crs *BRI* BN1 ....28 A1
arlin Hl *BRI* BN1 ....28 B2
rey Down *PEAHV* BN10.........62 D4
arisbrooke Cl
  LAN/SOMP BN15 ....39 G2
arisbrooke Dr *SALV* BN13 ......35 H5
arisbrooke Rd *ROTT* BN2 ....46 D3
arlisle Rd *HOVE* BN3 ....44 B4
arlton Cl *SEAF* BN25 ....70 B4
arlton Hl *ROTT* BN2 ....3 J4
arlton Rd *SEAF* BN25 ....70 B4
arlton Ter *HOVE* BN3 ....43 G2
arlyle Av *ROTT* BN2 ....46 D1
arlyle St *ROTT* BN2 ....46 C3
arnegie Cl *FIN/BW* BN14 ....37 G5
arnegie Gdns *LAN/SOMP* BN14....37 G5
arnegie Rd *FIN/BW* BN14 ....37 G5
arnforth Rd *LAN/SOMP* BN15 ..38 D5
arol Cl *BRI* BN1 ....27 H1
aroline Cl *SEAF* BN25 ....70 B3
aron Cl *LAN/SOMP* BN15........39 G3
arol Cl *BRI* BN1 ....27 H1
astle Banks *LEWES* BN7 ....17 E3
astle Cl *SALV* BN13 ....54 D1
  STEY/UB BN44 ....7 G1
astle Ditch La *LEWES* * BN7....17 E3
astle La *STEY/UB* BN44 ....7 G2
astle Precincts *LEWES* BN7 ....17 E3
astle Rd *SALV* BN13 ....54 D1
astle Sq *BRI* BN1 ....3 G5
astle St *BRI* BN1 ....2 D4
astle Ter *LEWES* * BN7 ....17 E3
astle Wy *SALV* BN13 ....54 D1
  STEY/UB BN44 ....7 G1
atherine V *ROTT* BN2 ....48 C2
he Causeway *FERR* BN12 ....54 B2
  ROTT BN2 ....46 D4
  SEAF BN25 ....72 C1
avell Av *PEAHV* BN10 ....66 D1
avell Av North *PEAHV* BN10....63 E5
avendish Cl *FERR* BN12 ....54 B2
  PEAHV BN10 ....62 D5
avendish Ms *HOVE* * BN3 ....2 B4
  WTHG * BN11 ....4 C6
avendish Pl *BRI* BN1 ....2 E3
avendish St *ROTT* BN2 ....3 J5
ecilian Av *FIN/BW* BN14 ....55 H1
ecil Pashley Wy *SHOR* BN43 ...40 C3
ecil Rd *LAN/SOMP* BN15........57 G1
edar Av *SALV* BN13 ....36 D4
edar Cl *FERR* BN12 ....53 E4
  LAN/SOMP BN15 ....57 F1
  SALV BN13 ....36 D4
he Cedars *BRI* * BN1 ....27 G4
  PEAHV BN10 ....63 E4
  ROTT * BN2 ....46 B2
edars Gdns *BRI* BN1 ....27 F4
edarwell Cl *NEWHV* BN9 ....64 B3
entral Av *FIN/BW* BN14 ....18 D4
  PEAHV BN10 ....66 C1
entrecourt Cl *FIN/BW* BN14......4 D1
entrecourt Rd *FIN/BW* BN14 ....4 D1
enturion Rd *BRI* BN1 ....2 E3
hadborn Cl *ROTT* BN2 ....58 D1
haffinch Cl *SALV* BN13 ....36 A5
hailey Av *ROTT* BN2 ....61 E4
hailey Crs *ROTT* BN2 ....62 A4
hailey Rd *BRI* BN1 ....29 E3
halet Cl *FERR* BN12 ....53 E5
halet Gdns *FERR* BN12 ....53 E4
halet Rd *FERR* BN12 ....53 E4
halfont Dr *HOVE* BN3 ....27 E4
halfont Wy *SALV* BN13 ....36 B5
halkland Ri *ROTT* BN2 ....48 C2
halky Rd *PTSD* BN41 ....24 D4
halloners Cl *ROTT* BN2 ....60 D1
halloners Ms *ROTT* BN2 ....60 D3
halvington Cl *BRI* BN1 ....29 E1
  SEAF BN25 ....70 D2
hampions Rw *HOVE* * BN3 .....45 F3
hanctonbury Dr *SHOR* BN43 ...41 G1
hanctonbury Rd *HOVE* BN3 ....45 G3
hancton Cl *HOVE* BN3 ....45 G3
hancton View Rd *WTHG* BN11 ..54 D2
handlers Wy *STEY/UB* BN44 .....7 E1
handos Rd *WTHG* BN11 ....1 E6
hannel Vw *STHW* BN42 ....42 C3
hannel View Rd *ROTT* BN2 .....47 H2
hantry Rd *SALV* BN13 ....37 G4
hapel Cl *SEAF* BN25 ....70 C4
hapel Hl *LEWES* BN7 ....17 G3
hapel Ms *HOVE* BN3 ....2 B4
hapel Pl *PTSD* BN41 ....43 F3
hapel Rd *PTSD* BN41 ....43 E3
  WTHG BN11 ....4 E3
hapel St *NEWHV* BN9 ....68 D1

ROTT BN2 ....3 J5
Chapel Ter *ROTT* BN2 ....58 D1
Chappell Cft *WTHG* * BN11 ......4 B4
Charlecote Rd *WTHG* BN11 ......5 C4
Charles Cl *HOVE* BN3 ....26 C4
  SEAF BN25 ....70 B3
Charles St *ROTT* BN2 ....3 H6
Charlotte St *ROTT* BN2 ....3 K6
Charlston Av *NEWHV* BN9 ....68 A3
The Charltons *BRI* BN1 ....28 D1
Charlton St *STEY/UB* BN44 ....7 E1
Charmandean La
  FIN/BW BN14 ....37 H2
Charmandean Rd
  FIN/BW BN14 ....37 H4
Chartfield *HOVE* BN3 ....26 C5
Chartfield Wy *HOVE* * BN3 ......26 D5
Chartwell Cl *SEAF* BN25 ....70 C2
Chartwell Rd *LAN/SOMP* BN15 ..39 F5
The Chase *FIN/BW* BN14 ....18 C2
Chatham Pl *BRI* BN1 ....2 E1
  SEAF BN25 ....72 C1
Chatham Rd *WTHG* BN11 ....56 C2
Chatsmore Crs *FERR* BN12 .....53 G2
Chatsworth Av *PEAHV* BN10 ...62 C4
Chatsworth Cl *PEAHV* BN10 ....62 C5
Chatsworth Pk *PEAHV* BN10 ...62 D4
Chatsworth Rd *BRI* BN1 ....45 G2
  WTHG BN11 ....5 F5
Chatsworth Sq *HOVE* BN3 ....2 A1
Chaucer Rd *WTHG* BN11 ....4 B3
Cheal Cl *SHOR* BN43 ....41 G4
Cheapside *BRI* BN1 ....3 G2
Chelston Av *HOVE* BN3 ....43 H3
Cheltenham Pl *BRI* BN1 ....3 H3
Chelwood Av *FERR* BN12 ....54 A4
Chelwood Cl *BRI* BN1 ....28 C1
Chene Rd *PEAHV* BN10 ....67 H2
Chepstow Ct *BRI* * BN1 ....29 F2
Cherry Gdns *SALV* BN13 ....36 C1
Cherry Tree Cl *SALV* BN13 ......36 B3
Cherry Wk *SALV* BN13 ....36 C1
Cherwell Rd *SALV* BN13 ....36 A2
Chesham Cl *FERR* BN12 ....54 C3
Chesham Pl *ROTT* BN2 ....58 D1
Chesham Rd *ROTT* BN2 ....58 D1
Chesham St *ROTT* BN2 ....58 D1
Chesley Cl *SALV* BN13 ....36 A4
Chesswood Cl *WTHG* BN11 ......5 K1
Chesswood Rd *WTHG* BN11 .....5 H2
Chester Av *LAN/SOMP* BN15 ..57 G1
  WTHG BN11 ....5 K2
Chesterfield Rd *FERR* BN12 ....54 B2
Chester Ter *BRI* BN1 ....46 A1
Chesterton Av *SEAF* BN25 ......71 F5
Chesterton Dr *SEAF* BN25 ......71 F5
Chestnut Cl *ANG/EP* BN16 ......52 A4
The Chestnuts *ROTT* * BN2 .....46 B2
Chestnut Wk *FERR* BN12 ....53 H1
Chestnut Wy *NEWHV* BN9 ....68 B3
Cheviot Cl *ANG/EP* BN16.........52 A3
  SALV BN13 ....36 C2
Cheviot Rd *SALV* BN13 ....36 C2
Chichester Cl *HOVE* BN3 ....26 A3
  PEAHV BN10 ....67 H1
  ROTT * BN2 ....58 D1
  ROTT BN2 ....61 G4
Chichester Ct *WTHG* * BN11 ...55 E4
Chichester Dr East *ROTT* BN2 ..61 G5
Chichester Dr West *ROTT* BN2..61 F4
Chichester Pl *ROTT* BN2 ....58 D1
Chichester Rd *SEAF* BN25 ....70 C5
Chichester Ter *ROTT* BN2 ....58 D1
Chiddingley Cl *ROTT* BN2 ....47 F5
Chilgrove Cl *FERR* BN12 ....53 H2
Chiltern Cl *ANG/EP* BN16 ....52 A3
  SHOR BN43 ....42 A2
Chiltern Crs *SALV* BN13 ....36 C2
Chiltington Cl *ROTT* BN2 ....61 G3
Chiltington Wy *ROTT* BN2 ....61 G3
Chippers Cl *SALV* BN13 ....54 D1
Chippers Rd *SALV* BN13 ....36 D5
Chippers Wk *SALV* * BN13 ......54 D1
Chorley Av *ROTT* BN2 ....61 F3
Chrisdory Rd *PTSD* BN41 ....24 C4
Christchurch Rd *WTHG* BN11 ....4 E3
Christie Rd *LEWES* BN7 ....16 C3
Church Cl *BRI* BN1 ....27 H2
  LAN/SOMP BN15 ....39 G2
  SALV BN13 ....35 F1
  STEY/UB BN44 ....8 A1
Church Farm Wk
  STEY/UB BN44 ....8 A1
Church Gn *SHOR* BN43 ....42 A3
Church Hl *BRI* BN1 ....27 G1
  NEWHV BN9 ....68 C1
Church House Cl *STHW* BN42 ..42 C1
Churchill Rd *LEWES* BN7 ....16 D1

Churchill Sq *BRI* * BN1 ....2 E4
Church La *FERR* BN12 ....53 E3
  LAN/SOMP BN15 ....38 C3
  LEWES BN7 ....17 E2
  LEWES BN7 ....31 H1
  SEAF BN25 ....72 C1
  STEY/UB BN44 ....7 F1
  STEY/UB BN44 ....8 A2
  STHW BN42 ....42 A2
Church Pl *ROTT* BN2 ....59 E1
Church Rd *HOVE* BN3 ....44 D4
  PTSD BN41 ....43 F3
  SALV BN13 ....37 E5
Church Rw *LEWES* * BN7 ....17 E3
Church St *BRI* BN1 ....2 E3
  PTSD BN41 ....43 F3
  SEAF BN25 ....70 C5
  SHOR BN43 ....41 F3
  STEY/UB BN44 ....7 F1
Church Wk *WTHG* BN11 ....5 K4
Church Way *SALV* BN13 ....37 E5
Church Way Cl *SALV* BN13 ......37 E5
Chute Av *SALV* BN13 ....36 C1
Chute Wy *SALV* BN13 ....36 C1
Chyngton Av *SEAF* BN25 ....71 F4
Chyngton Gdns *SEAF* BN25 .....71 F4
Chyngton La *SEAF* BN25 ....71 G5
Chyngton La North *SEAF* BN25..71 G5
Chyngton Pl *SEAF* BN25 ....73 F1
Chyngton Rd *SEAF* BN25 ....73 E1
Chyngton Wy *SEAF* BN25 ....73 G1
Cinquefoil *PEAHV* BN10 ....63 E5
Cinque Ports Wy *SEAF* BN25 ...71 H4
The Circle *ANG/EP* BN16 ....52 A5
Circus St *ROTT* BN2 ....3 H4
Cissbury Av *FIN/BW* BN14 ....18 D5
  PEAHV BN10 ....67 G2
Cissbury Crs *ROTT* BN2 ....62 A4
Cissbury Dr *FIN/BW* BN14 ....18 D5
Cissbury Gdns *FIN/BW* BN14 ...19 E4
Cissbury Rd *FERR* BN12 ....53 E2
  FIN/BW BN14 ....37 G4
  HOVE BN3 ....45 F3
Clapham Cl *SALV* BN13 ....35 F1
Clapham Common *SALV* BN13 ..35 E2
Claremont Rd *NEWHV* BN9 ......65 F4
  SEAF BN25 ....70 B5
Clarence Gdns *BRI* BN1 ....2 D4
Clarence Ms *SEAF* * BN25 ......70 C5
Clarence Sq *BRI* BN1 ....2 E4
Clarendon Pl *PTSD* BN41 ....43 G4
  ROTT BN2 ....58 C1
Clarendon Rd *FIN/BW* BN14 ....38 A4
  HOVE BN3 ....44 C3
  SHOR BN43 ....42 A3
Clarendon Ter *ROTT* BN2 ....58 D1
Clarendon Vls *HOVE* BN3 ....44 C3
Clare Rd *LEWES* BN7 ....16 C2
Clarke Av *HOVE* BN3 ....26 B4
Clayfields *PEAHV* BN10 ....66 D1
Clays Hl *STEY/UB* BN44 ....7 G2
Clayton Rd *ROTT* BN2 ....46 D3
Clayton Wy *HOVE* BN3 ....26 B4
Clementine Av *SEAF* BN25 ......70 B3
Clermont Rd *BRI* BN1 ....27 F5
Clermont Ter *BRI* BN1 ....27 G5
Cleveland Cl *SALV* BN13 ....36 B2
Cleveland Rd *BRI* BN1 ....46 A1
  SALV BN13 ....36 A2
Cleve Ter *LEWES* BN7 ....16 D4
The Cliff *ROTT* BN2 ....59 F1
Cliff Ap *ROTT* BN2 ....59 F1
Cliff Av *PEAHV* BN10 ....67 G3
Cliff Cl *SEAF* BN25 ....72 D2
Cliffe High St *LEWES* BN7 ....17 F3
Cliff Gdns *PEAHV* BN10 ....62 B5
  SEAF BN25 ....72 D2
Cliff Park *PEAHV* BN10 ....67 H1
Cliff Rd *ROTT* BN2 ....59 F2
  STEY/UB BN44 ....7 F2
Clifton Ct *WTHG* * BN11 ....4 D3
Clifton Gdns *WTHG* * BN11 ....4 D3
Clifton Hl *BRI* BN1 ....2 D3
Clifton Ms *BRI* * BN1 ....2 D3
Clifton Pl *BRI* BN1 ....2 D3
Clifton Rd *NEWHV* BN9 ....68 D1
  WTHG BN11 ....2 D3
Clifton St *BRI* BN1 ....3 F2
Clifton Ter *BRI* BN1 ....2 D3
Clifton Wy *PEAHV* BN10 ....62 C5
Clinton La *SEAF* BN25 ....70 C5
Clinton Pl *SEAF* BN25 ....70 C5
Clive Av *FERR* BN12 ....54 B3
Clivedale Gdns *STEY/UB* BN44...7 F1
Cloisters *NEWHV* BN9 ....68 C1
The Close *BRI* BN1 ....27 F2

LAN/SOMP BN15 ....57 H1
NEWHV BN9 ....65 F3
SEAF BN25 ....72 D1
SHOR BN43 ....41 F2
Clover La *FERR* BN12 ....53 E4
Clovers End *BRI* BN1 ....14 B5
Clover Wy *PTSD* BN41 ....25 F5
Club Wk *ANG/EP* BN16 ....52 A5
Cluny St *LEWES* BN7 ....17 E4
Clyde Cl *SALV* BN13 ....36 A2
Clyde Rd *BRI* BN1 ....46 A2
  SALV BN13 ....36 A3
Clyde Ter *STEY/UB* * BN44 ....7 G1
Coach House Ms *WTHG* BN11 ...4 D5
Coastal Rd *ANG/EP* BN16 ....52 B5
Cobden Rd *ROTT* BN2 ....46 C3
  WTHG BN11 ....4 C4
Cobton Dr *HOVE* BN3 ....26 C4
Cockshut Rd *LEWES* BN7 ....17 E5
Cokeham Gdns
  LAN/SOMP BN15 ....39 E4
Cokeham La *LAN/SOMP* BN15..39 E3
Cokeham Rd *LAN/SOMP* BN15..39 E3
Colbourne Av *ROTT* BN2 ....28 C5
Colbourne Rd *HOVE* BN3 ....2 C1
Coldean La *BRI* BN1 ....14 C4
Coldharbour La *SALV* BN13 .....34 D1
Colebrook Cl *WTHG* BN11 ....5 K2
Colebrook Rd *BRI* BN1 ....27 F5
  STHW BN42 ....42 D3
Coleman Av *HOVE* BN3 ....44 A3
Coleman St *ROTT* BN2 ....3 K1
Coleridge Cl *FERR* BN12 ....53 H2
Coleridge Crs *FERR* BN12 ....53 G2
Coleridge Rd *FERR* BN12 ....53 H2
Coleridge St *HOVE* BN3 ....44 C2
Colgate Cl *ROTT* BN2 ....47 F4
Colindale Rd *FERR* BN12 ....53 E3
Colindale Rd North *FERR* BN12..53 E3
College Cl *PTSD* BN41 ....24 D4
College Gdns *ROTT* BN2 ....58 C1
  WTHG BN11 ....5 E3
College Hl *STEY/UB* BN44 ....7 F1
College Pl *ROTT* BN2 ....58 C1
College Rd *ROTT* BN2 ....58 C1
  SEAF BN25 ....72 C1
  STEY/UB BN44 ....8 C3
College St *ROTT* BN2 ....58 C1
College Ter *ROTT* BN2 ....46 C5
Collingwood Cl *PEAHV* BN10 ...63 E4
Collingwood Ct *SHOR* BN43 ....41 F4
Collingwood Rd *ROTT* BN2 ......54 A1
Colne Cl *SALV* BN13 ....36 A2
Columbia Dr *SALV* BN13 ....36 A4
Colvill Av *SHOR* BN43 ....40 D2
Combe Dr *STEY/UB* BN44 ....7 F4
Commerce Wy
  LAN/SOMP BN15 ....39 E5
Compass Ct *PTSD* * BN41 ....24 D4
Compton Av *BRI* BN1 ....2 E2
  FERR BN12 ....53 H3
Compton Rd *BRI* BN1 ....45 F3
The Compts *PEAHV* BN10 ....62 D4
Coney Furlong *PEAHV* BN10 ...63 F4
Congreve Rd *FIN/BW* BN14 .....56 A1
Coniston Cl *LAN/SOMP* BN15 ..39 E4
Coniston Rd *FERR* BN12 ....54 A1
Connaught Av *SHOR* BN43 ......41 E2
Connaught Rd *HOVE* BN3 ....44 C4
  SEAF BN25 ....70 A5
Connaught Ter *HOVE* BN3 ....44 D3
Connell Dr *ROTT* BN2 ....48 C3
Convent Gdns *FIN/BW* BN14 ...18 C1
Conway Pl *HOVE* BN3 ....44 D2
Conway St *HOVE* BN3 ....44 D2
Cooksbridge Rd *ROTT* BN2 .....47 E4
Coolham Dr *ROTT* BN2 ....47 E4
Coombe Dro *STEY/UB* BN44 .....7 F2
Coombe Lea *HOVE* * BN3 ....45 E4
Coombe Ri *FIN/BW* BN14 ....19 E3
  ROTT BN2 ....61 H2
Coombe Rd *LEWES* * BN7 ....17 G2
  ROTT BN2 ....46 D1
  STEY/UB BN44 ....7 E2
Coombes Rd *LAN/SOMP* BN15..22 A1
Coombe Ter *ROTT* BN2 ....46 C1
Coombe V *ROTT* BN2 ....61 H2
Copse Hl *BRI* BN1 ....27 F2
Copthorne Cl *SALV* BN13 ....37 E3
Copthorne Hl *SALV* BN13 ....36 D3
Corbyn Crs *SHOR* BN43 ....41 G3
Cordons *LEWES* BN7 ....31 H4
Corfe Cl *SALV* BN13 ....35 H5
Cornelius Av *NEWHV* BN9 ....68 A3
Corner Garth *FERR* BN12 ....53 F4
Cornfield Cl *SEAF* BN25 ....70 D5
Cornfield Rd *SEAF* BN25 ....70 D5
Cornford Cl *PTSD* BN41 ....25 F5

Cornwall Av PEAHV BN10 ......67 C3
Cornwall Gdns BRI BN1 ......27 G4
Coronation St ROTT BN2 ......46 C3
Corsica Cl SEAF BN25 ......72 D2
Corsica Rd SEAF BN25 ......72 D2
Cortis Av FIN/BW BN14 ......37 C5
Cote St SALV BN13 ......36 A1
Cotswold Cl SALV BN13 ......36 C2
Cotswold Pl ROTT * BN2 ......47 F5
Cotswold Rd SALV BN13 ......36 D3
The Cotswolds STHW BN42 ......42 C3
Cotswold Wy LAN/SOMP BN6 ......52 A3
Cottage Bush Cl PTSD BN41 ......25 G5
Cottage Cl NEWHV BN9 ......64 D4
Cottenham Rd WTHG BN11 ......5 J2
County Oak Av BRI BN1 ......28 B1
The Course LEWES BN7 ......16 B4
Court Cl BRI BN1 ......13 G5
Court Farm Cl NEWHV BN9 ......64 B2
Court Farm Rd HOVE BN3 ......26 B5
  NEWHV BN9 ......68 C3
  ROTT BN2 ......60 C2
Courtfields LAN/SOMP BN15 ......39 F5
Courtlands Cl FERR BN12 ......54 C4
Courtlands Wy FERR BN12 ......54 C4
Court Ord Rd ROTT BN2 ......60 C2
Court Rd LEWES BN7 ......17 F4
The Courtyard WTHG * BN11 ......4 A3
Coventry Ct WTHG * BN11 ......55 E3
Coventry St BRI BN1 ......45 G2
The Covers SEAF BN25 ......72 D1
Cowden Rd ROTT BN2 ......61 H5
Cowdens Cl HOVE BN3 ......25 H3
Cowdray Cl FERR BN12 ......54 B4
Cowdray Ct FERR * BN12 ......53 H5
Cowdray Dr FERR BN12 ......54 B4
Cowfold Rd ROTT BN2 ......47 E5
Cowley Dr LAN/SOMP BN15 ......39 H5
  ROTT BN2 ......48 C4
Cowper Rd WTHG BN11 ......4 B4
Cowper St HOVE BN3 ......44 C3
Crabtree Ar LAN/SOMP * BN15 ......39 G4
Crabtree Av BRI BN1 ......28 A2
Crabtree La LAN/SOMP BN15 ......39 G4
Cradle Hill Rd SEAF BN25 ......71 G2
Cradock Rd SALV BN13 ......36 B2
Craignair Av BRI BN1 ......13 H5
Cranbourne St BRI BN1 ......2 E4
Cranedown LEWES BN7 ......16 C5
Cranleigh Av ROTT BN2 ......61 F4
Cranleigh Rd FIN/BW BN14 ......37 F5
Cranmer Av HOVE BN3 ......44 B1
Cranmer Cl LEWES BN7 ......17 F2
Cranmer Rd SALV BN13 ......55 E2
Cranworth Rd WTHG BN11 ......5 J2
Craven Pl ROTT * BN2 ......46 D5
Craven Rd ROTT BN2 ......46 D4
Crawley Rd BRI BN1 ......28 D1
Crayford Rd ROTT BN2 ......47 E5
The Crescent ANG/EP * BN16 ......52 A5
  LAN/SOMP BN15 ......57 C1
  NEWHV BN9 ......65 F4
  ROTT BN2 ......29 E5
  STEY/UB BN44 ......7 F2
  STHW BN42 ......42 D2
Crescent Cl ROTT BN2 ......48 C2
Crescent Dr North ROTT BN2 ......48 C3
Crescent Dr South ROTT BN2 ......48 C4
Crescent Pl ROTT BN2 ......58 C1
Crescent Rd ROTT BN2 ......46 B2
  WTHG BN11 ......4 D5
Crespin Wy BRI BN1 ......46 C1
Cresta Rd NEWHV BN9 ......68 A2
Crest Rd NEWHV BN9 ......65 F4
Crest Wy PTSD BN41 ......25 F4
The Crestway BRI BN1 ......46 C1
Crestway Pde BRI * BN1 ......28 C5
Cricketers Pde FIN/BW * BN14 ......37 H4
Cricketfield Rd SEAF BN25 ......72 C1
Cripps Av PEAHV BN10 ......63 F4
Cripps La STEY/UB BN44 ......7 C1
Crisp Rd LEWES BN7 ......16 C1
Crockhurst Hl SALV BN13 ......36 D2
Crocks Dean PEAHV BN10 ......63 F3
Croft Av STHW BN42 ......42 D3
Croft Ct SEAF BN25 ......70 C5
Croft Dr ROTT BN2 ......48 C4
Crofters Wd STEY/UB BN44 ......7 H2
The Croft ANG/EP BN16 ......52 A4
  BRI * BN1 ......45 G2
Croft La SEAF BN25 ......70 C5
Croft Rd BRI BN1 ......27 G4
Cromleigh Wy STHW BN42 ......24 C5
Cromwell Rd HOVE BN3 ......45 E3
Cromwell St ROTT BN2 ......46 C3
Crooked La SEAF BN25 ......72 D1
Crosby Cl SALV BN13 ......36 B4
Croshaw Cl LAN/SOMP BN15 ......39 F5

Crossbush Rd ROTT BN2 ......47 E4
Cross La FIN/BW BN14 ......18 C1
Cross Rd STHW BN42 ......42 B2
Crossroad Cl STHW BN42 ......42 B2
Cross St BRI BN1 ......46 A3
  HOVE BN3 ......2 B4
  WTHG BN11 ......4 D2
Cross Wy LEWES BN7 ......16 C3
The Crossway BRI BN1 ......28 B5
  PTSD BN41 ......25 E5
Crossways ANG/EP BN16 ......52 B3
Crossways Av FERR BN12 ......53 G1
Crouchfield Cl SEAF * BN25 ......72 D1
Crouch La SEAF BN25 ......72 C1
Crowborough Dr FERR BN12 ......53 H3
Crowborough Rd ROTT BN2 ......61 H5
Crowhurst Rd BRI BN1 ......14 B5
Crown Buildings
  LAN/SOMP * BN15 ......57 E1
Crown Cl HOVE * BN3 ......2 A2
Crown Gdns BRI * BN1 ......3 F3
Crown Hl SEAF BN25 ......70 C2
Crown Rd PTSD BN41 ......43 E2
  SHOR BN43 ......41 H2
Crown St BRI BN1 ......3 F3
Cubitt Ter ROTT * BN2 ......58 D1
Cuckfield Crs SALV BN13 ......36 D4
Cuckmere Rd NEWHV BN9 ......68 A3
  SEAF BN25 ......73 F1
Cuckmere Wy BRI BN1 ......28 B2
Cuilfail LEWES BN7 ......17 G3
Culpepper Cl ROTT BN2 ......28 D5
Culver Rd LAN/SOMP BN15 ......39 G4
Cumberland Av FERR BN12 ......36 B5
Cumberland Dr BRI BN1 ......27 G5
Cumberland Rd ANG/EP BN16 ......34 A5
  BRI BN1 ......27 G5
Cumbrian Cl SALV BN13 ......36 C3
The Curlews SHOR BN43 ......41 G2
Curvins Wy LAN/SOMP BN15 ......39 H5
Curwen Pl BRI BN1 ......27 G4
Curzon Cl SALV BN13 ......36 D4
Cuthbert Rd ROTT BN2 ......46 C4
The Cygnets SHOR BN43 ......41 F2
Cypress Av SALV BN13 ......36 A5
Cypress Cl SHOR BN43 ......41 F1

D

Dacre Rd NEWHV BN9 ......68 D1
Dagmar St WTHG BN11 ......5 F2
Dale Av BRI BN1 ......27 H2
Dale Crs BRI BN1 ......27 H1
Dale Dr BRI BN1 ......27 H1
Dale Rd LEWES BN7 ......16 C4
  WTHG BN11 ......56 D1
Dale Vw HOVE BN3 ......25 H5
Dale View Gdns HOVE BN3 ......25 H5
Dallington Rd HOVE BN3 ......44 A2
Damon Cl PEAHV BN10 ......67 E1
Dana Ldg PEAHV * BN10 ......66 C1
Dane Cl SEAF BN25 ......72 B1
Danehill Rd ROTT BN2 ......47 F5
Dane Rd SEAF BN25 ......72 B1
Dankton Gdns LAN/SOMP BN15 ......38 D3
Dankton La LAN/SOMP BN15 ......38 D3
Dapper's La ANG/EP BN16 ......34 A4
Darcey Dr BRI BN1 ......28 A1
Dart Cl SALV BN13 ......36 B2
Dartmouth Cl ROTT BN2 ......47 F1
Dartmouth Crs ROTT BN2 ......47 E1
Darwall Dr SEAF BN25 ......71 E5
Davey Dr BRI BN1 ......46 B1
Davey's La LEWES BN7 ......17 G2
Davigdor Rd HOVE BN3 ......2 B1
Dawes Av WTHG BN11 ......5 K2
Dawes Cl WTHG BN11 ......5 K2
Dawlish Cl ROTT BN2 ......47 E1
Dawn Cl STEY/UB BN44 ......8 B3
Dawn Crs STEY/UB BN44 ......8 A3
Dawson Ter ROTT BN2 ......46 C4
Deacons Dr PTSD BN41 ......25 F5
Deacons Wy STEY/UB BN44 ......8 A2
Deal Av SEAF BN25 ......71 G3
Dean Cl PTSD BN41 ......25 G5
Dean Court Rd ROTT BN2 ......61 E3
Deanery Cl LEWES BN7 ......17 F1
Dean Gdns PTSD BN41 ......25 G5
Dean Rd SEAF BN25 ......72 D1
Deans Cl ROTT BN2 ......48 C2
Dean St BRI BN1 ......2 D4
Deanway HOVE BN3 ......26 D4
Deborah Ter PEAHV * BN10 ......66 C1
De Braose Wy STEY/UB BN44 ......7 G2

De Courcel Rd ROTT BN2 ......59 E2
Decoy Rd FIN/BW BN14 ......38 B5
Deerswood Cl SALV BN13 ......35 H5
The Deeside BRI BN1 ......14 A5
De Grey Cl LEWES BN7 ......17 F2
Delaware Rd LEWES BN7 ......16 C4
De La Warr Gn LEWES * BN7 ......16 D1
De Montfort Rd LEWES BN7 ......16 C3
  ROTT BN2 ......46 C3
Dencher Rd LEWES BN7 ......32 A4
Deneside BRI BN1 ......27 F2
The Dene HOVE BN3 ......25 H4
Dene V BRI BN1 ......27 F2
The Deneway BRI BN1 ......27 F3
  LAN/SOMP BN15 ......39 E4
Denmark Rd PTSD BN41 ......43 G3
Denmark Ter BRI BN1 ......2 D2
Denmark Vls HOVE BN3 ......44 D3
Dennis Hobden Cl ROTT BN2 ......47 E1
Denton Cl FERR BN12 ......53 H2
Denton Dr BRI BN1 ......28 A2
  NEWHV BN9 ......65 E4
Denton Island NEWHV BN9 ......64 C5
Denton Ri NEWHV BN9 ......65 E3
Denton Rd NEWHV BN9 ......65 E4
Derek Av HOVE BN3 ......43 H4
Derek Rd LAN/SOMP BN15 ......39 F2
Derwent Cl LAN/SOMP BN15 ......39 E5
Derwent Dr FERR BN12 ......36 B5
Desmond Wy ROTT BN2 ......47 F4
Devil's Dyke Rd HOVE BN3 ......26 B1
  POY/PYE BN45 ......11 F2
Devonian Cl ROTT * BN2 ......46 B3
Devonport Pl WTHG BN11 ......56 C2
Devonport Rd WTHG BN11 ......56 C2
Devonshire Ct HOVE * BN3 ......45 E2
Devonshire Pl ROTT BN2 ......3 J6
De Warrenne Rd LEWES BN7 ......16 D3
Dewe Rd ROTT BN2 ......46 C1
The Dewpond PEAHV BN10 ......62 D4
Ditchling Cl FERR BN12 ......53 H1
Ditchling Crs BRI BN1 ......28 C2
Ditchling Gdns BRI BN1 ......46 A1
Ditchling Ri BRI BN1 ......46 A2
Ditchling Rd BRI BN1 ......14 C1
  ROTT BN2 ......3 H1
Dog La STEY/UB BN44 ......7 F1
Dolphin Ms ROTT * BN2 ......3 H6
  SHOR * BN43 ......41 G3
Dolphin Rd SHOR BN43 ......41 H3
Dolphin Wy SHOR BN43 ......41 H3
Dominion Buildings
  FIN/BW * BN14 ......56 B1
Dominion Cl FIN/BW BN14 ......56 A1
Dominion Rd FIN/BW BN14 ......38 A5
Dominion Wy FIN/BW BN14 ......38 B5
Dominion Wy West
  FIN/BW BN14 ......38 B5
Donald Hall Rd ROTT BN2 ......46 D5
Donkey Ms HOVE BN3 ......2 B4
Donnington Rd ROTT BN2 ......48 C4
Doone End FERR BN12 ......53 F5
Dorchester Gdns WTHG BN11 ......55 E3
Dorothy Av PEAHV BN10 ......67 E3
Dorothy Av North PEAHV BN10 ......63 E5
Dorothy Rd HOVE BN3 ......43 H2
Dorset Gdns ROTT BN2 ......3 J5
Dorset Ms ROTT * BN2 ......3 J5
Dorset Pl ROTT BN2 ......3 J5
  SALV * BN13 ......37 E5
Dorset Rd LEWES * BN7 ......17 F4
Dorset St ROTT BN2 ......3 H5
Douglas Av WTHG BN11 ......54 D3
Douglas Cl WTHG BN11 ......54 D3
Dovecote Ms LAN/SOMP BN15 ......39 E2
Dover Cl SEAF BN25 ......71 G3
Dover Rd BRI BN1 ......28 A5
  WTHG BN11 ......55 E4
Dower Cl ROTT BN2 ......60 B1
Downash Cl ROTT BN2 ......47 E4
Downland Av PEAHV BN10 ......67 G2
  STHW BN42 ......42 B1
Downland Cl FIN/BW BN14 ......18 C1
  ROTT BN2 ......47 H2
  STEY/UB BN44 ......8 B2
  STHW BN42 ......42 B1
Downland Crs HOVE BN3 ......26 A4
Downland Dr HOVE BN3 ......26 A4
Downland Rd ROTT BN2 ......47 H2
  STEY/UB BN44 ......8 B2
Downlands Av FIN/BW BN14 ......37 H3
Downlands Cl LAN/SOMP BN15 ......39 E3
Downlands Gdns FIN/BW BN14 ......38 A3
Downlands Pde
  FIN/BW * BN14 ......38 A3
Downs Cl LAN/SOMP BN15 ......40 B4
  LEWES BN7 ......16 C2
Downscroft STEY/UB BN44 ......8 B3

Downside HOVE BN3 ......26 D
  LEWES BN7 ......16 C
  SHOR BN43 41
Downside Av FIN/BW BN14 ......18 D
Downside Cl FIN/BW BN14 ......18 C
  SHOR BN43 ......41 F
Downs Link STEY/UB BN44 ......8 A
Downs Md LAN/SOMP * BN15 ......39 E
Downs Rd SEAF BN25 ......71 E
Downs Valley Rd ROTT BN2 ......48 C
Downsview HOVE BN3 ......25 H
Downs Vw PEAHV BN10 ......63 F
Downsview Av ROTT BN2 ......48 A
Downsview Rd ANG/EP BN16 ......52 D
  PTSD BN41 ......25 E
  SEAF BN25 ......71 E
The Down HOVE BN3 ......25 G
Downs Wk PEAHV BN10 ......62 D
Downsway ROTT BN2 ......48 B
  SHOR BN43 ......41 F
  STHW BN42 ......24 D
Down Ter ROTT BN2 ......46 C
Downview Av FERR BN12 ......53 E
Downview Rd FERR BN12 ......53 E
Down View Rd WTHG BN11 ......55 E
Drake Av FERR BN12 ......54 B
Drakes Cl LAN/SOMP BN15 ......40 B
Draxmont Wy BRI BN1 ......27 H
Draycliff Cl FERR BN12 ......53 E
The Driftway STEY/UB BN44 ......8 B
The Drive ANG/EP BN16 ......52 D
  HOVE BN3 ......45 E
  LAN/SOMP BN15 ......40 B
  LAN/SOMP BN15 ......57 F
  NEWHV BN9 ......68 C
  SHOR BN43 ......41 F
  STHW BN42 ......42 C
  WTHG BN11 ......54 D
The Driveway SHOR BN43 ......41 F
The Drove BRI BN1 ......30 A
  BRI BN1 ......45 F
  NEWHV BN9 ......65 E
Drove Av ROTT BN2 ......30 B
Drove Crs PTSD BN41 ......25 E
Drove Rd NEWHV BN9 ......65 E
  PTSD BN41 ......43 E
  ROTT BN2 ......47 G
Drovers Cl PTSD BN41 ......25 G
The Droveway HOVE BN3 ......26 C
Drummond Ct FERR * BN12 ......54 B
Drummond Rd FERR BN12 ......54 C
Duchess Dr SEAF BN25 ......70 C
Dudley Rd BRI BN1 ......46 B
Dudwell Rd ROTT BN2 ......48 C
Dukes Cl SEAF BN25 ......70 B
Dukes La BRI * BN1 ......3 F
Duke's Mound ROTT BN2 ......58 D
Duke St BRI BN1 ......3 F
Dukes Yd STEY/UB BN44 ......7 F
Dulwich Cl SEAF BN25 ......71 F
Dunster Cl BRI BN1 ......46 B
Dunvan Cl LEWES BN7 ......17 E
Durham Cl ROTT BN2 ......47 G
Durrington Gdns FERR * BN12 ......54 B
Durrington Hl SALV BN13 ......36 B
Durrington La SALV BN13 ......36 B
Dyke Cl HOVE BN3 ......26 D
Dyke Rd BRI BN1 ......2 E
  HOVE BN3 ......27 F
Dyke Road Av HOVE BN3 ......26 D
Dyke Road Dr BRI BN1 ......45 G
Dyke Road Pl HOVE BN3 ......27 E
Dymchurch Cl SEAF BN25 ......71 F
Dymock Cl SEAF BN25 ......71 G

E

Earls Cl SEAF BN25 ......70 A3
East Albany Rd SEAF BN25 ......70 C4
East Av FERR BN12 ......54 D4
Eastbank STHW BN42 ......42 D
Eastbourne Rd ROTT BN2 ......46 D7
  SEAF BN25 ......71 G5
Eastbourne Ter SEAF * BN25 ......71 E
Eastbridge Rd NEWHV BN9 ......69 E
Eastbrook Rd PTSD BN41 ......43 F
Eastbrook Wy STHW BN42 ......43 E
Eastcourt Rd FIN/BW BN14 ......4 D
East Dean Ri SEAF BN25 ......71 E
East Dr ROTT BN2 ......46 C
Eastergate Cl FERR BN12 ......53 F
Eastergate Rd ROTT BN2 ......29 F
Eastern Av SHOR BN43 ......41 G
Eastern Cl ANG/EP BN16 ......52 D
  SHOR BN43 ......41 G
Eastern Pl ROTT BN2 ......59 E

stern Rd *ROTT* BN2 ...... 3 K5
stern Rd *ROTT* BN2 ...... 58 D1
stgate St *LEWES* BN7 ...... 17 F3
stgate Whf *LEWES* * BN7 ...... 17 F3
st Highland Furlong
  SEAF * BN25 ...... 70 D4
sthill Dr *PTSD* BN41 ...... 25 F5
sthill Wy *PTSD* BN41 ...... 43 F1
sting Ct *FIN/BW* BN14 ...... 38 B5
st Md *FERR* BN12 ...... 53 F4
st Meadway *SHOR* BN43 ...... 41 G4
st Onslow Ct *FERR* BN12 ...... 53 E3
stport La *LEWES* BN7 ...... 17 E4
st St *BRI* BN1 ...... 3 G6
  BRI BN1 ...... 30 A1
  LAN/SOMP BN15 ...... 57 G1
  LEWES BN7 ...... 17 F3
  PTSD BN41 ...... 43 G4
  SEAF BN25 ...... 70 C5
  SHOR BN43 ...... 41 F3
st Tyne *SALV* BN13 ...... 36 B4
st Wy *LEWES* BN7 ...... 16 B2
stwick Cl *BRI* BN1 ...... 14 B5
ton Gdns *HOVE* BN3 ...... 45 E3
ton Gv *HOVE* BN3 ...... 45 E3
ton Mnr *HOVE* * BN3 ...... 45 E3
ton Pl *ROTT* BN2 ...... 58 D1
ton Rd *HOVE* BN3 ...... 45 E4
ton Vls *HOVE* BN3 ...... 44 D3
burton Av *BRI* BN1 ...... 46 A1
burton Gdns *SHOR* BN43 ...... 41 F1
dgehill Cl *SALV* BN13 ...... 36 D3
dgehill Wy *PTSD* BN41 ...... 24 D5
dinburgh Rd *ROTT* BN2 ...... 46 B2
  SEAF BN25 ...... 70 B5
dith Av *PEAHV* BN10 ...... 66 D2
dith Av North *PEAHV* BN10 ...... 63 E5
dmonton Rd *SALV* BN13 ...... 36 A4
dward Av *HOVE* BN3 ...... 26 C4
  ROTT BN2 ...... 61 H2
dward Cl *HOVE* BN3 ...... 26 C4
  SEAF BN25 ...... 69 G2
dwards Ter
  LAN/SOMP * BN15 ...... 38 B3
dward St *LEWES* BN7 ...... 17 F3
  ROTT BN2 ...... 3 J5
dwin Cl *LAN/SOMP* BN15 ...... 39 E4
ffingham Ct *ROTT* BN2 ...... 61 G3
gginton Rd *BRI* BN1 ...... 29 G2
gginton Rd *BRI* BN1 ...... 29 F3
gmont Rd *HOVE* BN3 ...... 43 H1
gremont Pl *ROTT* BN2 ...... 3 K5
ghth Av *LAN/SOMP* BN15 ...... 39 E4
leen Av *ROTT* BN2 ...... 61 F4
rene Av *FERR* BN12 ...... 54 D4
rene Av *FERR* BN12 ...... 54 C4
der Cl *PTSD* BN41 ...... 25 F5
der Pl *BRI* BN1 ...... 46 A3
don Rd *WTHG* BN11 ...... 5 J3
dred Av *BRI* BN1 ...... 27 F2
ley Crs *ROTT* BN2 ...... 60 C2
ley Dr *ROTT* BN2 ...... 60 C1
gin Gdns *SEAF* BN25 ...... 70 B3
gin Rd *LAN/SOMP* BN15 ...... 52 B3
izabeth Av *HOVE* BN3 ...... 26 C4
izabeth Cl *HOVE* BN3 ...... 26 C4
  SEAF BN25 ...... 70 B3
izabeth Pl *LAN/SOMP* BN15 ...... 39 E5
izabeth Rd *SHOR* BN43 ...... 42 A2
  WTHG BN11 ...... 4 D4
len St *HOVE* BN3 ...... 44 D3
  PTSD BN41 ...... 43 G3
lis Av *SALV* BN13 ...... 36 C2
m Av *ANG/EP* BN16 ...... 52 A4
m Cl *HOVE* BN3 ...... 27 E5
  SEAF BN25 ...... 71 G5
  SHOR BN43 ...... 41 F1
m Ct *NEWHV* BN9 ...... 68 B1
m Dr *HOVE* BN3 ...... 44 A1
m Gv *LAN/SOMP* BN15 ...... 39 F5
  ROTT BN2 ...... 46 C3
  WTHG BN11 ...... 5 D2
m Grove La *STEY/UB* BN44 ...... 7 F1
mhurst Rd *ANG/EP* BN16 ...... 34 A4
more Rd *ROTT* BN2 ...... 3 J3
m Pk *FERR* BN12 ...... 53 F2
m Ri *FIN/BW* BN14 ...... 18 C1
m Rd *PTSD* BN41 ...... 43 F2
  WTHG BN11 ...... 5 C5
ms Dr *LAN/SOMP* BN15 ...... 39 F4
ms Lea Av *BRI* BN1 ...... 27 G4
mstone Cl *LAN/SOMP* BN15 ...... 39 F4
m Vls *SEAF* * BN25 ...... 72 C1
phick Rd *NEWHV* BN9 ...... 64 C5
rington Rd *HOVE* BN3 ...... 45 E1
sie Rd *WTHG* BN11 ...... 4 B6
lsted Crs *BRI* BN1 ...... 28 C1

Elverlands Cl *FERR* BN12 ...... 53 F5
Elvin Crs *ROTT* BN2 ...... 60 C1
Ely Cl *SALV* BN13 ...... 54 D1
Ely Rd *SALV* BN13 ...... 54 D1
Emerald Quay *SHOR* BN43 ...... 41 G4
English Cl *HOVE* BN3 ...... 44 A2
English Pas *LEWES* * BN7 ...... 17 F3
Ennerdale Dr *LAN/SOMP* BN15 ...... 38 D3
Enterprise Ct *FERR* * BN12 ...... 54 A2
E Plan Est *NEWHV* * BN9 ...... 64 D5
Eridge Gn *LEWES* BN7 ...... 16 D2
Eridge Rd *HOVE* BN3 ...... 26 C5
Eriskay Ct *SALV* BN13 ...... 35 H4
Eriswell Rd *WTHG* BN11 ...... 4 D5
Erringham Rd *SHOR* BN43 ...... 41 E2
Erroll Rd *HOVE* BN3 ...... 43 G4
Esher Cl *SEAF* BN25 ...... 70 D4
Eskbank Av *BRI* BN1 ...... 14 A5
The Esplanade *PEAHV* BN10 ...... 66 C1
  WTHG BN11 ...... 5 J5
Esplanade Ct *SEAF* * BN25 ...... 72 C1
Esplanade Ct *WTHG* * BN11 ...... 5 K5
Esplanade Ms *SEAF* BN25 ...... 72 C1
Essenhigh Dr *SALV* BN13 ...... 35 H4
Essex Ms *NEWHV* * BN9 ...... 68 C1
Essex Pl *NEWHV* * BN9 ...... 68 C1
  ROTT * BN2 ...... 58 C1
Essex St *ROTT* BN2 ...... 58 C1
Estate Rd *NEWHV* BN9 ...... 64 D4
  NEWHV BN9 ...... 65 E5
  NEWHV BN9 ...... 68 D1
Ethelred Rd *SALV* BN13 ...... 55 E1
Ethel St *HOVE* BN3 ...... 44 D3
Ethelwulf Rd *SALV* BN13 ...... 55 E1
Etherton Wy *SEAF* BN25 ...... 71 E4
Eton Cl *SEAF* BN25 ...... 71 E4
Eton Rd *WTHG* BN11 ...... 55 E2
Evelyn Av *NEWHV* BN9 ...... 68 C1
Evelyn Rd *FIN/BW* BN14 ...... 55 H1
  LEWES BN7 ...... 16 D2
Evelyn Ter *ROTT* BN2 ...... 46 C5
Evershed Ct *PEAHV* * BN10 ...... 66 B1
Evershed Wy *SHOR* BN43 ...... 41 H3
Ewart St *ROTT* BN2 ...... 3 K2
Ewhurst Rd *ROTT* BN2 ...... 46 C2
Exceat Cl *ROTT* BN2 ...... 47 E4
The Excelsior *BRI* * BN1 ...... 27 F3
Exeter Ct *WTHG* * BN11 ...... 55 E4
Exeter St *BRI* BN1 ...... 45 C2
Exmoor Cl *SALV* BN13 ...... 36 B3
Exmoor Crs *SALV* BN13 ...... 36 C3
Exmoor Dr *SALV* BN13 ...... 36 C2

F

Fairdene *STHW* BN42 ...... 42 D1
Fairfield *PEAHV* * BN10 ...... 66 D1
Fairfield Cl *SHOR* BN43 ...... 41 H1
Fairfield Gdns *PTSD* BN41 ...... 43 F1
Fairfields *SALV* BN13 ...... 37 E5
Fairholme Rd *NEWHV* BN9 ...... 65 H4
Fairhurst *PEAHV* * BN10 ...... 66 B1
Fairlawn Dr *FIN/BW* BN14 ...... 55 H1
Fairlawns *SHOR* BN43 ...... 41 G2
Fairlie Gdns *BRI* BN1 ...... 27 G4
Fairlight Av *PEAHV* BN10 ...... 66 B1
Fairlight Pl *ROTT* BN2 ...... 46 C2
Fairview Av *FERR* BN12 ...... 54 A4
Fairview Ri *BRI* BN1 ...... 27 F2
Fairview Rd *LAN/SOMP* BN15 ...... 39 G2
The Fairway *LAN/SOMP* BN15 ...... 40 A3
  NEWHV BN9 ...... 68 A4
Fairway Crs *PTSD* BN41 ...... 25 G5
Fairways Cl *SEAF* BN25 ...... 73 E1
Fairways Rd *SEAF* BN25 ...... 73 F1
Falaise Rd *NEWHV* BN9 ...... 65 F4
Falcon Cl *SEAF* BN25 ...... 42 A4
Fallowfield Cl *HOVE* BN3 ...... 26 B5
Fallowfield Crs *HOVE* BN3 ...... 26 A5
Falmer Av *FERR* BN12 ...... 53 H4
  ROTT BN2 ...... 61 F3
Falmer Cl *FERR* BN12 ...... 54 A4
Falmer Gdns *ROTT* BN2 ...... 48 B2
Falmer House Rd *BRI* BN1 ...... 15 H5
Falmer Rd *ROTT* BN2 ...... 30 B5
Faraday Cl *SALV* BN13 ...... 36 A4
Farman St *HOVE* BN3 ...... 2 B4
Farm Cl *PTSD* BN41 ...... 25 E5
  SEAF BN25 ...... 71 F4
Farm Hl *ROTT* BN2 ...... 48 A2
Farm Ms *HOVE* BN3 ...... 2 A3
Farm Rd *HOVE* BN3 ...... 2 B3
Farm Wy *STHW* BN42 ...... 43 E3
Farmway Cl *HOVE* BN3 ...... 25 H5
Farncombe Rd *LEWES* BN7 ...... 17 G3
  WTHG BN11 ...... 5 J3

Fereday Cl *LAN/SOMP* BN15 ...... 39 G4
Ferndale Rd *HOVE* BN3 ...... 45 F3
Ferndale Wk *ANG/EP* BN15 ...... 34 A4
Fernhurst Crs *BRI* BN1 ...... 28 B2
Fernhurst Dr *FERR* BN12 ...... 53 G3
Fernwood Ri *BRI* BN1 ...... 27 F2
Ferrers Rd *LEWES* BN7 ...... 16 D2
Ferring Cl *FERR* BN12 ...... 53 E5
Ferring Grange Gdns
  FERR BN12 ...... 53 E3
Ferringham La *FERR* BN12 ...... 53 E4
Ferringham Wy *FERR* BN12 ...... 53 E5
Ferring La *FERR* BN12 ...... 53 F2
Ferring Marine *FERR* BN12 ...... 53 F5
Ferring St *FERR* BN12 ...... 53 E3
Ferry Rd *SHOR* BN43 ...... 41 F4
Fetherston Rd
  LAN/SOMP BN15 ...... 53 E3
Feversham Cl *SHOR* BN43 ...... 41 H4
Field Cl *LAN/SOMP* BN15 ...... 39 F5
  SEAF BN25 ...... 73 F1
Field Place Pde *FERR* * BN12 ...... 54 A2
Field Rw *WTHG* BN11 ...... 4 E5
Fifth Av *FIN/BW* BN14 ...... 37 G2
  LAN/SOMP BN15 ...... 39 C5
The Finches *SHOR* BN43 ...... 41 G2
Finches Cl *LAN/SOMP* BN15 ...... 39 F5
Findon Av *ROTT* BN2 ...... 62 A4
Findon By-Pass *FIN/BW* BN14 ...... 18 B4
Findon Cl *HOVE* BN3 ...... 26 B4
  SEAF BN25 ...... 70 D4
Findon Rd *FIN/BW* BN14 ...... 18 D3
  ROTT BN2 ...... 47 F5
Finsbury Rd *ROTT* BN2 ...... 3 K2
Fir Cl *ROTT* BN2 ...... 48 D3
Fircroft Cl *BRI* BN1 ...... 27 G4
Fircroft Cl *BRI* BN1 ...... 27 G4
Firle Cl *SEAF* BN25 ...... 70 C3
Firle Crs *LEWES* BN7 ...... 16 B2
Firle Dr *SEAF* BN25 ...... 70 C3
Firle Gra *SEAF* BN25 ...... 70 C3
Firle Rd *LAN/SOMP* BN15 ...... 39 F1
  PEAHV BN10 ...... 62 D4
  ROTT BN2 ...... 46 D4
  SEAF BN25 ...... 70 C4
Firsdown Cl *SALV* BN13 ...... 18 C5
Firsdown Rd *SALV* BN13 ...... 18 C5
First Av *FIN/BW* BN14 ...... 37 G2
  HOVE BN3 ...... 45 E5
  LAN/SOMP BN15 ...... 39 G2
  NEWHV BN9 ...... 68 C2
Fishergate Cl *PTSD* BN41 ...... 43 F1
Fishermans Wk *SHOR* BN43 ...... 40 D4
Fishersgate Ter *PTSD* BN41 ...... 43 E3
Fisher St *LEWES* BN7 ...... 17 E3
Fitch Dr *ROTT* BN2 ...... 47 E1
Fittleworth Cl *FERR* BN12 ...... 53 G1
Fitzgerald Av *SEAF* BN25 ...... 72 C1
Fitzgerald Pk *SEAF* BN25 ...... 72 C1
Fitzgerald Rd *LEWES* BN7 ...... 17 F1
Fitzherbert Dr *ROTT* BN2 ...... 46 D2
Fitzjohns Rd *LEWES* BN7 ...... 16 D2
Fitzroy Rd *LEWES* BN7 ...... 16 D2
Flag Sq *SHOR* BN43 ...... 41 F4
Fletcher Rd *FIN/BW* BN14 ...... 38 A5
Fletching Cl *ROTT* BN2 ...... 47 E4
Flimwell Cl *ROTT* BN2 ...... 47 E4
The Flints *LEWES* BN7 ...... 32 A2
Flint Cl *PTSD* BN41 ...... 25 F5
  SEAF BN25 ...... 70 C2
Florence Av *HOVE* BN3 ...... 43 H2
Florence Pl *BRI* BN1 ...... 46 B1
Florence Rd *BRI* BN1 ...... 46 A2
The Florets *STEY/UB* * BN44 ...... 8 B3
Florida Cl *FERR* BN12 ...... 53 F5
Florida Gdns *FERR* * BN12 ...... 53 F5
Florida Rd *FERR* BN12 ...... 53 F5
Florlandia Cl *LAN/SOMP* BN15 ...... 38 D5
Foamcourt Waye *FERR* BN12 ...... 53 E4
Folkestone Cl *SEAF* BN25 ...... 71 G3
Fonthill Rd *HOVE* BN3 ...... 44 D2
Fontwell Cl *FIN/BW* BN14 ...... 37 G2
Foredown Cl *PTSD* BN41 ...... 25 F5
Foredown Dr *PTSD* BN41 ...... 43 F1
Foredown Rd *PTSD* BN41 ...... 25 F3
Forest Rd *BRI* BN1 ...... 29 E2
  FIN/BW BN14 ...... 37 H4
Forge Cl *PTSD* BN41 ...... 25 F5
Fort Hvn *SHOR* BN43 ...... 42 A4
Fort Ri *NEWHV* BN9 ...... 68 D3
Fort Rd *NEWHV* BN9 ...... 68 D3
Forward Cl *NEWHV* BN9 ...... 65 G3
The Fosse *LEWES* * BN7 ...... 17 E3
Foster Cl *SEAF* BN25 ...... 70 C4
Foundry La *LEWES* BN7 ...... 17 G3
Foundry St *BRI* BN1 ...... 3 G3
Foundry Ter *LEWES* * BN7 ...... 17 G3

Fountains Cl *BRI* BN1 ...... 28 B5
Founthill Av *ROTT* BN2 ...... 61 F4
Founthill Rd *ROTT* BN2 ...... 61 F4
Fourth Av *FIN/BW* BN14 ...... 37 H3
  HOVE BN3 ...... 44 D5
  LAN/SOMP BN15 ...... 39 G3
Fowey Cl *SHOR* BN43 ...... 41 H4
Foxdown Rd *ROTT* BN2 ...... 48 D3
Foxglove Wk *FERR* BN12 ...... 54 A1
Foxhill *PEAHV* BN10 ...... 63 E4
Foxhunters Rd *PTSD* BN41 ...... 24 D4
Fox Lea *FERR* BN14 ...... 18 C2
Foxley La *SALV* BN13 ...... 36 D2
Fox Wy *PTSD* BN41 ...... 25 E4
Framfield Cl *BRI* BN1 ...... 29 E1
Frampton Ct *FERR* * BN12 ...... 54 A3
Frampton Rd *ROTT* BN2 ...... 40 D2
The Framptons *ANG/EP* BN16 ...... 52 B4
France La *SALV* BN13 ...... 34 D2
Francis St *BRI* BN1 ...... 3 H1
Franklands Cl *FIN/BW* BN14 ...... 36 D1
Franklin Rd *PTSD* BN41 ...... 43 G3
  ROTT BN2 ...... 46 C3
  SALV BN13 ...... 36 C3
  SHOR BN43 ...... 42 A2
Franklin St *ROTT* BN2 ...... 46 C3
Frant Rd *HOVE* BN3 ...... 26 C5
Frederick Gdns *BRI* * BN1 ...... 3 G2
Frederick Pl *BRI* * BN1 ...... 3 G2
Frederick St *BRI* BN1 ...... 3 F3
Frederick Ter *BRI* * BN1 ...... 3 G2
Freehold St *SHOR* BN43 ...... 41 E3
Freehold Ter *ROTT* BN2 ...... 46 B1
Freeland Cl *SEAF* BN25 ...... 69 H2
Freemans Rd *PTSD* BN41 ...... 43 E2
Freshbrook Cl
  LAN/SOMP BN15 ...... 39 G5
Freshbrook Rd
  LAN/SOMP BN15 ...... 39 H5
Freshfield Pl *ROTT* BN2 ...... 46 C5
Freshfield Rd *ROTT* BN2 ...... 46 C5
Freshfields Cl *LAN/SOMP* BN15 ...... 39 F4
Freshfields Dr *LAN/SOMP* BN15 ...... 39 F4
Freshfield St *ROTT* BN2 ...... 46 C5
Freshfield Wy *ROTT* BN2 ...... 46 C5
Friar Cl *BRI* BN1 ...... 28 A3
Friar Crs *BRI* BN1 ...... 27 H4
Friar Rd *BRI* BN1 ...... 28 A3
Friars' Av *PEAHV* BN10 ...... 67 G3
Friars' Wk *LEWES* BN7 ...... 17 F3
Friar Wk *BRI* BN1 ...... 27 H3
  SALV BN13 ...... 54 D2
Frimley Cl *ROTT* BN2 ...... 48 C3
Friston Cl *ROTT* BN2 ...... 29 F3
  SEAF BN25 ...... 70 A4
Frith Rd *HOVE* BN3 ...... 44 C2
Frobisher Cl *FERR* BN12 ...... 54 B1
Frobisher Wy *FERR* BN12 ...... 54 B1
Fulbeck Av *SALV* BN13 ...... 35 H4
Fuller Rd *LEWES* BN7 ...... 16 C1
Fullwood Av *NEWHV* BN9 ...... 68 B1
Fulmar Cl *HOVE* BN3 ...... 45 F1
The Furlongs *STEY/UB* BN44 ...... 7 F2
Furze Cl *SALV* BN13 ...... 18 B5
Furze Hl *HOVE* BN3 ...... 2 B5
Furzeholme *SALV* BN13 ...... 18 C5
Furze Vw *SALV* BN13 ...... 18 B5

G

Gableson Av *BRI* BN1 ...... 26 D3
Gainsborough Av *FIN/BW* BN14 ...... 38 A3
Gainsborough Ldg
  FIN/BW * BN14 ...... 55 G1
Gaisford Cl *FIN/BW* BN14 ...... 4 C1
Gaisford Rd *FIN/BW* BN14 ...... 55 F1
Galliers Cl *BRI* BN1 ...... 28 B1
The Gallops *LEWES* BN7 ...... 16 C3
Galsworthy Cl *FERR* BN12 ...... 53 H2
Galsworthy Rd *FERR* BN12 ...... 53 H2
Gannon Rd *WTHG* BN11 ...... 5 K3
Garden Cl *ANG/EP* BN16 ...... 34 A3
  LAN/SOMP BN15 ...... 39 E4
  PTSD BN41 ...... 43 G2
  SHOR BN43 ...... 41 H1
The Gardens *PTSD* BN41 ...... 43 G2
  STHW BN42 ...... 42 D3
Gardener St *PTSD* BN41 ...... 43 F3
Garden St *LEWES* BN7 ...... 17 E4
Gardner Rd *PTSD* BN41 ...... 43 E3
Gardner St *BRI* BN1 ...... 3 G4
Garrick Rd *FIN/BW* BN14 ...... 55 H1
Gatcombe Cl *SALV* * BN13 ...... 35 H5
Gatewycke Ter *STEY/UB* * BN44 ...... 7 F1
Geneva Rd *NEWHV* BN9 ...... 68 C2
George St *PTSD* BN41 ...... 43 E3

ROTT BN2 ....3 J5
George V Av *LAN/SOMP* BN15 ....40 B5
  WTHG BN11 ....54 C2
Georgia Av *FIN/BW* BN14 ....55 H1
Gerald Rd *SEAF* BN25 ....72 E2
  WTHG BN11 ....54 D4
Gerard St *BRI* BN1 ....46 A2
Ghyllside *ROTT* BN2 ....47 E1
Gibbon Rd *NEWHV* BN9 ....68 B2
Gildredge Rd *SEAF* BN25 ....70 D5
Gladstone PI *ROTT* BN2 ....46 C2
Gladstone Rd *PTSD* BN41 ....43 F3
Gladstone Ter *ROTT* BN2 ....46 C2
Gladys Av *PEAHV* BN10 ....67 F2
Gladys Rd *ROTT* BN2 ....43 H2
Glastonbury Rd *HOVE* BN3 ....43 H4
Glebe CI *LAN/SOMP* BN15 ....39 C3
  LEWES BN7 ....16 C4
  STHW BN42 ....42 D3
Glebe Dr *SEAF* BN25 ....70 C5
Glebelands CI *SHOR* BN43 ....41 H2
Glebe Rd *SALV* BN13 ....37 E5
Glebeside Av *FIN/BW* BN14 ....37 E5
Glebeside CI *FIN/BW* BN14 ....37 E5
Glebe Vls *HOVE* BN3 ....43 H3
Glebe Wy *LAN/SOMP* BN15 ....39 C3
The Glen *SALV* BN13 ....37 E3
Glenbarrie Wy *FERR* BN12 ....52 D2
Glendale Rd *HOVE* BN3 ....45 F3
Glendor Rd *HOVE* BN3 ....44 A4
Gleneagles CI *SEAF* BN25 ....69 G2
Glenfalls Av *BRI* BN1 ....14 A5
Glen Gdns *FERR* BN12 ....53 F3
Glen Ri *BRI* BN1 ....26 D2
Glen Rise CI *BRI* BN1 ....26 D2
Gleton Av *HOVE* BN3 ....25 H5
Gloucester Ms *BRI* * BN1 ....3 H3
Gloucester Pas *BRI* BN1 ....3 H3
Gloucester PI *ROTT* BN2 ....3 H3
Gloucester Rd *BRI* BN1 ....3 G3
Gloucester St *BRI* BN1 ....3 H3
Glynde Av *FERR* BN12 ....53 F3
  ROTT BN2 ....61 G3
Glyndebourne Av *ROTT* BN2 ....61 G4
Glynde CI *FERR* BN12 ....53 F3
  NEWHV BN9 ....64 D3
Glynde Rd *ROTT* BN2 ....46 D4
Glynn Ri *PEAHV* BN10 ....62 D4
Glynn Rd *PEAHV* BN10 ....62 D4
Godfrey CI *LEWES* BN7 ....17 E1
Godstalls La *STEY/UB* BN44 ....7 E1
Godwin Rd *HOVE* BN3 ....43 H2
Golden Acre *ANG/EP* BN16 ....52 B5
Golden Av *ANG/EP* BN16 ....52 B4
Golden Avenue CI *ANG/EP* BN16 ..52 B5
Golden La *HOVE* * BN3 ....2 B4
Gold La *PEAHV* BN10 ....63 E3
Goldsmith Rd *FIN/BW* BN14 ....56 A1
Goldstone CI *HOVE* BN3 ....26 D4
Goldstone Crs *HOVE* BN3 ....26 C5
Goldstone La *HOVE* BN3 ....44 D2
Goldstone Rd *HOVE* BN3 ....44 D3
Goldstone St *HOVE* BN3 ....44 D3
Goldstone Vls *HOVE* BN3 ....44 D3
Goldstone Wy *HOVE* BN3 ....26 C5
Golf Dr *BRI* BN1 ....28 B4
Goodwood Rd *SALV* BN13 ....37 E3
Goodwood Wy *ROTT* BN2 ....29 E4
Gordon Av *SHOR* BN43 ....41 G3
Gordon Rd *BRI* BN1 ....27 H5
  LAN/SOMP BN15 ....39 F4
  PTSD BN41 ....43 E3
  SHOR BN43 ....41 F3
  WTHG BN11 ....5 F3
Gorham Av *ROTT* BN2 ....61 E3
Gorham CI *ROTT* BN2 ....61 E3
Gorham Wy *PEAHV* BN10 ....62 A5
Goring Cha *FERR* BN12 ....53 G1
Goring Rd *FERR* BN12 ....54 A3
  STEY/UB BN44 ....7 F2
Goring St *FERR* BN12 ....53 G1
Goring Wy *FERR* BN12 ....53 F3
Gorringe CI *SHOR* BN43 ....42 B3
Gorse Av *FIN/BW* BN14 ....37 F4
Gorse CI *PTSD* BN41 ....24 D3
Gorse Dr *SEAF* BN25 ....70 D2
Gorse La *SALV* BN13 ....18 C5
Gorse Vw *ANG/EP* * BN16 ....52 C5
Gowscroft *LEWES* * BN7 ....32 A2
Graffham CI *ROTT* BN2 ....47 E4
Grafton Dr *LAN/SOMP* BN15 ....39 E4
Grafton Gdns *LAN/SOMP* BN15 .....39 E4
Grafton PI *WTHG* BN11 ....4 E5
Grafton Rd *WTHG* BN11 ....4 E5
Grafton St *ROTT* BN2 ....3 K6
Graham Av *BRI* BN1 ....27 G3
  PTSD BN41 ....24 D3
Graham Crs *PTSD* BN41 ....24 D3

Graham Rd *WTHG* BN11 ....4 E5
Grand Av *HOVE* BN3 ....45 E4
  LAN/SOMP BN15 ....39 G3
  SEAF BN25 ....70 A3
  WTHG BN11 ....55 E3
Grand Crs *ROTT* BN2 ....61 E4
Grand Junction Rd *BRI* BN1 ....3 G6
Grand Pde *ROTT* BN2 ....3 H3
Grand Parade Ms *ROTT* BN2 ....3 H4
Grange CI *BRI* BN1 ....45 G1
  FERR BN12 ....53 E4
Grange Ct *FERR* * BN12 ....53 E3
Grange Park Rd *FERR* BN12 ....53 E4
Grange Rd *HOVE* BN3 ....44 A3
  LEWES BN7 ....17 E4
  PTSD BN41 ....42 C3
Grangeways *BRI* BN1 ....27 G2
Grantham Rd *BRI* BN1 ....46 A1
Grantsmead *LAN/SOMP* BN15 ......39 G3
Grant St *ROTT* BN2 ....3 K1
Granville Rd *HOVE* BN3 ....2 C2
The Graperies *ROTT* BN2 ....46 C5
Grasmere Av *LAN/SOMP* BN15 .....38 D4
Grassmere Av *PEAHV* BN10 ....62 B5
Cratwicke Rd *WTHG* BN11 ....4 D5
Gravelly Crs *LAN/SOMP* BN15 ....39 H4
Great College St *ROTT* BN2 ....58 C1
Greatham Rd *FIN/BW* BN14 ....36 D1
The Green *HOVE* BN3 ....27 E5
  ROTT BN2 ....60 D3
Greenacres *BRI* * BN1 ....45 H1
  PEAHV BN10 ....63 F3
  SHOR BN43 ....41 E2
  STEY/UB BN44 ....7 F2
Greenbank Av *ROTT* BN2 ....61 G4
Green CI *STHW* BN42 ....42 C3
Green Ct *STHW* * BN42 ....42 C3
Greenfield CI *BRI* BN1 ....28 A2
Green Field CI *STHW* BN42 ....42 C2
Greenfield Crs *BRI* BN1 ....27 H2
Green Ga *PEAHV* BN10 ....63 E4
Greenhill Wy *PEAHV* BN10 ....63 E3
Greenland CI *SALV* BN13 ....36 C3
Greenland Rd *SALV* BN13 ....36 C4
Green La *LEWES* BN7 ....17 E4
  ROTT BN2 ....48 C4
  SEAF BN25 ....72 C1
Greenleas *HOVE* BN3 ....25 H5
Greenoaks *LAN/SOMP* BN15 ....39 F2
Green Pk *FERR* BN12 ....53 F2
Green Rdg *BRI* BN1 ....26 D2
Greentrees *LAN/SOMP* BN15 ....39 E4
Greentrees CI *LAN/SOMP* BN15 ....39 E4
Greentrees Crs *LAN/SOMP* BN15 ..39 E4
Green Wk *SEAF* BN25 ....73 F1
The Green Wy *FERR* BN12 ....53 H1
Greenways *PTSD* * BN41 ....43 F1
  ROTT BN2 ....60 B1
  STHW BN42 ....42 D1
Greenways Cnr *ROTT* * BN2 ....60 B1
Greenways Crs *FERR* BN12 ....53 F1
  SHOR BN43 ....41 H1
Greenwell CI *SEAF* BN25 ....71 E4
Greenwich Wy *PEAHV* BN10 ....67 E1
Greet Rd *LAN/SOMP* BN15 ....39 F3
Grenville Av *FERR* BN12 ....54 B2
Grenville CI *FERR* BN12 ....54 A2
Grenville St *BRI* BN1 ....2 E4
Greyfiars *HOVE* BN3 ....45 F2
Greyfriars CI *SALV* BN13 ....37 E4
Greystoke Ms *FERR* BN12 ....53 E3
Greystoke Rd *FERR* BN12 ....53 E3
Greystone Av *SALV* BN13 ....36 D5
Griffith's Av *LAN/SOMP* BN15 ....39 F2
Grinstead Av *LAN/SOMP* BN15 .....39 G4
Grinstead La *LAN/SOMP* BN15 .....39 G4
Grinstead Mt *ROTT* * BN2 ....47 F5
Grosvenor Rd *SEAF* BN25 ....70 C4
  WTHG BN11 ....4 E4
Grosvenor St *ROTT* BN2 ....3 J5
The Grove *FERR* BN12 ....53 E3
  NEWHV BN9 ....65 E3
Grove Bank *ROTT* * BN2 ....3 J3
Grove HI *ROTT* BN2 ....3 J3
The Grovelands
  LAN/SOMP BN15 ....57 G1
Grover Av *LAN/SOMP* BN15 ....39 F3
Grove Rd *FIN/BW* BN14 ....37 G4
  SEAF BN25 ....70 D5
Grove St *ROTT* BN2 ....3 K2
Guardswell PI *SEAF* BN25 ....70 C5
Guernsey Rd *FERR* BN12 ....53 F5
Guildford CI *FIN/BW* BN14 ....55 E1
Guildford Rd *BRI* BN1 ....3 F2
  FIN/BW BN14 ....55 E1
Guildford St *BRI* BN1 ....3 F2
Gundreda Rd *LEWES* BN7 ....16 D2

H

Haddington CI *HOVE* BN3 ....44 D4
Haddington St *HOVE* BN3 ....44 D3
Hadley Av *FIN/BW* BN14 ....37 H3
Hadlow CI *ROTT* BN2 ....46 D4
Hadlow Wy *LAN/SOMP* BN15 ....39 H4
Haig Av *BRI* BN1 ....28 D1
Haigh CI *LAN/SOMP* BN15 ....40 B4
Hailsham Av *ROTT* BN2 ....61 H2
Hailsham CI *ANG/EP* BN16 ....52 B2
Hailsham Rd *WTHG* BN11 ....54 D4
Hairpin Cft *PEAHV* BN10 ....63 E4
Halewick CI *LAN/SOMP* BN15 ....39 E2
Halewick La *LAN/SOMP* BN15 ......39 E2
Half Moon La *SALV* BN13 ....36 D2
Half Moon Pde *SALV* * BN13 ....36 D3
Halifax Dr *SALV* BN13 ....36 A4
Halland Rd *ROTT* BN2 ....29 F3
Hallett Rd *ROTT* BN2 ....37 E3
Hall CI *FIN/BW* BN14 ....37 E3
Hallett Rd *ROTT* BN2 ....46 D3
Hallyburton Rd *HOVE* BN3 ....43 H2
Halsbury CI *WTHG* BN11 ....5 J2
Halsbury Rd *WTHG* BN11 ....5 J2
Hamble Gdns *SALV* BN13 ....36 A3
Hamble Rd *LAN/SOMP* BN15 ....38 D4
Hamble Wy *SALV* BN13 ....36 A3
Ham CI *FIN/BW* BN14 ....56 C1
  PTSD BN41 ....25 E4
Hamilton Ct *FERR* * BN12 ....54 B2
Hamilton Ms *LAN/SOMP* * BN15 ...39 E3
Hamilton Rd *BRI* BN1 ....45 H2
  LAN/SOMP BN15 ....39 F3
Hamsey CI *ROTT* BN2 ....47 F5
Hamsey Crs *LEWES* BN7 ....16 C2
Hamsey La *SEAF* BN25 ....73 G1
Hamsey Rd *ROTT* BN2 ....61 H5
Hangleton CI *HOVE* BN3 ....25 H5
Hangleton Gdns *HOVE* BN3 ....43 H1
Hangleton Gra *FERR* BN12 ....53 E2
Hangleton La *FERR* BN12 ....52 C1
  HOVE BN3 ....25 G5
Hangleton Manor CI *HOVE* BN3 ...25 G5
Hangleton Rd *HOVE* BN3 ....26 A5
Hangleton Valley Dr *HOVE* BN3 ....25 G4
Hangleton Wy *HOVE* BN3 ....25 H5
Hanover CI *SEAF* BN25 ....69 H2
Hanover Crs *ROTT* BN2 ....3 J1
Hanover Ms *ROTT* BN2 ....3 K1
Hanover PI *ROTT* BN2 ....3 K1
Hanover St *ROTT* BN2 ....3 K1
Hanover Ter *ROTT* BN2 ....3 K1
Hanson Rd *NEWHV* BN9 ....68 B2
Harbour View CI *SEAF* * BN25 ......69 H2
Harbour View Rd *NEWHV* BN9 ......68 B3
Harbour Wy *SHOR* BN43 ....41 G4
Hardwick Rd *HOVE* BN3 ....26 A4
Hardwick Wy *HOVE* BN3 ....26 A3
Hardy St *SHOR* BN43 ....41 F4
Harebell Dr *PTSD* BN41 ....25 E4
Harefield Av *SALV* BN13 ....54 D1
Harfield CI *NEWHV* BN9 ....65 F3
Harison Rd *SEAF* BN25 ....71 E4
Harlech CI *SALV* BN13 ....35 H5
Harmsworth Crs *HOVE* BN3 ....26 A4
Harpers Rd *NEWHV* BN9 ....68 C1
Harrington PI *BRI* BN1 ....28 B5
Harrington Rd *BRI* BN1 ....28 B5
Harrington Vls *BRI* BN1 ....27 H5
Harrison Ct *FIN/BW* BN14 ....38 A5
Harrison Rd *FIN/BW* BN14 ....38 A5
Harrow CI *SEAF* BN25 ....71 E4
Harrow Rd *WTHG* BN11 ....4 A2
Hartfield Av *BRI* BN1 ....28 A3
Hartfield Rd *ROTT* BN2 ....61 H4
  SEAF BN25 ....71 E5
Harting CI *FERR* BN12 ....53 H1
Hartington PI *ROTT* BN2 ....46 C2
Hartington Rd *ROTT* BN2 ....46 C2

Hartington Ter *ROTT* BN2 46
Hartington Vls *HOVE* BN3 44
Harvard CI *LEWES* BN7 17
Harvest CI *PEAHV* BN10 62
Harvey Rd *FERR* BN12 54
Harveys Wy *LEWES* BN7 17
Harwood Av *FERR* BN12 54
Hastings Av *SEAF* BN25 71
Hastings Rd *ROTT* BN2 46
  WTHG BN11 55
The Haven *LAN/SOMP* * BN15 57
Havelock Rd *BRI* BN1 45
Haven Brow *SEAF* BN25 71
Havenside *SHOR* BN43 40
Hawkenbury Wy *LEWES* BN7 16
Hawkhurst CI *PEAHV* BN10 62
Hawkhurst PI *BRI* * BN1 28
Hawkhurst Rd *BRI* BN1 28
Hawkins CI *SHOR* BN43 42
Hawkins Crs *SHOR* BN43 42
Hawkins Rd *SHOR* BN43 42
Hawth CI *SEAF* BN25 70
Hawth Crs *SEAF* BN25 70
Hawth Gv *SEAF* BN25 70
Hawth HI *SEAF* BN25 69
Hawthorn Bank *ROTT* * BN2 29
Hawthorn CI *ROTT* BN2 61
Hawthorn Crs *FIN/BW* BN14 37
Hawthorn Gdns *FIN/BW* BN14 37
Hawthorn Ri *NEWHV* BN9 68
Hawthorn Rd *FIN/BW* BN14 37
Hawthorn Wy *PTSD* BN41 25
Hawth Park Rd *SEAF* BN25 70
Hawth Ri *SEAF* BN25 70
Hawth Wy *SEAF* BN25 70
Haybourne CI *ROTT* BN2 47
Haybourne Rd *ROTT* BN2 47
Hayes CI *PTSD* BN41 43
Hayley Rd *LAN/SOMP* BN15 39
Hayling Gdns *SALV* BN13 36
Hayling Ri *SALV* BN13 36
Haynes Rd *FIN/BW* BN14 55
Haynes Wy *FIN/BW* BN14 4
Hayward Rd *LEWES* BN7 16
Haywards Rd *BRI* BN1 28
Hazel CI *NEWHV* BN9 68
  PTSD BN41 25
Hazeldene *SEAF* BN25 71
Hazeldene Meads *BRI* BN1 27
Hazelhurst Crs *FIN/BW* BN14 18
Hazelmead Dr *ANG/EP* BN16 52
Hazelwood CI *FIN/BW* BN14 38
Headland Av *SEAF* BN25 71
Headland Cnr *SEAF* * BN25 73
Headlands CI *PEAHV* BN10 67
Heathdown CI *PEAHV* BN10 63
Heather La *SALV* BN13 37
Heatherstone Rd *WTHG* BN11 56
Heathfield Av *ROTT* BN2 61
Heathfield CI *SALV* BN13 36
Heathfield Crs *PTSD* BN41 24
Heathfield Dr *PTSD* BN41 24
Heathfield Rd *SEAF* BN25 70
Heath Hill Av *ROTT* BN2 47
Heathy Brow *PEAHV* BN10 62
Hebe Rd *SHOR* BN43 41
Heene PI *WTHG* BN11 4
Heene Rd *WTHG* BN11 4
Heene Ter *WTHG* BN11 4
Heene Wy *WTHG* BN11 4
Heighton Crs *NEWHV* BN9 64
Heighton Rd *NEWHV* BN9 65
The Heights *BRI* BN1 26
  FIN/BW BN14 37
Helena CI *PTSD* BN41 43
Helena Rd *ROTT* BN2 48
Hellingly CI *ROTT* BN2 47
Hempstead Rd *ROTT* BN2 61
Hendon St *ROTT* BN2 46
Henfield CI *FERR* BN12 53
  ROTT BN2 59
Henfield Rd *STEY/UB* BN44 8
Henfield Wy *HOVE* BN3 26
Henge Wy *PTSD* BN41 25
Henley Rd *ROTT* BN2 59
Henty Rd *FERR* BN12 53
  FIN/BW BN14 4
Herbert Rd *BRI* BN1 27
  LAN/SOMP BN15 38
Hereford St *ROTT* BN2 3
Hereward Wy *LEWES* BN7 17
Hermione CI *FERR* BN12 52
Hermit Ter *FIN/BW* * BN14 18
Herm Rd *FERR* BN12 53
The Herons *LAN/SOMP* * BN15 52
Heronsdale Rd *ROTT* BN2 48
Hertford Rd *BRI* BN1 28
  WTHG BN11 4
Heston Av *BRI* BN1 13

Knole Rd *ROTT* BN2 .... 61 E4
Knoll Cl *HOVE* BN3 .... 43 H1
Knoyle Rd *BRI* BN1 .... 27 G5

L

Laburnum Av *HOVE* BN3 .... 44 A1
Laburnum Cl *FERR* BN12 .... 53 F4
  LAN/SOMP BN15 .... 57 F1
Laburnum Gv *BRI* * BN1 .... 28 B4
Ladies Mile Cl *BRI* BN1 .... 27 H1
Ladies' Mile Rd *BRI* BN1 .... 27 G1
Ladycross Cl *SEAF* BN25 .... 71 F5
Ladydell Rd *WTHG* BN11 .... 5 J1
Ladysmith Rd *ROTT* BN2 .... 46 D2
Laine Cl *BRI* BN1 .... 27 G4
Laines Rd *STEY/UB* BN44 .... 7 E2
Lake Dr *PEAHV* BN10 .... 62 D5
Lambert Pl *LEWES* BN7 .... 17 F1
Lambleys La *FIN/BW* BN14 .... 38 B3
Lambourne Cl *BRI* BN1 .... 28 C5
Lambourne Rd *BRI* BN1 .... 28 C5
Lamorna Gdns *FERR* BN12 .... 53 F5
Lamorna Gv *FIN/BW* BN14 .... 37 G4
Lancaster Rd *BRI* BN1 .... 45 H3
  FERR BN12 .... 54 C4
Lancaster St *LEWES* BN7 .... 17 E3
Lancing Cl *LAN/SOMP* BN15 .... 39 F4
Lancing Pk *LAN/SOMP* BN15 .... 57 F1
Landport *LEWES* BN7 .... 16 C1
Landport Rd *LEWES* BN7 .... 16 D1
Landsdown Rd *SEAF* BN25 .... 71 G3
Landseer Rd *HOVE* BN3 .... 44 C2
Lanfranc Rd *HOVE* BN3 .... 4 A1
Langbury Cl *FERR* BN12 .... 52 D2
Langbury La *FERR* BN12 .... 52 C2
Langdale Cl *LAN/SOMP* BN15 .... 39 E5
Langdale Gdns *HOVE* BN3 .... 44 B4
Langdale Rd *HOVE* BN3 .... 44 B4
Langham Gdns *WTHG* BN11 .... 55 E3
Langley Crs *ROTT* BN2 .... 48 B1
Langridge Dr *PTSD* BN41 .... 25 E5
Langton Rd *FIN/BW* BN14 .... 4 E1
Lansdowne Ct *WTHG* BN11 .... 55 E3
Lansdowne Ms *HOVE* BN3 .... 2 A3
Lansdowne Pl *HOVE* BN3 .... 2 A4
  WTHG BN11 .... 55 E3
Lansdowne Rd *HOVE* BN3 .... 2 B3
  WTHG BN11 .... 55 E3
Lansdowne Sq *HOVE* BN3 .... 2 A4
Lansdowne St *HOVE* BN3 .... 2 A3
Lansdown Pl *LEWES* BN7 .... 17 F4
Lapierre Rd *NEWHV* BN9 .... 68 B1
Larch Cl *ROTT* BN2 .... 48 D3
Larke Cl *SHOR* BN43 .... 42 A3
Larkfield Cl *LAN/SOMP* BN15 .... 39 H5
Larkfield Wy *BRI* BN1 .... 28 A3
Lark Hi *HOVE* BN3 .... 26 A4
Lashmar Rd *ANG/EP* BN16 .... 52 A4
Latimer Rd *WTHG* BN11 .... 54 D4
Laughton Rd *ROTT* BN2 .... 48 D2
Laurel Cl *SALV* BN13 .... 36 A5
The Laurels *ROTT* * BN2 .... 46 B2
Lauriston Rd *BRI* BN1 .... 27 G5
Lavant Cl *FERR* BN12 .... 53 G1
Lavender Hi *SHOR* BN43 .... 41 H1
Lavender St *ROTT* BN2 .... 3 K6
Lavington Rd *FIN/BW* BN14 .... 37 F4
Lavinia Ct *FERR* BN12 .... 54 A2
Lavinia Wy *ANG/EP* BN16 .... 52 A4
Lawes Av *NEWHV* BN9 .... 68 C1
The Lawns *LAN/SOMP* BN15 .... 39 E3
Lawrence Rd *HOVE* BN3 .... 44 B3
Laylands Rd *PTSD* BN41 .... 43 E3
Leahurst Ct *BRI* * BN1 .... 27 G4
Leahurst Court Rd *BRI* BN1 .... 27 G4
Lea Rd *PEAHV* BN10 .... 62 D5
The Leas *PEAHV* BN10 .... 67 H3
Leconfield Rd *LAN/SOMP* BN15 .... 39 E5
Leeds Cl *SALV* BN13 .... 35 H5
Lee Rd *LEWES* BN7 .... 16 D2
Leeward Rd *SALV* BN13 .... 36 D5
Leeward Rd *SALV* BN13 .... 36 D5
Lee Wy *NEWHV* BN9 .... 64 B5
Leicester Rd *LEWES* BN7 .... 16 D3
Leicester St *ROTT* BN2 .... 3 K5
Leicester Vls *HOVE* BN3 .... 43 H3
Leigh Rd *WTHG* BN14 .... 37 H4
Leighton Av *FIN/BW* BN14 .... 38 A4
Leighton Rd *HOVE* BN3 .... 44 C2
Lenham Av *ROTT* BN2 .... 61 F4
Lenham Rd East *ROTT* BN2 .... 61 F4
Lenham Rd West *ROTT* BN2 .... 61 E4
Lenhurst Wy *SALV* BN13 .... 36 D5
Lennox Rd *HOVE* BN3 .... 44 B2
  SHOR BN43 .... 41 H2

WTHG BN11 .... 5 F3
Lennox St *ROTT* BN2 .... 3 K4
Leopold Rd *BRI* BN1 .... 2 E5
Lesser Foxholes *SHOR* BN43 .... 40 D1
Letchworth Cl *FERR* BN12 .... 53 E4
Lewes Cl *ROTT* BN2 .... 62 A4
Lewes Crs *ROTT* BN2 .... 59 E1
Lewes Ms *ROTT* * BN2 .... 59 E1
Lewes Rd *BRI* BN1 .... 29 G1
  NEWHV BN9 .... 64 B5
  ROTT BN2 .... 3 J2
Lewes St *ROTT* BN2 .... 3 J2
Lewin Cl *LAN/SOMP* BN15 .... 39 H3
Lewis Cl *NEWHV* BN9 .... 65 F3
Lewis Ct *SALV* BN13 .... 35 H5
Lewis Rd *LAN/SOMP* BN15 .... 39 F2
Lewry Cl *NEWHV* BN9 .... 68 B1
Lexden Ct *SEAF* * BN25 .... 71 E4
Lexden Dr *SEAF* BN25 .... 70 D3
Lexden Rd *SEAF* BN25 .... 70 D3
Leybourne Cl *ROTT* BN2 .... 47 G1
Leybourne Rd *ROTT* BN2 .... 29 G5
Library Pl *WTHG* BN11 .... 5 G5
Lichfield Ct *WTHG* * BN11 .... 55 E4
Lilac Cl *SALV* BN13 .... 35 H5
Limbrick Cl *FERR* BN12 .... 54 A2
Limbrick Cnr *FERR* * BN12 .... 54 A1
Limbrick La *FERR* BN12 .... 54 A2
Limbrick Wy *FERR* BN12 .... 53 H1
The Limes *ROTT* * BN2 .... 46 B2
Lime Tree Av *FIN/BW* BN14 .... 18 D5
Limney Rd *ROTT* BN2 .... 47 E3
Lincett Av *SALV* BN13 .... 54 D1
Lincett Dr *SALV* BN13 .... 54 D2
Linchmere Av *ROTT* BN2 .... 61 G4
Lincoln Av *PEAHV* BN10 .... 66 C1
Lincoln Av South *PEAHV* BN10 .... 66 C1
Lincoln Cottages *ROTT* BN2 .... 3 K2
Lincoln Rd *PTSD* BN41 .... 43 F3
  SALV BN13 .... 54 D1
Lincoln St *ROTT* BN2 .... 3 K2
The Lindens *ROTT* * BN2 .... 46 B3
Lindfield *PTSD* * BN41 .... 43 E1
Lindfield Av *SEAF* BN25 .... 73 C1
Lindfield Cl *ROTT* BN2 .... 61 F3
Lindum Rd *SALV* BN13 .... 36 D5
Lindum Wy *SALV* BN13 .... 36 D5
Lingfield Cl *SALV* BN13 .... 36 D4
Links Av *NEWHV* BN9 .... 68 A1
Links Cl *PTSD* BN41 .... 43 G2
  SEAF BN25 .... 71 E5
Links Rd *FIN/BW* BN14 .... 37 G2
  LAN/SOMP BN15 .... 39 H4
  PTSD BN41 .... 43 G2
  SEAF BN25 .... 73 E1
The Linkway *BRI* BN1 .... 28 B5
  WTHG * BN11 .... 4 C3
Linthouse Cl *PEAHV* BN10 .... 63 F3
Linton Rd *HOVE* BN3 .... 44 B2
Lions Ct *ROTT* * BN2 .... 47 E5
Lions Dr *SEAF* BN25 .... 72 D1
Liphook Cl *BRI* BN1 .... 46 C1
Lisher Rd *LAN/SOMP* BN15 .... 39 H3
Little Crs *ROTT* BN2 .... 61 F4
Little Dr *FERR* BN12 .... 53 E4
Little Dro *STEY/UB* BN44 .... 7 F3
Little East St *BRI* * BN1 .... 3 G6
  LEWES BN7 .... 17 F3
Little Gables *SALV* BN13 .... 36 D4
Littlehampton Rd *ANG/EP* BN16 .... 52 C2
Little High St *SHOR* BN43 .... 41 E3
  WTHG BN11 .... 5 F3
Little Md *FERR* * BN12 .... 54 A3
Little Paddocks Wy *FERR* BN12 .... 53 F4
Little Pembrokes *WTHG* BN11 .... 55 E2
Little Preston St *BRI* BN1 .... 2 D5
Littlestone Rd *SALV* BN13 .... 36 C4
Little Western St *BRI* BN1 .... 2 B4
Littleworth Cl *ROTT* BN2 .... 48 D3
Liverpool Gdns *WTHG* BN11 .... 5 F5
Liverpool Rd *WTHG* BN11 .... 5 F5
Liverpool Ter *WTHG* BN11 .... 5 F5
Livesay Crs *FIN/BW* BN14 .... 55 H1
Livingstone Rd *HOVE* BN3 .... 44 D3
Livingstone St *ROTT* BN2 .... 46 D5
Lloyd Cl *HOVE* BN3 .... 45 E2
Lloyd Rd *HOVE* BN3 .... 45 F2
Lloyds Bank Chambers
  SEAF BN25 .... 70 C5
Lockitt Wy *LEWES* BN7 .... 32 A2
Locks Crs *PTSD* BN41 .... 43 F2
Locks Hi *PTSD* BN41 .... 43 F1
Lockwood Cl *ROTT* BN2 .... 48 C3
Lockwood Crs *ROTT* BN2 .... 48 C3
Loddon Cl *SALV* BN13 .... 36 A2
Loder Gdns *FIN/BW* BN14 .... 37 G5
Loder Pl *BRI* BN1 .... 27 H5
Loder Rd *BRI* BN1 .... 27 H5

Lodge Cl *LEWES* BN7 .... 16 C4
  PTSD BN41 .... 24 D5
Lodge Ct *SHOR* BN43 .... 41 E1
Lodsworth Cl *ROTT* BN2 .... 47 F3
Lomond Av *BRI* BN1 .... 14 A5
London Rd *BRI* BN1 .... 13 F5
London St *WTHG* BN11 .... 4 C2
London Ter *BRI* BN1 .... 46 A3
Longfellow Rd *WTHG* BN11 .... 4 B3
Long Furlong *SALV* BN13 .... 35 E1
Longhill Cl *ROTT* BN2 .... 60 C1
Longhill Rd *ROTT* BN2 .... 60 B1
Longlands *FIN/BW* BN14 .... 37 H2
Longlands Gld *FIN/BW* BN14 .... 37 H2
Longlands Spinney
  FIN/BW BN14 .... 37 H2
Long Meadow *FIN/BW* BN14 .... 18 D3
Longridge Av *ROTT* BN2 .... 61 G5
The Lookout *PEAHV* BN10 .... 63 E2
Loose La *FIN/BW* BN14 .... 38 C5
The Lords *SEAF* BN25 .... 70 C2
Lorna Rd *HOVE* BN3 .... 45 F3
Lorne Rd *BRI* BN1 .... 46 A2
Lorraine Rd *NEWHV* BN9 .... 68 D1
Lotts La *LAN/SOMP* BN15 .... 39 E4
Lover's Wk *BRI* BN1 .... 45 H2
Lovers Walk Cottages *BRI* BN1 .... 45 H2
Lovett Ct *FERR* * BN12 .... 54 A1
Lower Beach Rd *SHOR* BN43 .... 41 F4
Lower Bevendean Av
  ROTT BN2 .... 47 E1
Lower Chalvington Pl
  ROTT BN2 .... 47 E5
Lower Dr *SEAF* BN25 .... 70 D3
  STHW BN42 .... 42 C1
Lower Market St *HOVE* BN3 .... 2 B4
Lower Pl *NEWHV* BN9 .... 68 C1
Lower Rock Gdns *ROTT* BN2 .... 3 K6
Lowther Rd *BRI* BN1 .... 28 A5
  SALV BN13 .... 36 D3
Loxley Gdns *FIN/BW* * BN14 .... 4 C1
Loxwood Av *FIN/BW* BN14 .... 52 B2
Loxwood Av *FIN/BW* BN14 .... 37 F5
Lucerne Cl *PTSD* BN41 .... 43 F1
Lucerne Rd *BRI* BN1 .... 45 H1
Lucraft Rd *ROTT* BN2 .... 29 F2
Ludlow Ri *ROTT* BN2 .... 47 G1
Lulham Cl *PEAHV* BN10 .... 62 D5
Lullington Av *HOVE* BN3 .... 44 B2
Lullington Cl *SEAF* BN25 .... 73 F1
Lustrells Cl *ROTT* BN2 .... 61 F3
Lustrells Crs *ROTT* BN2 .... 61 F3
Lustrells Rd *ROTT* BN2 .... 61 F3
Lustrells V *ROTT* BN2 .... 61 F3
Luther St *ROTT* BN2 .... 46 C3
Lyminster Av *BRI* BN1 .... 28 A2
Lynchet Cl *BRI* BN1 .... 28 C5
Lynchet Down *BRI* BN1 .... 28 C5
The Lynchets *LEWES* BN7 .... 17 G1
Lynchets Crs *HOVE* BN3 .... 25 H4
The Lynchette *SHOR* BN43 .... 41 F1
Lynchmere Av *LAN/SOMP* BN15 .... 39 F2
Lynchet Wk *BRI* BN1 .... 28 C5
Lyndhurst Cnr *HOVE* * BN3 .... 45 F3
Lyndhurst Rd *HOVE* BN3 .... 45 F3
  WTHG BN11 .... 5 G4
Lyn Rd *SALV* BN13 .... 36 A4
Lynton St *ROTT* BN2 .... 46 C3
Lynwood Rd *ROTT* BN2 .... 61 G5
Lyon Cl *HOVE* BN3 .... 2 B1
Lyons Wy *FIN/BW* BN14 .... 38 A2

M

Mackie Av *BRI* BN1 .... 27 H1
Madehurst Cl *ROTT* BN2 .... 46 D5
Madeira Av *WTHG* BN11 .... 5 H4
Madeira Dr *ROTT* BN2 .... 3 H6
Madeira Pl *ROTT* BN2 .... 3 J6
Mafeking Rd *ROTT* BN2 .... 46 C2
Magnolia Cl *SALV* BN13 .... 35 H5
Mainstone Rd *HOVE* BN3 .... 44 B3
Major Cl *BRI* BN1 .... 46 B1
Malcolm Cl *FERR* BN12 .... 53 E4
Maldon Rd *BRI* BN1 .... 27 F5
Malines Av *PEAHV* BN10 .... 66 D1
Malines Av South *PEAHV* BN10 .... 66 C1
Mallett Cl *SEAF* BN25 .... 72 C1
Malling *LEWES* BN7 .... 16 D1
Malling Cl *LEWES* BN7 .... 17 F1
Malling Down *LEWES* BN7 .... 17 G1
Malling Hl *LEWES* BN7 .... 17 G1
The Mallings *LEWES* * BN7 .... 17 G3
Malling St *LEWES* BN7 .... 17 G3
Mallory Rd *HOVE* BN3 .... 27 E5

The Malthouse *LEWES* * BN7 17
Malthouse Cl *LAN/SOMP* BN15 38
Malthouse La *ROTT* BN2 3
Malvern Cl *WTHG* BN11 56
Malvern St *HOVE* BN3 44
Manchester St *ROTT* BN2 3
Manitoba Wy *SALV* BN13 36
The Manor *WTHG* * BN11 4
Manor Cl *LAN/SOMP* BN15 39
  LAN/SOMP BN15 40
  ROTT BN2 47
  SEAF BN25 71
  STHW BN42 42
  WTHG BN11 4
Manor Ct *LAN/SOMP* * BN15 39
  SEAF * BN25 71
  STHW * BN42 43
Manor Crs *ROTT* BN2 47
Manor Dr *PEAHV* BN10 62
Manor Field Ct *FIN/BW* * BN14 37
Manor Gdns *ROTT* BN2 47
Manor Gn *ROTT* BN2 47
Manor Hall Rd *STHW* BN42 42
Manor Hl *ROTT* BN2 47
Manor Lea *WTHG* * BN11 4
Manor Paddock *ROTT* BN2 59
Manor Pde *SALV* * BN13 36
Manor Pl *ROTT* BN2 47
Manor Rd *ANG/EP* BN16 52
  LAN/SOMP BN15 39
  PTSD BN41 43
  ROTT BN2 59
  SEAF BN25 71
  STEY/UB BN44 8
  WTHG BN11 4
Manor Rd North *SEAF* BN25 71
Manor Ter *LEWES* * BN7 17
Manor View Ct *FIN/BW* * BN14 37
Manor Wy *LAN/SOMP* BN15 39
  ROTT BN2 47
Mansell Rd *SHOR* BN43 41
Mansfield Cl *WTHG* BN11 56
Mansfield Rd *HOVE* BN3 44
  WTHG BN11 56
Manton Rd *ROTT* BN2 47
Maple Cl *ROTT* BN2 48
  SALV BN13 36
Maple Gdns *HOVE* BN3 44
Maplehurst Rd *PTSD* BN41 43
Maple Leaf Cl *NEWHV* BN9 68
The Maples *FERR* BN12 53
Maple Wk *LAN/SOMP* BN15 38
Mardale Rd *SALV* BN13 36
Mardyke *SHOR* BN43 40
Maresfield Rd *ROTT* BN2 47
Margaret St *ROTT* BN2 3
Margery Rd *HOVE* BN3 43
Marina Wy *ROTT* BN2 59
Marine Av *HOVE* BN3 43
Marine Cl *ROTT* BN2 61
  WTHG BN11 55
Marine Ct *PEAHV* * BN10 66
Marine Crs *SEAF* BN25 54
  SEAF BN25 72
Marine Dr *FERR* BN12 53
  ROTT BN2 59
  SEAF BN25 69
Marine Gdns *ROTT* BN2 3
Marine Pde *ROTT* BN2 3
  SEAF BN25 69
  WTHG BN11 4
Marine Pl *WTHG* BN11 5
The Mariners *LAN/SOMP* * BN15 57
Mariners Cl *SHOR* BN43 40
Marine Sq *ROTT* BN2 58
Marine Vw *NEWHV* BN9 68
  ROTT BN2 3
Marjoram Pl *SHOR* BN43 41
Mark Cl *SEAF* BN25 73
Market Fld *STEY/UB* BN44 7
Market La *LEWES* BN7 17
Market St *BRI* BN1 3
  LEWES BN7 17
  WTHG BN11 5
Markwick Ms *WTHG* BN11 5
Marlborough Ms *BRI* BN1 2
Marlborough Pl *BRI* BN1 3
Marlborough Rd *FERR* BN12 54
  LAN/SOMP BN15 57
Marlborough St *BRI* BN1 2
Marlborough Wy *FERR* * BN12 54
The Marlinspike *SHOR* BN43 41
Marlowe Rd *FIN/BW* BN14 38
Marlow Rd *ROTT* BN2 59
Marmion Rd *HOVE* BN3 44
Marshall Av *FIN/BW* BN14 18
Marshalls Rw *BRI* BN1 3
  ROTT BN2 46

'rshall Wy *HOVE* BN3................44 B1
'rston Rd *FIN/BW* BN14.........56 A1
rtello Ms *SEAF* * BN25............72 C1
rtello Rd *SEAF* BN25...............72 C1
tha Gunn Rd *ROTT* BN2..........46 D1
tin Rd *PEAHV* BN3..................43 H1
Martins *PEAHV* BN10..............62 D4
Martlet *HOVE* BN3..................45 F2
Martlets *LAN/SOMP* BN15......39 E4
HOVE BN7...............................17 F1
HOR BN43................................41 F2
rtlets Wy *FERR* BN12..............54 A2
rtyn's Cl *ROTT* BN2................60 C1
son Rd *SEAF* BN25.................70 D4
clock Rd *BRI* BN1..................45 F1
dlin La *STEY/UB* BN44.............7 F3
udlyn Cl *STEY/UB* BN44............7 G3
udlyn Pk *STEY/UB* BN44...........7 F3
udlyn Pkwy *STEY/UB* BN44.......7 F3
urice Rd *SEAF* BN25...............72 D2
y Av *SEAF* BN25......................71 F5
ybridge Crs *FERR* BN12..........54 A2
ybridge Sq *FERR* BN12...........54 A1
y Cl *FERR* BN12......................54 A1
y Cottages *ROTT* * BN2...........46 C2
yfield *ANG/EP* BN16...............52 A2
y Pk *PEAHV* BN10..................67 F2
yfield Cl *BRI* BN1...................27 H2
FIN/BW BN14...........................57 E2
yfield Crs *BRI* BN1.................27 H2
yflower Wy *ANG/EP* BN16.....52 A2
yhew Wy *LEWES* BN7.............17 F1
yo Rd *ROTT* BN2....................46 B2
y Rd *ROTT* BN2......................46 D3
y Tree Av *FIN/BW* BN14.........18 D4
ytree Cl *LAN/SOMP* BN15.......38 D4
ytree Wk *HOVE* BN3...............44 A1
kerchar Cl *LAN/SOMP* BN15....39 H3
adow Cl *HOVE* BN3................26 D4
adow La *LAN/SOMP* BN15......39 G5
adow Pde *ROTT* BN2..............60 D2
adow Pk *ANG/EP* BN16..........52 B4
adow Rd *WTHG* BN11..............56 C2
e Meadows *HOVE* BN3...........25 G4
adowside *ANG/EP* BN16.........34 A4
adowside Ct *FERR* * BN12......53 E3
LEWES BN7..............................17 C1
adow Sweet Cl *SALV* * BN13...35 C5
adowview Rd *ROTT* BN2.........47 E1
adowview Rd
LAN/SOMP BN15.....................39 F2
adow Wy *FERR* BN12.............53 E3
SEAF BN25..............................71 E3
e Meads *BRI* BN1..................28 D2
ads Av *HOVE* BN3.................25 G4
ads Rd *SEAF* BN25................25 G4
adway Ct *SALV* * BN13.........54 C1
STHW BN42..............................42 B2
adway Crs *HOVE* BN3...........26 B5
e Meadway *ROTT* BN2...........47 F5
SHOR BN43..............................41 F4
ealla Cl *LEWES* BN7..............17 E1
easham Ct *FERR* BN12...........53 F4
edina Pl *HOVE* BN3...............44 D3
edina Ter *HOVE* BN3.............44 D5
edina Vls *HOVE* BN3.............44 D5
edmerry Hl *ROTT* BN2...........29 E5
edway Ct *SALV* BN13............36 B5
eeching Pl *NEWHV* * BN9.......68 C1
eeching Ri *NEWHV* BN9.........68 C1
eeching Rd *NEWHV* BN9........68 D1
eeting House La *BRI* BN1..........3 G5
elbourne Av *FERR* BN12.........54 A3
elbourne Rd *FERR* BN12.........54 A3
elbourne St *ROTT* BN2...........46 C2
elrose Av *PTSD* BN41............43 E1
SALV BN13...............................54 C1
elrose Cl *BRI* BN1.................28 C5
SALV BN13...............................54 C1
elville Rd *HOVE* BN3...............2 D1
elville Wy *FERR* BN12...........54 A1
endip Cl *ANG/EP* BN16..........52 A3
endip Crs *SALV* BN13............36 C3
endip Rd *SALV* BN13.............36 C3
ercroad St *SEAF* BN25...........70 D5
eredith Rd *FIN/BW* BN14.........5 J1
erevale *BRI* BN1....................28 B5
erianci Rd *LEWES* BN7..........16 C3
eriandian Wy *PEAHV* BN10.....66 D1
erlin Cl *HOVE* BN3................45 F2
erryfield Crs *ANG/EP* BN16....34 A4

Mersey Cl *SALV* BN13............36 A3
Mersey Rd *SALV* BN13............36 A3
Mersham Gdns *FERR* BN12......54 A3
Merston Cl *ROTT* BN2.............48 C4
Merton Rd *WTHG* BN11.............5 J5
Metcalfe Av *NEWHV* BN9.........64 B5
Meyners Cl *HOVE* BN3............25 G4
The Mews *WTHG* * BN11............4 C4
Middle Furlong *SEAF* BN25......70 D5
Middle Onslow Cl *FERR* * BN12..53 E2
Middle Rd *BRI* BN1.................45 G1
LAN/SOMP BN15......................39 G5
SHOR BN43..............................41 H3
Middle St *BRI* BN1....................3 F6
BRI BN1...................................43 F4
PTSD BN41..............................43 F4
SHOR BN43..............................41 F4
Middleton Av *HOVE* BN3.........43 H4
Middleton Rd *BRI* BN1............29 E2
Middle Tyne *SALV* BN13.........36 B5
Midhurst Wy *ANG/EP* BN16.....16 C3
LEWES BN7..............................16 C3
Midhurst Cl *SALV* BN13..........53 F3
Midhurst Dr *FERR* BN12..........53 F3
Midhurst Ri *BRI* BN1...............28 B4
Midhurst Wk *HOVE* BN3..........26 B4
Midway Rd *ROTT* BN2.............48 A2
Mighell St *ROTT* BN2................3 J4
Milbury Cl *FERR* BN12............53 F5
Milcote Av *HOVE* BN3.............44 B2
Mildmay Rd *LEWES* BN7..........16 C3
Mile Oak Crs *STHW* BN42........45 G1
Mile Oak Gdns *PTSD* BN41......43 E1
Mile Oak Rd *PTSD* BN41..........43 E1
LEWES BN7..............................16 C3
Millberg Rd *SEAF* BN25..........71 F4
Mill Cl *PTSD* BN41.................43 G1
Mill Ct *WTHG* * BN11.................4 B4
Millcroft *BRI* BN1...................27 E2
Millcroft Av *STHW* BN42..........42 C1
Millcroft Gdns *STHW* BN42......42 C1
Millcross Rd *PTSD* BN41..........43 F1
Milldown Rd *SEAF* BN25..........70 D4
Mill Dr *HOVE* BN3..................26 C4
SEAF BN25..............................71 E5
Mill Dro *SEAF* BN25...............69 F3
Millennium La *LAN/SOMP* BN15..40 B4
Miller Rd *BRI* BN1..................45 G1
Miller's Rd *BRI* BN1................45 G1
Millfield *LAN/SOMP* BN15........39 E3
STEY/UB * BN44.........................8 A2
Millfield Cl *SEAF* BN25...........71 E4
Millfield Cottages *ROTT* BN2....58 D1
Mill Hl *SHOR* BN43.................23 E1
Mill Hill Cl *SHOR* BN43...........41 E1
Mill Hill Dr *SHOR* BN43...........41 E1
Mill Hill Gdns *SHOR* BN43.......41 E1
Mill House Gdns *WTHG* BN11....55 E3
Mill La *LEWES* BN7.................51 E3
PTSD BN41...............................25 F5
SALV BN13...............................18 D5
Mill Ri *BRI* BN1......................27 E2
Mill Rd *BRI* BN1.....................27 E1
LAN/SOMP BN15......................39 E1
LEWES BN7..............................17 G1
PTSD BN41..............................43 F3
STEY/UB BN44............................7 E1
WTHG BN11................................4 B4
Mill Rw *BRI* * BN1....................27 E1
Millyard Crs *ROTT* BN2...........48 B3
Milner Rd *BRI* BN1.................46 C1
Milnthorpe Rd *HOVE* BN3........44 A2
Milton Cl *LAN/SOMP* BN15......39 G5
Milton Dr *STHW* BN42.............42 D2
Milton Rd *ROTT* BN2.................3 K1
WTHG BN11................................4 C6
Milton St *WTHG* BN11.............28 D2
Mitchelldean *PEAHV* BN10.......62 D4
Moat Wy *FERR* BN12..............54 C4
Modena Rd *HOVE* BN3............44 B2
Molesworth St *HOVE* BN3........44 B2
Monarch Gdns *SEAF* * BN25.....71 E4
Monarchs Wy *HOVE* BN3.........45 E3
PTSD BN41..............................25 H1
SHOR BN44................................9 C5
STEY/UB BN44............................6 C4
STEY/UB BN44............................7 G3
STHW BN42..............................24 C4
Monckton Wy *LEWES* BN7.......32 A2
Monk Cl *BRI* BN1...................29 E1
Monks Av *LAN/SOMP* BN15.....39 H4
Monks Cl *LAN/SOMP* BN15......39 H4
Monks La *LEWES* * BN7...........17 E4
Monks Wk *STEY/UB* BN44..........8 B1
Monmouth St *HOVE* BN3.........44 D3
Montacute Rd *LEWES* BN7.......16 C4
Montague Cl *SHOR* BN43.........42 B3

Montague Pl *ROTT* BN2............58 C1
WTHG BN11...............................5 F6
Montague St *ROTT* BN2...........58 C1
WTHG BN11................................5 F6
Montefiore Rd *HOVE* BN3...........2 C1
Montford Cl *SHOR* BN43..........42 B2
Montgomery St *HOVE* BN3.......44 B3
Montpelier Crs *BRI* BN1.............2 C3
Montpelier Pl *BRI* BN1...............2 C3
Montpelier Rd *ANG/EP* BN16....52 A4
BRI BN1.....................................2 C4
Montpelier St *BRI* BN1..............2 D3
Montpelier Ter *BRI* BN1..............2 D3
Montpelier Vls *BRI* BN1.............2 D3
Montreal Rd *ROTT* BN2..............3 K3
Montreal Wy *SALV* BN13..........36 A4
Montrose Cl *FERR* BN12...........54 A2
Monument Vw *ROTT* BN2.........46 D3
Moore Cl *SALV* BN13...............35 H4
Moorfoot Rd *SALV* BN13..........36 D3
The Moorings *LAN/SOMP* BN15..39 H2
LEWES * BN7............................17 G3
SHOR BN43..............................42 A4
Morecambe Rd *BRI* BN1..........28 A1
Morestead *PEAHV* BN10..........63 F4
Morland Av *FIN/BW* BN14.......38 A3
Morley Cl *LEWES* BN7.............16 D5
Morley St *ROTT* BN2..................3 H5
Morningside Cl *SEAF* BN25.......70 D4
Mornington Crs *HOVE* BN3.......43 H3
Mornington Man *HOVE* * BN3...43 H3
Morris Rd *LEWES* * BN7...........17 G3
Mortimer Rd *HOVE* BN3...........44 B2
Moulsecoomb Pl *ROTT* * BN2....28 D5
Moulsecoomb Wy *ROTT* BN2....29 E4
Mount Caburn Crs *PEAHV* BN10..63 E3
Mount Cl *NEWHV* BN9..............65 F5
Mount Dr *ROTT* BN2................61 H3
Mountfield Rd *LEWES* BN7.......17 H4
Mountfields *BRI* BN1...............28 C5
Mount Harry Rd *LEWES* BN7.....16 C2
Mount Pl *LEWES* BN7..............17 E3
Mount Pleasant *ROTT* BN2.........3 K5
Mount Rd *NEWHV* BN9.............65 F5
Mount St *LEWES* BN7..............17 E4
Mountview Rd *LAN/SOMP* BN15..39 E2
Mountway *LAN/SOMP* BN15......39 C1
Mount Zion Pl *BRI* BN1..............3 F5
Moyne Cl *HOVE* BN3...............44 A1
Muirfield Cl *SALV* BN13...........36 B4
Muirfield Rd *SALV* BN13...........36 B4
Mulberry Cl *HOVE* BN3............27 H4
FERR BN12...............................53 E3
FERR BN12...............................54 A2
LAN/SOMP BN15......................39 G4
SHOR BN43...............................42 B1
Mulberry Ct *FERR* * BN12.........54 A3
Mulberry Gdns *FERR* BN12......54 A3
Mulberry La *FERR* BN12...........54 A3
Murray Av *NEWHV* BN9...........68 C1
Mushroom Fld *LEWES* BN7.......32 A2
Myrtle Crs *LAN/SOMP* BN15.....39 E5
Myrtle Rd *LAN/SOMP* BN15......39 E5

N

Namrik Ms *HOVE* BN3..............44 C4
Nanson Rd *BRI* BN1................28 D1
Natal Rd *ROTT* BN2................28 D5
Navarino Wy *WTHG* BN11........56 C2
Neill's Cl *NEWHV* BN9.............68 C1
Nelson Cl *LAN/SOMP* BN15......39 F2
Nelson Rd *FERR* BN12.............54 B1
Nelson Rw *ROTT* BN2................3 J4
Nepcote La *FIN/BW* BN14........18 C1
Nepfield Cl *FIN/BW* BN14.........18 C1
Nesbitt Rd *ROTT* BN2..............46 D1
Netherfield Gn *ROTT* BN2.........48 D2
Nevill Av *HOVE* BN3................26 A5
Nevill Cl *HOVE* BN3.................26 A5
Nevill Crs *LEWES* BN7.............16 D5
Neville Rd *PEAHV* BN10...........67 F2
Nevill Gdns *HOVE* BN3............26 A5
Nevill Pl *HOVE* BN3.................26 A5
Nevill Rd *HOVE* BN3................26 A5
LEWES BN7...............................16 C2
ROTT BN2................................60 D4
Nevill Ter *LEWES* BN7..............16 C2
Nevill Wy *HOVE* BN3...............26 A5
Newark Pl *ROTT* BN2.................3 J2
New Barn Cl *PTSD* BN41..........25 F5
SHOR * BN43...........................41 H1
New Barn Rd *ROTT* BN2...........60 D2
SHOR BN43...............................41 H1
New Broadway *FIN/BW* * BN14..55 E2
New Church Rd *HOVE* BN3.......43 H3

New Coastguard Cottages
SEAF * BN25............................70 A4
New Dorset St *BRI* BN1..............3 F3
Newells Cl *ROTT* BN2..............48 C1
New England Ri *PTSD* BN41......25 E5
New England Rd *BRI* BN1...........2 E1
New England St *BRI* BN1............3 G1
Newfield La *NEWHV* BN9.........68 C1
Newfield Rd *NEWHV* BN9.........68 C1
New Gdns *FIN/BW* BN14..........38 B3
Newham Cl *STEY/UB* BN44.........7 E1
Newham La *STEY/UB* BN44.........6 D2
Newhaven Fort *NEWHV* * BN9...68 D3
Newhaven Hts *NEWHV* * BN9....68 C3
Newhaven Rd *SEAF* BN25.........69 C3
Newhaven Sq *NEWHV* BN9.......68 D1
Newhaven St *ROTT* BN2.............3 J2
Newick Cl *SEAF* BN25..............73 C1
Newick Rd *BRI* BN1.................29 E3
Newland Rd *STEY/UB* BN44........8 B2
WTHG BN11................................5 F2
Newlands Rd *ROTT* BN2...........61 E4
Newland St *WTHG* BN11............5 F2
Newling Wy *SALV* BN13...........36 C1
Newman's Gdns
LAN/SOMP BN15......................38 D3
Newmarket Rd *ROTT* BN2.........46 C2
New Pde *WTHG* BN11................5 J5
Newport Ms *WTHG* BN11..........56 D2
Newport St *ROTT* BN2.............46 B3
New Rd *BRI* BN1......................3 G4
LEWES BN7...............................17 E3
NEWHV BN9.............................36 D4
SALV BN13...............................36 A3
SHOR BN43..............................41 F3
STEY/UB BN44.............................8 B3
New Salts Farm Rd *SHOR* BN43..40 C4
New Steine *ROTT* BN2................3 J6
New Steine Ms *ROTT* BN2...........3 J6
New St *WTHG* BN11...................4 E6
Newtimber Av *FERR* BN12........53 H2
Newtimber Dr *PTSD* BN41.........43 E1
Newtimber Gdns *SHOR* BN43....41 F1
Newton Rd *LEWES* BN7............16 D2
PEAHV BN10............................67 E1
Newtown Rd *HOVE* BN3............44 D2
Nicolson Dr *SHOR* BN43...........41 F2
Nile St *BRI* BN1........................3 G5
Ninfield Pl *ROTT* BN2..............47 E3
Nizells Av *HOVE* BN3................2 B1
Nolan Rd *ROTT* BN2................48 C3
The Nookery *ANG/EP* BN16......52 A4
Norbury Cl *LAN/SOMP* BN15....39 H2
Norbury Dr *LAN/SOMP* BN15....39 G2
Nore Rd *NEWHV* BN9...............68 B2
Norfolk Buildings *BRI* BN1..........4 C3
Norfolk Ct *WTHG* * BN11............4 C3
Norfolk Rd *BRI* BN1...................2 C3
Norfolk Ms *BRI* BN1..................2 C4
Norfolk Sq *BRI* BN1...................2 C4
Norfolk St *BRI* BN1....................2 C5
WTHG BN11................................4 C3
Norfolk Ter *BRI* BN1..................2 C3
Norman Cl *SEAF* BN25.............69 H2
Norman Crs *SHOR* BN43...........41 F1
Normandy La *ANG/EP* BN16.....52 A5
Normandy Rd *FIN/BW* BN14......55 F1
Norman Rd *SEAF* BN25.............44 A4
NEWHV BN9.............................68 C1
Normansal Ct *SEAF* BN25.........71 E2
Normansal Park Av *SEAF* BN25..70 D4
Normans Ct *SHOR* * BN43.........41 F1
Normanton St *ROTT* BN2...........46 D3
North Av *FERR* BN12...............54 C4
Northbourne Cl *SHOR* BN43......41 F2
Northbrook Cl *FIN/BW* BN14......38 A4
Northbrook Rd *FIN/BW* BN14.....38 A4
North Camp La *SEAF* BN25.......70 D3
Northcliffe Ct *SEAF* BN25..........70 D4
North Cl *PTSD* BN41................25 H3
Northcote La *PEAHV* BN10........62 C4
North Ct *LEWES* BN7...............17 E3
Northcourt Rd *FIN/BW* BN14.......4 D1
Northdown Cl *NEWHV* BN9.......68 C1
Northdown Rd *NEWHV* BN9......68 B2
North Dr *ROTT* BN2................46 C4
Northease Cl *HOVE* BN3...........25 H5
Northease Dr *HOVE* BN3...........25 H5
Northease Gdns *HOVE* BN3.......26 A4
North Farm Rd
LAN/SOMP BN15......................39 G4
Northfield Cl *SEAF* BN25...........70 D3
Northfield Ri *HOVE* BN3............25 H3
ROTT BN2.................................61 E5
Northfield Rd *SALV* BN13.........37 E4
Northfield Wy *BRI* BN1............28 A3
North Gdns *BRI* BN1..................3 F3
Northgate Cl *LAN/SOMP* BN15..38 D4

ROTT BN2....................................60 D3
North La *ANG/EP* BN16............52 A4
  NEWHV * BN9..........................68 C1
  PTSD BN41...............................25 E5
North Pl *BRI* BN1.........................3 H4
North Quay Rd *NEWHV* BN9....64 D4
North Rd *BRI* BN1.........................3 G3
  LAN/SOMP BN15....................39 C4
  PTSD BN41...............................25 E5
North St *BRI* BN1.........................3 F4
  LEWES BN7...............................17 E2
  SHOR BN43...............................41 E3
  WTHG BN11.................................5 F3
North Street Qd *BRI* * BN1.........3 F4
Northview Ter *FIN/BW* * BN14....18 C1
North Wy *LEWES* BN7.................16 C2
  NEWHV BN9.............................64 D5
  NEWHV BN9.............................68 C1
  SEAF BN25...............................70 D3
Northwood Av *ROTT* BN2..........62 A4
Norton Cl *HOVE* BN3..................44 D4
Norton Dr *ROTT* BN2..................48 B1
Norton Rd *HOVE* BN3..................44 D4
  LAN/SOMP BN15....................39 F5
  NEWHV BN9.............................69 E1
Norton Ter *NEWHV* BN9............69 E1
Norway St *PTSD* BN41...............43 G3
Norwich Cl *ROTT* BN2................29 C5
Norwich Ct *WTHG* * BN11...........55 E4
Norwich Dr *ROTT* BN2................29 C5
Nunnery Stable *LEWES* BN7......16 D3
Nursery Cl *ANG/EP* BN16..........52 A5
  LAN/SOMP BN15....................39 F2
  PTSD BN41...............................24 C3
  SHOR BN43...............................41 H2
Nursery La *WTHG* BN11...............4 C6
Nutbourne Rd *FIN/BW* BN14......55 F1
Nuthurst Cl *ROTT* BN2...............47 F4
Nuthurst Pl *ROTT* BN2...............47 F5
Nutley Av *FERR* BN12................54 A4
  ROTT BN2.................................61 H5
Nutley Cl *FERR* BN12................54 A4
  HOVE BN3.................................26 B4
Nutley Crs *FERR* BN12..............54 A4
Nutley Dr *FERR* BN12................54 A4
Nyetimber Hl *ROTT* BN2.............29 E5

O

Oakapple Rd *STHW* BN42...........24 B5
Oak Cl *BRI* BN1.........................27 G4
  SALV BN13...............................36 C1
Oakdene Av *PTSD* BN41...........24 C4
Oakdene Cl *PTSD* BN41.............24 C4
Oakdene Crs *PTSD* BN41...........24 C4
Oakdene Gdns *PTSD* BN41........24 C4
Oakdene Ri *PTSD* BN41.............24 C4
Oakdene Wy *PTSD* BN41...........24 C4
Oaklands Av *ROTT* BN2.............61 G4
Oakleigh Cl *WTHG* BN11............56 C1
Oakleigh Rd *FIN/BW* BN14.........56 C1
Oakley Gdns *ANG/EP* BN16.......52 A5
Ocean Cl *FERR* BN12.................53 E5
Ocean Dr *FERR* BN12.................53 E5
Ocean Pde *FERR* * BN12............53 E4
Offham Cl *SEAF* BN25................70 D3
Offham Rd *LEWES* BN7..............16 C2
Offham Ter *LEWES* * BN7............17 E2
Offington Av *FIN/BW* BN14.........37 F3
Offington Ct *FIN/BW* BN14..........37 F3
Offington Dr *FIN/BW* BN14..........37 F3
Offington Gdns *FIN/BW* BN14.....37 E3
Offington La *FIN/BW* BN14..........37 E4
Old Barn Wy *STHW* BN42...........43 E3
Old Boat Wk *BRI* BN1.................14 B5
Old Court Cl *BRI* BN1.................27 H3
Olde Place Ms *ROTT* BN2...........60 D4
Old Farm Rd *BRI* BN1.................27 H2
Oldfield Crs *STHW* BN42............42 B3
Old Fort Rd *SHOR* BN43.............41 G4
Old London Rd *BRI* BN1.............27 G2
Old Malling Wy *LEWES* BN7.......17 E1
Old Market Sq *STEY/UB* * BN44....7 F1
Old Mill Cl *BRI* BN1...................27 G2
Old Parish La *ROTT* BN2............48 B2
Old Rectory Gdns *STHW* BN42....42 B3
Old Salts Farm Rd
  LAN/SOMP BN15....................39 H5
Old Shoreham Rd *HOVE* BN3.....45 E2
  LAN/SOMP BN15....................39 H3
  LAN/SOMP BN15....................40 C3
  STHW BN42.............................42 D2
Old Steine *BRI* BN1......................3 H5
Old Stocks *FIN/BW* * BN14..........18 C1
Old Tree Pde *SEAF* * BN25.........72 C1
Old Worthing Rd *ANG/EP* BN16....52 B3

Oliver Cl *ROTT* BN2....................46 C5
Olive Rd *HOVE* BN3....................44 A4
Onslow Dr *FERR* BN12................53 E3
Onslow Rd *HOVE* BN3................45 E1
Ontario Cl *SALV* BN13................36 A4
Ontario Gdns *SALV* BN13............36 A4
Ophir Rd *WTHG* BN11................56 C2
Orchard Av *FIN/BW* BN14...........37 E5
  HOVE BN3.................................44 C1
  LAN/SOMP BN15....................39 G3
Orchard Cl *FERR* BN12..............53 E2
  FIN/BW BN14...........................37 F5
  SHOR BN43...............................41 E2
  STHW BN42.............................42 D2
Orchard Gdns *HOVE* BN3...........44 D1
Orchard Ms *NEWHV* BN9............65 F3
Orchard Rd *ANG/EP* BN16..........52 A3
  HOVE BN3.................................44 C1
  LEWES BN7...............................17 G2
Orchard Wy *LAN/SOMP* BN15....39 G3
Orchid Vw *BRI* BN1...................28 C1
Oriental Pl *BRI* BN1.......................2 C5
Orient Rd *LAN/SOMP* BN15.........40 C5
Orkney Ct *SALV* BN13................35 H5
Orme Rd *WTHG* BN11...................4 C2
Ormonde Wy *SHOR* BN43..........40 D4
Orpen Rd *HOVE* BN3..................45 F1
Osborne Cl *LAN/SOMP* BN15......39 F4
Osborne Dr *LAN/SOMP* BN15......39 F4
Osborne Rd *BRI* BN1..................27 H5
Osborne Vls *HOVE* BN3..............44 D5
Osmonde Cl *FIN/BW* BN14...........4 D1
Osmond Rd *HOVE* BN3.................2 C1
Ousedale Cl *LEWES* BN7............16 D3
Outlook Av *PEAHV* BN10.............67 H2
The Oval *SALV* BN13.................36 D5
Oval Cl *PEAHV* BN10.................63 E3
Oval Waye *FERR* BN12...............53 E5
Overdown Ri *PTSD* BN41............24 D3
Overhill *STHW* BN42...................42 C1
Overhill Dr *BRI* BN1....................27 G2
Overhill Gdns *BRI* BN1...............27 G2
Overhill Wy *BRI* BN1..................27 G1
Overmead *SHOR* BN43...............41 E2
Over St *BRI* BN1...........................3 G2
Ovingdean Cl *ROTT* BN2............48 B3
Ovingdean Rd *ROTT* BN2...........60 B1
Oxen Av *SHOR* BN43..................41 F2
Oxford Ct *BRI* BN1.......................3 H1
Oxford Ms *HOVE* BN3.................45 E3
Oxford Pl *BRI* BN1........................3 H1
Oxford Rd *WTHG* BN11...............4 D3
Oxford St *BRI* BN1.......................3 H1
Oxford Ter *STEY/UB* * BN44........7 F1

P

The Paddock *HOVE* BN3.............45 E1
  SHOR BN43...............................40 D1
Paddock Cl *FIN/BW* * BN14.........55 F1
Paddock Fld *BRI* * BN1...............29 H2
Paddock La *LEWES* BN7.............17 E3
Paddock Rd *LEWES* BN7............17 E3
The Paddocks *LAN/SOMP* BN15...39 H5
  LEWES BN7...............................51 F2
  STEY/UB BN44...........................8 B1
Paddock Wy *FIN/BW* BN14.........18 C1
Pages La *WTHG* BN11................56 C2
Palace Pl *BRI* BN1........................3 H5
Palatine Rd *FERR* BN12..............54 A1
The Pallant *FERR* BN12..............53 H1
Palma Ct *WTHG* * BN11................4 A5
Palm Ct *SALV* BN13...................36 C3
Palmeira Av *HOVE* BN3..............45 E4
Palmeira Sq *HOVE* BN3..............45 E5
Palmerston Av *FERR* BN12.........54 A3
Palmerston Rd *NEWHV* BN9........65 G4
Palmers Wy *SALV* BN13.............36 B1
Pankhurst Av *ROTT* BN2.............46 C4
The Pantiles *FERR* BN12.............53 E4
The Parade *ANG/EP* * BN16........52 A5
  BRI * BN1.................................26 D3
  HOVE * BN3.............................26 A5
Parade Man *ANG/EP* * BN16.......52 A5
Parham Cl *FIN/BW* BN14............36 D1
  ROTT BN2.................................46 D5
Parham Rd *FIN/BW* BN14...........36 D1
Park Av *HOVE* BN3.....................44 A3
  PEAHV BN10.............................62 C5
  SHOR BN43...............................41 G2
  WTHG BN11.................................5 H1
Park Cl *BRI* BN1.........................29 E2
  FIN/BW BN14...........................37 E3
  HOVE BN3.................................26 A4
  PTSD BN41...............................43 F1
Park Crs *PTSD* BN41..................43 E2

ROTT * BN2...............................46 B3
ROTT BN2.................................60 D4
WTHG BN11...............................4 D4
Park Crescent Pl *ROTT* BN2........46 B3
Park Crescent Rd *ROTT* BN2.......46 B3
Park Crescent Ter *ROTT* BN2......46 B3
Park Dr *FERR* BN12...................53 F3
Park Drive Cl *NEWHV* BN9.........65 F3
Parkfield Ct *SALV* BN13..............55 E1
Parkfield Rd *SALV* BN13.............55 E1
Park Hl *ROTT* BN2........................3 K4
Parklands *SHOR* BN43...............42 A2
Parklands Av *FERR* BN12...........54 B4
Park La *STHW* BN42...................42 B3
Park Mnr *BRI* * BN1....................27 F4
Parkmore Ter *BRI* BN1................45 H2
Park Ri *HOVE* BN3......................26 A4
Park Rd *BRI* BN1........................29 E2
  LEWES BN7...............................17 E3
  PEAHV BN10.............................67 H3
  ROTT BN2.................................60 D4
  SEAF BN25...............................70 B5
  SHOR BN43...............................41 G2
  WTHG BN11.................................5 G2
Park Road Ter *ROTT* BN2.............3 K4
The Parks *PTSD* BN41................25 E4
Parkside *SHOR* BN43.................41 C1
  WTHG * BN11.............................5 H1
Parkside Rd *SEAF* BN25.............70 D4
Park St *BRI* BN1.........................30 A1
  ROTT BN2...................................3 K5
The Park *ROTT* BN2...................61 E4
Park View *PEAHV* BN10.............62 C4
Park View Ri *PEAHV* BN10..........62 C4
Park View Rd *HOVE* BN3............44 D1
Park View Ter *BRI* BN1...............45 C2
Park Wy *STHW* BN42..................42 D2
Park Way Cl *STHW* BN42............42 D2
Parochial Ms *ROTT* * BN2.............3 H5
Parochial Ter *ROTT* * BN2.............3 H5
Paston Pl *ROTT* BN2..................58 D1
Patcham By-Pass *BRI* BN1.........27 G2
Patcham Gra *BRI* BN1................27 G2
Patchdean *BRI* BN1....................27 H2
Patching Cl *FERR* BN12.............53 H1
Patricia Av *FERR* BN12..............54 B4
Patricia Cl *FERR* BN12...............54 B4
Pavilion Buildings *BRI* BN1...........3 G5
Pavilion Pde *ROTT* BN2................3 H4
  WTHG * BN11.............................5 F6
Pavilion Rd *FIN/BW* BN14............4 B2
Pavilion St *ROTT* BN2..................3 H5
Paxmead Crs *FIN/BW* BN14........38 B4
Payne Av *HOVE* BN3..................44 B2
Paythorne Cl *STHW* BN42...........42 B1
Peace Cl *BRI* BN1......................46 C1
Peacock La *BRI* BN1..................27 G3
Peak La *ANG/EP* BN16...............52 B2
Pearsons Retreat *WTHG* BN11....56 D2
Peckham Cl *LEWES* BN7............17 E1
Peel Rd *ROTT* BN2.....................59 F1
Pegler Av *NEWHV* BN9...............68 B2
Pelham Av *PEAHV* BN10.............63 F4
Pelham Pl *SEAF* * BN25.............72 C1
Pelham Ri *PEAHV* BN10.............63 E4
Pelham Rd *SALV* BN13...............36 D5
  SEAF BN25...............................72 C1
Pelham Sq *BRI* BN1.....................3 H3
Pelham Ter *LEWES* BN7.............17 E2
Pelham Yd *SEAF* * BN25.............72 C1
Pellbrook Rd *LEWES* BN7...........16 C1
Pemberton Cl *LAN/SOMP* BN15...39 G3
Pembroke Cl *HOVE* BN3.............44 C4
  WTHG BN11...............................54 D3
Pembroke Crs *HOVE* BN3...........44 C4
Pembroke Gdns *HOVE* BN3........44 C3
Pembury Cl *FIN/BW* BN14............4 F1
Pende Cl *LAN/SOMP* BN15.........39 F1
Pendine Av *WTHG* BN11.............56 C2
Pendragon Ct *HOVE* * BN3.........44 C2
Penfold Rd *FIN/BW* BN14...........38 A5
Penfold Wy *STEY/UB* BN44..........7 F2
Penhill Rd *LAN/SOMP* BN15........39 H5
Penhurst Pl *ROTT* BN2...............47 F4
Penland's Cl *STEY/UB* BN44.........7 F2
Penlands Ri *STEY/UB* BN44..........7 F2
Penlands V *STEY/UB* BN44...........7 F2
Penlands Wy *STEY/UB* BN44........7 F2
Penleigh Cl *LAN/SOMP* BN15......39 H5
Pennycress Av *FERR* BN12.........35 G5
Penstone Pk *LAN/SOMP* BN15....39 F4
Pentland Rd *SALV* BN13.............36 C3
Pepperscoombe La
  STEY/UB BN44............................8 A1
Percival Ter *ROTT* BN2...............58 D1
Perrots La *STEY/UB* BN44............7 E2
Perry Hl *ROTT* BN2.....................61 G3
Perth Cl *SEAF* BN25...................71 G5

Peter Rd *LAN/SOMP* BN15..........57
Pett Cl *ROTT* BN2.......................47
Petworth Av *FERR* BN12.............54
Petworth Rd *BRI* BN1..................28
Pevensey Cl *SEAF* BN25............71
Pevensey Gdn *WTHG* BN11........55
Pevensey Rd *NEWHV* BN9..........68
  ROTT BN2.................................46
  WTHG BN11...............................54
The Peverells *SEAF* BN25...........71
Peverel Rd *SALV* BN13...............55
The Peverels *SEAF* * BN25.........71
Peveril Cl *LAN/SOMP* BN15.........38
Peveril Dr *LAN/SOMP* BN15.........38
Phoenix Cswy *LEWES* BN7.........17
Phoenix Crs *STHW* BN42............42
Phoenix Pl *LEWES* * BN7............17
  ROTT BN2...................................3
Phoenix Ri *ROTT* BN2...................3
Phoenix Wy *STHW* BN42............42
Phrosso Rd *WTHG* BN11............54
Phyllis Av *PEAHV* BN10..............66
Picton St *ROTT* BN2...................46
Piddinghoe Av *PEAHV* BN10.......67
Piddinghoe Cl *PEAHV* BN10........67
Piddinghoe Md *NEWHV* BN9.......64
Pilgrims Ter *SALV* * BN13...........55
Pilgrims Wk *SALV* BN13.............55
Piltdown Rd *ROTT* BN2...............47
The Pines *ROTT* * BN2................46
Pines Av *FIN/BW* BN14..............37
Pinewood Cl *ANG/EP* BN16.........52
  SEAF BN25...............................70
Pinfold Cl *ROTT* BN2..................48
Pinwell Rd *LEWES* BN7..............17
Pipe Pas *LEWES* * BN7...............17
Pipers Cl *HOVE* BN3..................25
Pitt Dr *SEAF* BN25.....................71
Pitt Gdns *ROTT* BN2..................48
Place La *SEAF* BN25..................70
Plainfields Av *BRI* BN1...............14
Plaistow Cl *ROTT* BN2................47
The Plantation *ANG/EP* BN16......52
  SALV BN13...............................36
Plantation Cl *SALV* BN13............36
Plantation Ri *SALV* BN13............37
Plantation Wy *SALV* BN13..........36
Playden Cl *ROTT* BN2................59
Plaza Pde *WTHG* * BN11..............4
Plumpton Rd *ROTT* BN2..............46
Plymouth Av *ROTT* BN2..............62
Poling Cl *FERR* BN12.................53
Polperro Cl *FERR* BN12..............52
Pond La *SALV* BN13...................36
Pond Ms *SALV* * BN13................36
Pond Rd *SHOR* BN43.................41
Pony Farm *FIN/BW* BN14............18
Pool Va *BRI* BN1..........................3
The Poplars *ROTT* * BN2.............46
Poplar Av *HOVE* BN3.................26
Poplar Cl *BRI* BN1......................27
  HOVE BN3.................................26
Poplar Rd *SALV* BN13................36
Portfield Av *BRI* BN1..................28
Port Hall Av *BRI* BN1..................45
Port Hall Ms *BRI* BN1.................45
Port Hall Pl *BRI* BN1...................45
Port Hall Rd *BRI* BN1..................45
Port Hall St *BRI* BN1...................45
Portland Av *HOVE* BN3...............44
Portland Ms *ROTT* * BN2............58
Portland Pl *ROTT* BN2................58
Portland Rd *HOVE* BN3...............43
  WTHG BN11.................................4
Portland Sq *WTHG* * BN11............4
Portland St *BRI* BN1.....................3
Portland Vls *HOVE* BN3..............43
Port Vw *NEWHV* BN9.................65
Portway *STEY/UB* BN44................7
Potter's La *LEWES* BN7..............17
Poulter's La *FIN/BW* BN14..........37
Pound La *STEY/UB* BN44..............7
Powell Gdns *NEWHV* BN9...........64
Powis Gv *BRI* BN1........................2
Powis Rd *BRI* BN1........................2
Powis Sq *BRI* BN1........................2
Powis Vls *BRI* BN1........................2
Poynings Cl *SEAF* BN25.............73
Poynings Dr *HOVE* BN3..............26
Poynter Rd *HOVE* BN3................44
Pratton Av *LAN/SOMP* BN15.......39
Preston Circ *BRI* * BN1...............46
Preston Dro *BRI* BN1..................27
Preston Gra *BRI* * BN1...............45
Preston Pk *BRI* BN1....................27
Preston Park Av *BRI* BN1............45
Preston Rd *BRI* BN1....................27
Preston St *BRI* BN1......................2
Preston Village Ms *BRI* * BN1......45

stonville Rd BRI BN1 ......2 E1
ace Albert St BRI BN1 ......3 F5
ace Charles Cl STHW BN42 ...42 D1
ace Charles Rd LEWES BN7 ...17 G1
ace Edward's Rd LEWES BN7 ...16 D3
aces Av HOVE BN3 ......44 C4
aces Cl SEAF BN25 ......70 C4
aces Crs HOVE BN3 ......44 C4
OTT BN2 ......46 B2
ace's Pl BRI BN1 ......3 G5
ace's Rd ROTT BN2 ......46 B2
acess Av SALV BN13 ......54 D2
acess Dr SEAF BN25 ......70 B3
ace's St ROTT BN3 ......44 C4
ace's St ROTT BN2 ......3 H5
ace Ter ROTT BN2 ......59 E1
ace William Cl FIN/BW BN14 ...37 E2
nsep Rd HOVE BN3 ......44 C2
e Priory BRI * BN1 ......27 G2
ory Cl LAN/SOMP BN15 ...38 D3
ALV BN13 ......55 E1
ory Crs LEWES BN7 ......17 E4
ory Fld STEY/UB BN44 ......8 A2
ory St LEWES BN7 ......17 F4
ory Ter LEWES * BN7 ......17 E3
omenade PEAHV BN10 ......66 C2
ospect Pl WTHG BN11 ......4 E6
vidence Pl BRI BN1 ......3 G1
vidence Ter WTHG BN11 ......5 G4
borough Cl ROTT BN2 ......47 F3

Q

e Quadrangle FIN/BW BN14 ...18 C2
e Quadrant FERR BN12 ......54 A2
antock Cl SALV BN13 ......36 D2
antock Rd SALV BN13 ......36 D2
arry Bank Rd BRI BN1 ......28 B5
arry La SEAF BN25 ......71 E3
arry Rd NEWHV BN9 ......68 C3
e Quashetts FIN/BW BN14 ...5 F1
ebec St ROTT BN2 ......3 K3
een Alexandra Av HOVE BN3 ...26 C4
een Anne's Cl LEWES * BN7 ...17 E3
een Caroline Cl HOVE BN3 ...26 C4
een Mary Av HOVE BN3 ......26 C4
eensbury Ms BRI BN1 ......2 D5
eensdown School Rd
 BRI BN1 ......28 C4
een's Gdns BRI BN1 ......3 G3
HOVE BN3 ......45 E5
eens Pde LAN/SOMP * BN15 ...39 G4
een's Park Gdns SEAF BN25 ...70 C4
een's Park Ri ROTT BN2 ......46 C4
een's Park Rd ROTT BN2 ......3 K4
een's Park Ter ROTT BN2 ......46 C4
een's Pl BRI BN1 ......3 H2
HOVE BN3 ......45 E4
SHOR BN43 ......41 F3
een Sq BRI BN1 ......3 F4
een's St BRI BN1 ......3 F3
LAN/SOMP BN15 ......57 F1
LEWES BN7 ......17 F1
STHW BN42 ......42 C1
een St FIN/BW BN14 ......55 E1
eensway LAN/SOMP BN15 ...39 G4
ROTT BN2 ......46 D4
SEAF BN25 ......71 E3
een Victoria Av HOVE BN3 ...26 C4
erneby Cl SHOR BN43 ......42 B3

R

ckham Cl SALV BN13 ......36 D5
ckham Rd SALV BN13 ......36 D5
dinden Dr HOVE BN3 ......45 F1
dinden Manor Rd HOVE BN3 ...45 G2
dnor Cl SALV * BN13 ......54 D1
dnor Rd SALV BN13 ......54 D1
glan Av SALV BN13 ......36 C5
ilway Ap NEWHV BN9 ......68 D1
WTHG BN11 ......4 D2
ilway La LEWES BN7 ......17 F3
ilway Rd NEWHV BN9 ......68 C3
ilway St BRI BN1 ......3 F2
aleigh Rd SHOR BN43 ......41 E4
aleigh Crs FERR BN12 ......54 B2
aleigh Wy FERR BN12 ......54 A1
melagh Vls HOVE BN3 ......44 B3
aphael Rd HOVE BN3 ......44 B3
avensbourne Av SHOR BN43 ...41 F1

Ravensbourne Cl SHOR BN43 ...41 F1
Raven's Rd SHOR BN43 ......41 F3
Ravenswood Dr ROTT BN2 ...48 D4
Rayford Cl PEAHV BN10 ......67 E1
Raymond Cl SEAF BN25 ......71 E3
Reading Rd ROTT BN2 ......59 F1
Rectory Cl HOVE * BN3 ......43 H3
 NEWHV BN9 ......68 C2
 SHOR BN43 ......42 B3
Rectory Farm Rd
 LAN/SOMP BN15 ......38 D3
Rectory Gdns FIN/BW BN14 ...37 C3
Rectory Rd FIN/BW BN14 ......55 E3
 NEWHV BN9 ......68 C1
 SHOR BN43 ......42 A3
Rectory Wk LAN/SOMP BN15 ...38 D3
Redcross St BRI BN1 ......3 H2
Redhill Cl BRI BN1 ......27 E2
Redhill Dr BRI BN1 ......27 E3
Redvers Rd ROTT BN2 ......46 D4
Redwood Cl SALV BN13 ......36 A5
Reeves Hl BRI BN1 ......28 D2
Regency Ms BRI BN1 ......2 D4
Regency Rd SALV BN13 ......36 C5
Regency Sq BRI BN1 ......2 D5
Regent Ar BRI BN1 ......2 E5
Regent Cl LAN/SOMP BN15 ...40 B4
Regent Hl BRI BN1 ......2 E4
Regent Rw BRI BN1 ......2 E4
Regents Cl SEAF BN25 ......70 C3
Regent St BRI BN1 ......3 G4
Reigate Rd BRI BN1 ......45 F1
 WTHG BN11 ......54 D3
Reynolds Rd HOVE BN3 ......44 B3
Richardson Rd HOVE BN3 ......44 B3
Richington Wy SEAF BN25 ...71 F3
Richmond Ct WTHG BN11 ......4 C4
Richmond Pde ROTT BN2 ......3 H3
Richmond Pl ROTT BN2 ......3 H3
Richmond Rd ROTT BN2 ......46 B2
 SEAF BN25 ......70 B5
 WTHG BN11 ......4 B5
Richmond St ROTT BN2 ......3 K3
Richmond Ter ROTT BN2 ......3 J1
 SEAF BN25 ......70 C5
Ridge Cl PTSD BN41 ......25 E3
Ridge Rd BRI BN1 ......15 H4
Ridgeside Av BRI BN1 ......27 G2
Ridge Vw BRI BN1 ......29 E2
The Ridgeway SEAF BN25 ...70 D4
Ridgeway PTSD BN41 ......42 D1
Ridgeway Cl STHW BN42 ......42 D1
Ridgeway Gdns ROTT BN2 ...48 B3
Ridgewood Av ROTT BN2 ......61 G2
The Ridgway ROTT BN2 ......48 B2
Ridgway Cl ROTT BN2 ......48 B2
Ridgway Paddock LEWES BN7 ...31 H1
The Ridings PEAHV BN10 ......62 D4
 ROTT BN2 ......60 A1
 SEAF BN25 ......70 D3
 STEY/UB BN44 ......7 F3
Rifeside Gdns FERR BN12 ......53 E2
Rife Wy FERR BN12 ......53 E3
Rigden Rd HOVE BN3 ......45 E2
Riley Rd ROTT BN2 ......46 C1
Ringmer Cl BRI BN1 ......29 E1
Ringmer Rd BRI BN1 ......29 F3
 NEWHV BN9 ......68 B2
 SALV BN13 ......36 C5
 SEAF BN25 ......72 C1
Ring Rd LAN/SOMP BN15 ...39 G1
Ripley Rd WTHG BN11 ......54 D2
Ripon Ct WTHG * BN11 ......55 E3
The Rise PTSD BN41 ......24 D5
River Cl SHOR BN43 ......41 E4
Riverdale LEWES BN7 ......17 E2
Riverside NEWHV BN9 ......68 D1
 PTSD BN41 ......42 C4
 SHOR BN43 ......41 F4
 STEY/UB BN44 ......8 A2
Riverside Rd SHOR BN43 ......41 F4
Roadean Cl SEAF BN25 ......71 E4
Robertson Rd BRI BN1 ......27 F5
Roberts Rd LAN/SOMP BN15 ...57 G1
Robert St BRI BN1 ......3 G3
Robin Davis Cl ROTT BN2 ...47 E2
Robin Dene ROTT BN2 ......59 E1
Robinson Cl LAN/SOMP BN15 ...39 G4
Robinson Rd NEWHV BN9 ......64 C5
Robson Ct WTHG * BN11 ......54 C2
Robson Rd WTHG BN11 ......54 C3
Rochester Cl HOVE * BN3 ......2 A2
 SALV BN13 ......35 H5
Rochester Ct WTHG * BN11 ...54 C2
Rochester Gdns HOVE BN3 ......2 A2
Rochester St ROTT BN2 ......46 D5
Rochford Wy SEAF BN25 ...69 H2
Rock Gv ROTT BN2 ......58 D1

Rockingham Cl SALV BN13 ...36 C4
Rockingham Ct SALV * BN13 ...36 C4
Rock Pl ROTT BN2 ......3 K6
Rock St ROTT BN2 ......59 E1
Roderick Av PEAHV BN10 ......66 B2
Roderick Av North PEAHV BN10 ...63 E3
Rodmell Av ROTT BN2 ......61 H4
Rodmell Pl BRI * BN1 ......28 A1
Rodmell Rd SALV BN13 ......36 C5
 SEAF BN25 ......73 F1
Roedale Rd BRI BN1 ......46 B1
Roedean Crs ROTT BN2 ......59 G1
Roedean Hts ROTT BN2 ......59 G1
Roedean Pth ROTT BN2 ......59 H2
Roedean Rd ROTT BN2 ......59 F1
 SALV BN13 ......36 C4
Roedean V ROTT BN2 ......59 H2
Roedean Wy ROTT BN2 ......59 G2
Rogate Cl LAN/SOMP BN15 ...38 D3
 SALV BN13 ......37 E4
Rogate Rd SALV BN13 ......37 E4
Roger's La FIN/BW BN14 ......18 C3
Roman Cl SEAF BN25 ......69 H2
Roman Crs STHW BN42 ......42 C2
Roman Rd HOVE BN3 ......43 H4
 STEY/UB BN44 ......7 G2
 STHW BN42 ......42 C2
Roman Wk LAN/SOMP BN13 ...38 D3
Roman Wy STHW BN42 ......42 C2
Romany Cl PTSD BN41 ......43 F2
Romany Rd SALV BN13 ......35 H5
Romney Cl SEAF BN25 ......71 G4
Romney Rd ROTT BN2 ......61 E4
 WTHG BN11 ......54 D4
Romsey Cl BRI BN1 ......28 B5
Rookery Cl BRI BN1 ......45 G3
 NEWHV BN9 ......65 E3
Rookery Wy NEWHV BN9 ......65 E3
 SEAF BN25 ......69 H3
Ropetackle SHOR BN43 ......41 G3
Rope Wk SHOR BN43 ......41 G3
Rosebery Av FERR BN12 ......54 C3
 ROTT BN2 ......48 A2
Rosecroft Cl LAN/SOMP BN15 ...39 G2
Rosedene Cl ROTT BN2 ......48 C4
Rose Hill Cl BRI BN1 ......46 A3
Rose Hill Ter BRI BN1 ......46 A3
Rosemary Av STEY/UB BN44 ...7 G1
Rosemary Cl PEAHV BN10 ......63 E5
 STEY/UB BN44 ......7 G1
Rosemary Dr SHOR BN43 ......41 H1
Rosemount Cl ROTT BN2 ......69 G2
The Rose Wk NEWHV BN9 ......68 C1
Rose Wk FERR BN12 ......54 C3
 SEAF BN25 ......70 D4
Rose Walk Cl NEWHV BN9 ......68 B1
Rossiter Rd LAN/SOMP BN15 ...39 G2
Rosslyn Av SHOR BN43 ......41 G3
Rosslyn Cl SHOR BN43 ......41 G3
Rosslyn Rd SHOR BN43 ......41 F3
Rothbury Rd HOVE BN3 ......43 H3
Rotherfield Cl BRI BN1 ......28 B1
Rotherfield Crs BRI BN1 ......28 B2
Rother Rd SEAF BN25 ......73 E1
Rothesay Cl SALV BN13 ......54 C1
Rothwell Ct NEWHV BN9 ......68 A1
Rotten Rw LEWES BN7 ......16 D4
Rottingdean Pl ROTT * BN2 ...60 D4
The Rotyngs ROTT BN2 ......60 D3
Rough Brow SEAF BN25 ......71 E4
Roundhay Av PEAHV * BN10 ...67 G2
Roundhill Crs ROTT BN2 ......46 B2
Round Hill Rd ROTT BN2 ......46 B2
Round Hill St ROTT BN2 ......46 B2
Roundstone Dr ANG/EP BN16 ...52 A3
Roundstone La ANG/EP BN16 ...52 A2
Roundway BRI BN1 ......29 E2
Rowan Av HOVE BN3 ......44 A1
Rowan Cl PTSD BN41 ......42 D1
 SEAF BN25 ......71 G5
The Rowans WTHG BN11 ......55 E3
Rowans Ct LEWES BN7 ......17 E3
Rowan Wy ROTT BN2 ......60 C2
Rowe Av PEAHV BN10 ......62 D5
Rowlands Rd WTHG BN11 ......4 A6
Roxburgh Cl SALV BN13 ......36 D3
The Royal Ar WTHG BN11 ......5 F6
Royal Buildings
 LAN/SOMP * BN15 ......57 F1
Royal Crs ROTT BN2 ......58 C1
Royal Crescent Ms ROTT BN2 ...58 C1
Royal Dr SEAF BN25 ......70 C2
Royal George Pde SHOR BN43 ...41 H1
Royles Cl ROTT BN2 ......61 E3
Rudgwick Av FERR BN12 ......53 G3
Rudyard Cl ROTT BN2 ......48 C2
Rudyard Rd ROTT BN2 ......48 C2
Rufus Cl LEWES BN7 ......17 E3

Rugby Cl SEAF BN25 ......71 F4
Rugby Pl ROTT BN2 ......59 E1
Rugby Rd BRI BN1 ......46 A1
 WTHG BN11 ......55 E2
Rusbridge La LEWES BN7 ......17 G3
Rushlake Cl BRI BN1 ......29 E2
Rushlake Rd BRI BN1 ......29 E1
Ruskin Rd FIN/BW BN14 ......56 B1
 HOVE BN3 ......44 B2
Rusper Rd BRI BN1 ......28 D1
 SALV BN13 ......36 D5
Rusper Rd South SALV BN13 ...36 D5
Russell Cl FIN/BW BN14 ......38 A5
Russell Crs BRI BN1 ......45 H3
Russell Ms BRI BN1 ......2 D4
Russell Pl BRI BN1 ......2 E5
Russell Rd BRI BN1 ......2 D4
Russell Rw LEWES BN7 ......17 E1
Russell's Cl ANG/EP BN16 ......52 B3
Russells Dr LAN/SOMP BN15 ...39 C5
Russell Sq BRI BN1 ......2 D4
Rustic Cl ROTT BN2 ......62 D4
Rustic Rd PEAHV BN10 ......62 D3
Rustington Rd BRI BN1 ......28 A2
Rutland Gdns HOVE BN3 ......44 B3
Rutland Rd HOVE BN3 ......44 C3
Rycroft Cl FERR BN12 ......54 A4
Ryde Rd ROTT BN2 ......40 D3
Rye Cl ROTT BN2 ......62 A3
 SEAF BN25 ......71 G4
 WTHG BN11 ......55 E4
Ryecroft Gdns FERR BN12 ......54 A4
Ryelands Dr ROTT BN2 ......28 D4

S

Sackville Cl LEWES BN7 ......17 E3
Sackville Crs FIN/BW BN14 ...56 A1
Sackville Gdns HOVE BN3 ......44 B4
Sackville Rd FIN/BW BN14 ......5 C1
 HOVE BN3 ......44 C4
Sackville Wy FIN/BW BN14 ...5 H1
Sadler Wy ROTT BN2 ......47 F4
Saffron Cl SHOR BN43 ......42 A1
St Andrew's Cl FERR BN12 ......53 E3
St Andrew's Dr SEAF BN25 ...69 G2
St Andrews Gdns SALV * BN13...55 E1
St Andrew's La LEWES * BN7 ...17 E3
St Andrew's Rd BRI BN1 ......46 A1
 PTSD BN41 ......43 F3
 SALV BN13 ......54 D1
St Anne's Crs LEWES BN7 ......16 D4
St Annes Ter LEWES * BN7 ......16 D3
St Anselm's Rd FIN/BW BN14 ...4 A1
St Aubins Rd FERR BN12 ......53 F5
St Aubyns HOVE BN3......44 C4
St Aubyn's Crs PTSD BN41 ......43 F3
St Aubyn's Md ROTT BN2 ......61 E4
St Aubyn's Rd PTSD BN41 ......43 E3
St Aubyns South HOVE BN3......44 C4
St Bernards Ct LAN/SOMP BN15 ...39 G5
St Botolph's Rd WTHG BN11 ...4 A2
St Crispians SEAF BN25 ......70 B5
St Cuthmans Cl ROTT BN2 ......47 E3
St Dunstan's Rd SALV BN13 ...55 E2
St Elmo Rd FIN/BW BN14 ......4 B1
St Georges Gdns WTHG * BN11 ...5 J4
St George's Ms BRI BN1 ......3 H3
St George's Pl BRI BN1 ......3 H2
St George's Rd ROTT BN2 ......58 D1
 WTHG BN11 ......5 J3
St George's Ter ROTT BN2 ......58 C1
St Giles Cl SHOR BN43 ......41 H2
St Helen's Crs HOVE BN3 ......25 H4
St Helen's Dr HOVE BN3 ......25 H4
St Helen's Rd ROTT BN2 ......46 D3
St Helier Rd FERR BN12 ......53 F5
St Heliers Av HOVE BN3 ......44 A3
St James Av LAN/SOMP BN15 ...39 G2
St James's Av ROTT BN2 ......3 K6
St James's Pl ROTT BN2 ......3 H5
St James's St BRI BN1 ......3 H5
St James's Street Ms ROTT BN2 ...3 J5
St James St LEWES BN7 ......17 E4
St John's Av FERR BN12 ......54 B4
St John's Cl FERR BN12 ......54 A4
St John's Hl LEWES BN7 ......17 E3
St Johns Ms ROTT * BN2 ......58 C1
St John's Pl HOVE BN3 ......45 E4
 ROTT BN2 ......3 J4
St John's Rd HOVE BN3 ......45 E5
 SEAF BN25 ......72 C1
St John's Ter LEWES BN7 ......17 E3
St John St LEWES BN7 ......17 F3
St Joseph's Cl HOVE BN3 ......44 C2
St Julians Cl SHOR BN43 ......42 A3

St Julian's La *SHOR* BN43 ....**42** A3
St Keyna Av *HOVE* BN3 ....**43** H4
St Laurence Cl *PEAHV* * BN10 ......**62** C4
St Lawrence Av *FIN/BW* BN14 ......**55** F1
St Leonard's Av *FIN/BW* BN14 ......**55** G4
St Leonards Cl *NEWHV* BN9 ....**65** H5
St Leonard's Gdns *HOVE* BN3 ......**43** H4
St Leonard's Rd *HOVE* BN3 ....**43** G4
  NEWHV BN9 ....**65** H3
  ROTT BN2 ....**46** C2
St Louie Cl *STHW* BN42 ....**43** E2
St Luke's Cl *WTHG* BN11 ....**56** D1
St Luke's Rd *ROTT* BN2 ....**46** C4
St Luke's Ter *ROTT* BN2 ....**46** C4
St Malo Cl *FERR* BN12 ....**53** F5
St Margarets *ROTT* * BN2 ....**61** E4
St Margaret's Pl *BRI* BN1 ....**2** D5
St Margaret's Ri *SEAF* BN25 ....**69** G2
St Mark's Crs *WTHG* BN11 ....**56** D1
St Mark's St *ROTT* BN2 ....**59** E1
St Martins Crs *NEWHV* BN9 ....**64** D4
St Martin's Pl *ROTT* BN2 ....**46** B3
St Martin's St *ROTT* BN2 ....**46** B3
St Mary Magdalene St
  ROTT BN2................................**46** B2
St Marys Cl *LAN/SOMP* BN15 ......**38** C3
  SHOR BN43 ....**41** F3
St Mary's Pl *ROTT* BN2 ....**3** K6
St Mary's Rd *SHOR* BN43 ....**41** F3
St Mary's Sq *ROTT* BN2 ....**58** D1
St Matthew's Rd *WTHG* BN11 ....**4** C3
St Maur's Rd *FERR* BN12 ....**53** E3
St Michael's Ct *WTHG* BN11 ....**4** A5
St Michael's Pl *BRI* BN1 ....**2** D3
St Michael's Rd *PTSD* BN41 ....**43** F3
  WTHG BN11 ....**4** A5
St Michael's Ter *LEWES* BN7 ....**17** F2
St Nicholas La *LEWES* * BN7 ....**17** F3
St Nicholas Rd *BRI* BN1 ....**3** F3
  PTSD BN41 ....**43** F3
St Nicolas La *SHOR* BN43 ....**40** D2
St Osmund Rd *FERR* BN12 ....**52** D3
St Pancras Gdns *LEWES* BN7 ......**16** D4
St Pancras Gn *LEWES* BN7 ....**31** H2
St Pancras Rd *LEWES* BN7 ....**16** D4
St Patrick's Rd *HOVE* BN3 ....**44** C3
St Paul's Av *WTHG* BN11 ....**56** D1
St Paul's St *HOVE* BN3 ....**46** B2
St Peter's Av *PEAHV* BN10 ....**62** C5
St Peter's Cl *SEAF* BN25 ....**70** C3
St Peter's Pl *BRI* BN1 ....**3** H2
  LAN/SOMP * BN15 ....**57** E1
  LEWES * BN7 ....**17** E4
St Peter's Rd *PTSD* BN41 ....**43** F3
  SEAF BN25 ....**70** C3
St Peter's St *BRI* BN1 ....**3** H1
St Philips Ms *HOVE* BN3 ....**44** B3
St Raphael's Rd *WTHG* * BN11 .....**54** D3
St Richard's Rd *PTSD* BN41 ....**43** F3
St Swithun's Ter *LEWES* * BN7 .....**17** E4
St Thomas's Rd *FIN/BW* BN14 ......**55** F1
St Valerie Rd *WTHG* BN11 ....**55** H1
St Wilfred's Pl *SEAF* BN25 ....**73** F1
St Wilfred's Rd *FIN/BW* BN14 ......**55** H1
Salisbury Rd *HOVE* BN3 ....**45** E4
  SEAF BN25 ....**70** C5
  WTHG BN11 ....**4** A4
Saltdean Dr *ROTT* BN2 ....**61** F4
Saltdean Park Rd *ROTT* BN2 ....**61** G4
Saltdean V *ROTT* BN2 ....**61** G3
The Saltings *LAN/SOMP* BN15 .....**39** H5
  SHOR BN43 ....**40** D4
Saltings Wy *STEY/UB* BN44 ....**8** A2
Saltwood Rd *SEAF* BN25 ....**71** E4
Salvington Cl *SALV* BN13 ....**36** C3
Salvington Gdns *SALV* BN13 ....**36** D4
Salvington Hl *SALV* BN13 ....**36** C1
Salvington Rd *SALV* BN13 ....**36** C3
Samphire Dr *SALV* BN13 ....**35** G5
Sandgate Cl *SEAF* BN25 ....**71** G3
Sandgate Rd *BRI* BN1 ....**28** A5
Sandhurst Av *ROTT* BN2 ....**48** B1
Sandore Cl *SEAF* BN25 ....**71** E4
Sandore Rd *SEAF* BN25 ....**71** E4
Sandown Av *FERR* BN12 ....**54** A4
Sandown Cl *FERR* BN12 ....**54** A4
Sandown Rd *ROTT* BN2 ....**46** D3
  STHW BN42 ....**42** B2
Sandringham Cl *HOVE* BN3 ....**26** C4
  SEAF BN25 ....**71** E2
Sandringham Ct
  LAN/SOMP * BN15 ....**39** H5
Sandringham Dr *HOVE* BN3 ....**26** C4
Sandringham Ms
  FIN/BW * BN14 ....**37** H4
  SALV BN13 ....**36** B3
Sandwich Rd *WTHG* BN11 ....**54** D4
Sanyhils Av *BRI* BN1 ....**13** H5

Sark Gdns *FERR* BN12 ....**53** F4
Saunders Hl *BRI* BN1 ....**14** D5
Saunders Park Ri *ROTT* BN2 ....**46** C1
Saunders Park Vw *ROTT* BN2 ......**46** C1
Saxifrage Wy *SALV* BN13 ....**35** G5
Saxon Cl *ANG/EP* BN16 ....**52** B2
  ROTT BN2 ....**61** G3
Saxon La *SEAF* BN25 ....**72** C1
Saxon Rd *HOVE* BN3 ....**43** H4
  NEWHV BN9 ....**68** C1
  STEY/UB BN44 ....**7** H1
Saxons *SHOR* BN43 ....**41** F1
Saxony Rd *FIN/BW* BN14 ....**55** F1
Scarborough Rd *BRI* BN1 ....**45** F1
School Cl *STHW* BN42 ....**42** C3
School Hl *FIN/BW* BN14 ....**18** C1
School La *ROTT* BN2 ....**61** G3
  STEY/UB BN44 ....**7** F1
School Rd *HOVE* BN3 ....**44** B3
  STEY/UB BN44 ....**8** A2
School Ri *ROTT* BN2 ....**47** E4
Scotland St *ROTT* BN2 ....**3** K3
Scotney Cl *SALV* BN13 ....**35** H5
Scott Rd *HOVE* BN3 ....**44** B3
Seacliffe *PEAHV* * BN10 ....**66** B1
Sea Cl *FERR* BN12 ....**54** C3
Seadown Pde
  LAN/SOMP * BN15 ....**38** D5
Sea Dr *FERR* BN12 ....**53** F5
Seafield Av *FERR* BN12 ....**54** B5
Seafield Cl *SEAF* BN25 ....**71** F3
Seafield Rd *HOVE* BN3 ....**44** D5
Seaford Rd *HOVE* BN3 ....**43** G4
  NEWHV BN9 ....**69** F1
Seagrave Cl *SEAF* * BN25 ....**69** G2
Seagrove Wy *SEAF* BN25 ....**70** D2
Seahaven Gdns *SHOR* BN43 ....**40** C5
Sea La *ANG/EP* BN16 ....**52** D5
  FERR BN12 ....**53** F3
  FERR BN12 ....**54** A4
Sea Lane Cl *FERR* BN12 ....**53** F3
Sea Lane Gdns *FERR* BN12 ....**53** F4
Seamill Park Av *WTHG* BN11 ....**57** E2
Seamill Park Crs *WTHG* BN11 ......**56** D2
Seamill Wy *WTHG* BN11 ....**56** D2
Sea Pl *FERR* BN12 ....**54** C5
Searle Av *PEAHV* BN10 ....**67** G2
Sea Rd *ANG/EP* BN16 ....**52** A4
Seasaw Wy *ROTT* BN2 ....**47** F3
Seaside Av *LAN/SOMP* BN15 ....**39** H5
Seaside Cl *LAN/SOMP* BN15 ....**39** H5
Seaside Rd *LAN/SOMP* BN15 ....**39** H5
Seaview Av *ANG/EP* BN16 ....**52** A5
  ANG/EP BN16 ....**52** D5
  PEAHV BN10 ....**67** G3
Seaview Ct *LAN/SOMP* BN15 ....**57** F1
Seaview Rd *NEWHV* BN9 ....**65** F4
  PEAHV BN10 ....**67** G3
  ROTT BN2 ....**47** H2
Sea View Rd *WTHG* BN11 ....**4** A7
Seawaves Cl *ANG/EP* BN16 ....**52** A4
Second Av *FIN/BW* BN14 ....**37** H3
  HOVE BN3 ....**45** E5
  LAN/SOMP BN15 ....**39** G3
  NEWHV BN9 ....**68** C2
Second Rd *PEAHV* BN10 ....**66** C1
Sedbury Rd *LAN/SOMP* BN15 ......**39** E2
Sefton Cl *SALV* BN13 ....**36** B4
Sefton Rd *PTSD* BN41 ....**24** D4
Segrave Cl *LEWES* BN7 ....**16** D2
Selba Dr *ROTT* BN2 ....**29** E5
Selborne Pl *HOVE* BN3 ....**45** E3
Selborne Rd *HOVE* BN3 ....**45** E3
  WTHG BN11 ....**5** J2
Selden La *SALV* BN13 ....**34** B1
  WTHG BN11 ....**5** J4
Selden Pde *SALV* * BN13 ....**36** D3
Selden Rd *WTHG* BN11 ....**5** J3
Selden's Ms *SALV* BN13 ....**36** D4
Selden's Wy *SALV* BN13 ....**36** D4
Selham Cl *BRI* BN1 ....**28** D1
Selham Dr *BRI* BN1 ....**28** D1
Selham Pl *BRI* * BN1 ....**28** D1
Selhurst Rd *ROTT* BN2 ....**48** C4
Selkirk Cl *SALV* BN13 ....**54** C1
Selmeston Pl *ROTT* BN2 ....**47** F4
Selsey Cl *BRI* BN1 ....**29** E1
  SALV BN13 ....**36** D5
Selsfield Dr *ROTT* BN2 ....**28** D4
Semley Rd *BRI* BN1 ....**46** A1
Seniac Rd *NEWHV* BN9 ....**68** D1
Sevelands Cl *ROTT* BN2 ....**47** F3
Seventh Av *LAN/SOMP* BN15 ......**39** G2
Seville St *ROTT* BN2 ....**46** C3
Seymour Sq *ROTT* BN2 ....**58** D1
Shadwells Cl *LAN/SOMP* BN15 .....**39** H3
Shadwells Rd *LAN/SOMP* BN15 ....**39** H3
Shaftesbury Av *FERR* BN12 ....**54** C2

Shaftesbury Pl *BRI* BN1 ....**46** A2
Shaftesbury Rd *BRI* BN1 ....**46** A2
Shakespeare Rd *WTHG* BN11 ......**4** B3
Shakespeare St *HOVE* BN3 ....**44** C2
Shandon Gdns *FIN/BW* BN14 ......**37** H4
Shandon Rd *FIN/BW* BN14 ....**37** H4
Shandon Wy *FIN/BW* BN14 ....**37** H4
Shanklin Rd *ROTT* BN2 ....**46** C2
Shannon Cl *PEAHV* BN10 ....**62** C4
Sharpthorne Cl *PTSD* BN41 ....**25** C5
Sheepbell Cl *PTSD* BN41 ....**25** E4
Sheepfair *LEWES* BN7 ....**16** C2
Sheep Pen La *SEAF* BN25 ....**71** E5
  STEY/UB BN44 ....**7** F1
Sheep Wk *ROTT* BN2 ....**60** D4
Shelby Rd *SALV* BN13 ....**36** A4
Sheldon Ct *WTHG* * BN11 ....**4** A6
Shelldale Av *PTSD* BN41 ....**43** F3
Shelldale Crs *PTSD* BN41 ....**43** F3
Shelldale Rd *PTSD* BN41 ....**43** F2
Shelley Cl *LEWES* BN7 ....**16** D3
Shelley Rd *HOVE* BN3 ....**44** B3
  WTHG BN11 ....**4** C5
Shenfield Wy *BRI* BN1 ....**28** B5
Shepham Av *ROTT* BN2 ....**61** G4
Shepherds Cl *NEWHV* BN9 ....**64** B3
Shepherds Cot *PEAHV* * BN10 .....**63** F3
Shepherds Cft *BRI* BN1 ....**27** E4
Shepherds Md *FIN/BW* BN14 ......**19** E4
Sheppard Wy *PTSD* BN41 ....**25** E4
The Shepway *SEAF* BN25 ....**71** F4
Shepway Pde *SEAF* * BN25 ....**70** C5
Sherbourne Cl *HOVE* BN3 ....**25** H4
Sherbourne Rd *HOVE* BN3 ....**25** H4
Sherbourne Wy *HOVE* BN3 ....**25** H4
Sherbrooke Cl *SALV* BN13 ....**36** B4
Sheridan Rd *FIN/BW* BN14 ....**37** H5
Sheridan Ter *HOVE* BN3 ....**44** C2
Shermanbury Rd *FIN/BW* BN14 ...**4** B1
Sherrington Rd *ROTT* BN2 ....**48** D2
Sherwood Ri *SEAF* BN25 ....**70** D4
Sherwood Rd *SEAF* BN25 ....**70** D4
Shetland Ct *SALV* BN13 ....**35** H5
Shingle Rd *SHOR* BN43 ....**41** G4
Shipley Rd *ROTT* BN2 ....**48** C3
Ship St *BRI* BN1 ....**3** F5
  NEWHV BN9 ....**64** C5
  SHOR BN43 ....**41** E3
Ship Street Gdns *BRI* * BN1 ....**3** F5
Shirley Av *HOVE* BN3 ....**26** D5
Shirley Cl *FIN/BW* BN14 ....**37** F3
  SHOR BN43 ....**42** A2
Shirley Dr *FIN/BW* BN14 ....**37** F3
  HOVE BN3 ....**45** E1
Shirley Rd *HOVE* BN3 ....**45** E2
Shirley St *HOVE* BN3 ....**44** D3
Shopsdam Rd *LAN/SOMP* BN15 ...**57** H1
Shoreham By-Pass
  LAN/SOMP BN15 ....**40** C1
Shoreham Rd *STEY/UB* BN44 ....**8** B4
Short Brow *SEAF* BN25 ....**71** E4
Shortgate Rd *ROTT* BN2 ....**29** F3
Sidehill Dr *PTSD* BN41 ....**24** D5
Sillwood Pl *BRI* BN1 ....**2** C4
Sillwood Rd *BRI* BN1 ....**2** C4
Sillwood St *BRI* BN1 ....**2** C4
Sillwood Ter *BRI* BN1 ....**2** C4
Silver Birch Dr *SALV* BN13 ....**35** H5
Silverdale Av *HOVE* BN3 ....**45** F3
Silverdale Dr *LAN/SOMP* BN15 ....**39** E5
Silverdale Rd *HOVE* BN3 ....**45** F3
Singleton Cl *FERR* BN12 ....**53** F2
Singleton Crs *FERR* BN12 ....**53** F2
Singleton Rd *BRI* BN1 ....**28** A1
Sir George's Pl *STEY/UB* BN44 ....**7** E1
Skyline Vw *PEAHV* BN10 ....**63** F4
Slindon Av *PEAHV* BN10 ....**67** F2
Slindon Rd *FIN/BW* BN14 ....**37** H4
Slinford Cl *ROTT* BN2 ....**46** D5
Slonk Hill Rd *SHOR* BN43 ....**23** C5
Smugglers Wk *FERR* BN12 ....**54** C4
Snednore *LEWES* BN7 ....**32** B2
Solway Av *BRI* BN1 ....**13** H5
Somerhill Av *HOVE* BN3 ....**2** A1
Somerhill Rd *HOVE* BN3 ....**2** B2
Somerset Cl *SALV* BN13 ....**37** E5
Somerset Rd *ANG/EP* BN16 ....**52** B3
  FERR BN12 ....**53** F5
Somerset St *ROTT* BN2 ....**46** C5
Sompting Av *FIN/BW* BN14 ....**37** H5
Sompting By-Pass
  FIN/BW BN14 ....**38** A3
Sompting Cl *ROTT* BN2 ....**47** F3
Sompting Rd *FIN/BW* BN14 ....**38** A3
  LAN/SOMP BN15 ....**39** F4
Sopers La *STEY/UB* BN44 ....**6** D5
Southall Av *ROTT* BN2 ....**28** D5

Southampton St *ROTT* BN2 ....**3**
South Av *FERR* BN12 ....**54**
  ROTT BN2 ....**61**
South Beach *SHOR* * BN43 ....**41**
South Coast Rd *ROTT* BN2 ....**61**
Southcourt Rd *FIN/BW* BN14 ......**4**
Southdown Av *BRI* BN1 ....**46**
  LEWES BN7 ....**16**
  PEAHV BN10 ....**67**
  PTSD BN41 ....**43**
Southdown Cl *NEWHV* BN9 ....**68**
Southdown Cnr *SEAF* * BN25 ......**73**
Southdown Ms *ROTT* BN2 ....**46**
Southdown Pl *BRI* BN1 ....**46**
Southdown Rd *BRI* BN1 ....**46**
  NEWHV BN9 ....**68**
  PTSD BN41 ....**25**
  SEAF BN25 ....**70**
  SHOR BN43 ....**41**
  STHW BN42 ....**42**
South Downs Rd *LEWES* BN7 ......**17**
South Downs Wy *LEWES* BN7 .....**30**
  SHOR BN43 ....**41**
  STEY/UB BN44 ....**6**
Southdown Ter *STEY/UB* BN44 ....**7**
Southdown View Cl
  FIN/BW BN14 ....**38**
Southdown View Rd
  FIN/BW BN14 ....**38**
Southdown View Wy
  FIN/BW BN14 ....**38**
South Dr *FERR* BN12 ....**53**
Southey Rd *WTHG* BN11 ....**4**
South Farm Rd *FIN/BW* BN14 .....**37**
  FIN/BW BN14 ....**37**
South La *NEWHV* BN9 ....**68**
South Ldg *LAN/SOMP* * BN15 .....**39**
Southmount *ROTT* BN2 ....**46**
Southon Cl *PTSD* BN41 ....**24**
Southover High St *LEWES* BN7 ....**16**
Southover Pl *ROTT* BN2 ....**3**
Southover Rd *LEWES* BN7 ....**17**
Southover St *ROTT* BN2 ....**3**
South Rd *BRI* BN1 ....**45**
  NEWHV BN9 ....**68**
South Road Ms *BRI* BN1 ....**45**
Southsea Av *FERR* BN12 ....**54**
South Strd *ANG/EP* BN16 ....**52**
South St *BRI* BN1 ....**3**
  BRI BN1 ....**30**
  LAN/SOMP BN15 ....**39**
  LEWES BN7 ....**17**
  PTSD BN41 ....**43**
  SALV BN13 ....**37**
  SEAF BN25 ....**72**
  WTHG BN11 ....**5**
South Vw *ANG/EP* BN16 ....**52**
Southview Cl *SHOR* BN43 ....**42**
  STHW BN42 ....**42**
Southview Dr *WTHG* BN11 ....**55**
Southview Gdns *WTHG* BN11 ......**54**
Southview Rd *PEAHV* BN10 ....**63**
  STHW BN42 ....**42**
Southview Ter *NEWHV* * BN9 ......**65**
Southwater Cl *FERR* BN12 ....**53**
  ROTT BN2 ....**46**
South Wy *LEWES* BN7 ....**16**
  NEWHV BN9 ....**68**
  SEAF BN25 ....**73**
Southways Av *FIN/BW* BN14 ....**38**
Southwick Sq *STHW* BN42 ....**42**
Southwick St *STHW* BN42 ....**42**
Southwold Cl *SALV* BN13 ....**36**
South Woodlands *BRI* BN1 ....**27**
Sovereign Cl *SEAF* BN25 ....**71**
The Sparrows *PEAHV* BN10 ....**63**
Speedwell Cl *SALV* BN13 ....**35**
Spencer Av *HOVE* BN3 ....**25**
Spencer Rd *LAN/SOMP* BN15 ......**39**
Spences Fld *LEWES* BN7 ....**17**
Spences La *LEWES* BN7 ....**17**
Spey Cl *SALV* BN13 ....**36**
Spinnals Gv *STHW* BN42 ....**42**
The Spinney *ANG/EP* BN16 ....**52**
  HOVE BN3 ....**27**
The Spinneys *LEWES* BN7 ....**17**
Spital Rd *LEWES* BN7 ....**16**
Springate Rd *STHW* BN42 ....**42**
Springfield Av *PEAHV* BN10 ....**62**
Springfield Rd *BRI* BN1 ....**45**
Spring Gdns *BRI* BN1 ....**3**
  LEWES BN7 ....**17**
Spring St *BRI* BN1 ....**2**
Squadron Dr *SALV* BN13 ....**35**
The Square *FIN/BW* * BN14 ....**37**
Stable La *FIN/BW* BN14 ....**37**
Stafford Rd *BRI* BN1 ....**45**
  SEAF BN25 ....**70**

ndean Cl BRI BN1 .....28 D1
nford Av BRI BN1 .....45 H2
nford Cl HOVE BN3 .....45 E1
nford Rd BRI BN1 .....45 G2
nford Sq WTHG BN11 .....5 G5
nhope Rd WTHG BN11 .....4 E3
nley Av PTSD BN41 .....24 D4
nley Rd BRI BN1 .....46 A3
 EAHV BN10 .....62 D4
 TSD BN41 .....43 E2
nley St ROTT BN2 .....3 K4
 THG BN11 .....5 F3
nmer Av ROTT BN2 .....61 H2
nmer Park Rd BRI BN1 .....28 A5
nmer St BRI BN1 .....28 B5
nmer Vls BRI BN1 .....28 B4
nsfield Rd LEWES BN7 .....16 D2
nstead Crs ROTT BN2 .....48 D4
plefield Dr ROTT BN2 .....29 F4
pley Rd HOVE BN3 .....43 H2
tion Ap BRI BN1 .....29 H1
 EAF BN25 .....70 C5
tion Pde LAN/SOMP * BN15 .....39 G5
 VTHG * BN11 .....55 E2
tion Rd BRI BN1 .....27 H4
 EWES BN7 .....17 F4
 EWHV BN9 .....65 F4
 EAF BN25 .....69 I4
 TEY/UB BN44 .....7 G1
 THW BN42 .....42 C3
 VTHG BN11 .....5 F7
tion St BRI BN1 .....3 G2
ep Cl FIN/BW BN14 .....18 C2
epdown Rd LAN/SOMP BN15 .....39 E2
ep La FIN/BW BN14 .....18 C2
eple Vw SALV BN13 .....37 E5
ine Gdns ROTT BN2 .....3 H5
ine La BRI BN1 .....3 G5
ine St ROTT BN2 .....3 H6
phens Rd BRI BN1 .....28 B5
venson Rd ROTT BN2 .....46 C5
wards Inn La LEWES * BN7 .....17 E4
e Steyne SEAF * BN25 .....72 C1
 VTHG BN11 .....5 G5
yne Cl SEAF BN25 .....72 D1
yne Gdns WTHG BN11 .....5 G5
yne Rd SEAF BN25 .....72 C1
yning Av HOVE BN3 .....26 B4
 PEAHV BN10 .....67 E2
yning By-Pass STEY/UB BN44 .....7 H3
yning Cl FERR BN12 .....53 H2
 AN/SOMP BN15 .....39 F2
 EAF BN25 .....73 G1
yning Rd ROTT BN2 .....60 D4
 EAF BN25 .....73 G1
 HOR BN43 .....22 B1
rling Av SEAF BN25 .....71 G4
rling Cl SEAF BN25 .....71 G5
rling Pl HOVE BN3 .....44 C4
oke Abbott Rd WTHG BN11 .....4 E4
oke Cl SEAF BN25 .....71 F5
oke Manor Cl SEAF BN25 .....71 F5
one Cl SALV BN13 .....36 C4
onecroft Cl HOVE BN3 .....26 A3
onecross Rd ROTT BN2 .....29 F3
oneham Cl LEWES BN7 .....17 E1
oneham Rd HOVE BN3 .....44 B3
onehurst Ct ROTT BN2 .....46 C4
one La SALV BN13 .....36 D4
oneleigh Av BRI BN1 .....27 H1
oneleigh Cl BRI BN1 .....27 H1
onery Cl PTSD BN41 .....25 E5
onery Rd PTSD BN41 .....25 E5
one St BRI BN1 .....2 D4
onewood Cl SEAF BN25 .....71 G5
oney La SHOR BN43 .....42 A2
opham Cl FIN/BW BN14 .....37 E5
orrington Cl HOVE BN3 .....26 A5
orrington Ri FIN/BW BN14 .....18 D3
our Cl SALV BN13 .....36 A2
our Rd SALV BN13 .....36 A2
e Strand FERR BN12 .....53 H2
 FERR BN12 .....53 H2
 ROTT BN2 .....59 G2
and Pde FERR * BN12 .....54 C1
rathmore Cl SALV BN13 .....54 C1
rathmore Rd SALV BN13 .....54 C1
e Street LAN/SOMP BN15 .....39 G2
 EWES BN7 .....32 A2
 SALV BN13 .....35 E1
 HOR BN43 .....40 D1
 STEY/UB BN44 .....7 H3
ringer Wy BRI BN1 .....27 H4
uart Cl WTHG BN11 .....5 K1
deley Pl ROTT BN2 .....58 D1
deley Rd ROTT BN2 .....58 D1
deley Ter ROTT BN2 .....58 D1

Suffolk St HOVE BN3 .....44 B2
Sugden Rd WTHG BN11 .....5 J2
Sullington Cl ROTT BN2 .....29 F3
Sullington Gdns FIN/BW BN14 .....18 D3
Sullington Wy SHOR BN43 .....41 G2
Summer Cl PTSD BN41 .....43 E3
Summerdale Av HOVE BN3 .....25 H5
Summerdown Cl SALV BN13 .....35 H5
Summerfields FIN/BW BN14 .....18 C1
Summersdeane STHW BN42 .....42 D1
Sunningdale Cl SEAF BN25 .....71 G5
Sunningdale Ct FERR * BN12 .....54 A2
Sunningdale Rd SALV BN13 .....36 B4
Sunninghill Av HOVE BN3 .....26 A5
Sunninghill Cl HOVE BN3 .....26 A5
Sunny Cl FERR BN12 .....54 C4
Sunnydale Av BRI BN1 .....28 A1
Sunnydale Cl BRI BN1 .....28 A1
Sunset Cl PEAHV BN10 .....62 D4
Sun St LEWES BN7 .....17 E3
Sunview Av PEAHV BN10 .....67 F2
Surrenden Crs BRI BN1 .....27 H4
Surrenden Holt BRI BN1 .....27 H4
Surrenden Pk BRI BN1 .....28 A3
Surrenden Rd BRI BN1 .....27 H4
Surrey Rd SEAF BN25 .....70 A4
Surrey Ct BRI DN1 .....
Surry St SHOR BN43 .....41 F3
Sussex Border Pth BRI BN1 .....13 G2
 PTSD BN41 .....11 E3
Sussex Hts BRI * BN1 .....2 D5
Sussex Ms ROTT BN2 .....59 E1
Sussex Pl ROTT BN2 .....3 J3
Sussex Rd HOVE BN3 .....44 D5
 LAN/SOMP BN15 .....39 G5
 WTHG BN11 .....5 F3
Sussex Sq ROTT BN2 .....59 E1
Sussex St ROTT BN2 .....3 J4
Sussex Ter ROTT BN2 .....3 J5
Sussex Wy PEAHV BN10 .....66 B3
Sussex Whf SHOR * BN43 .....41 H4
Sutherland Rd ROTT BN2 .....46 C5
Sutton Av PEAHV BN10 .....62 D5
 SEAF BN25 .....73 E1
Sutton Av North PEAHV BN10 .....62 D5
Sutton Cl ROTT BN2 .....48 C1
Sutton Croft La SEAF BN25 .....70 C5
Sutton Dro SEAF BN25 .....70 D4
Sutton Park Rd SEAF BN25 .....70 D4
Sutton Pl SEAF * BN25 .....70 D4
Sutton Rd SEAF BN25 .....70 D5
The Swallows PEAHV BN10 .....62 D4
Swallows Cl LAN/SOMP BN15 .....40 C5
Swallows Green Dr SALV BN13 .....36 A5
Swanborough Dr ROTT BN2 .....47 F3
Swanborough Dro LEWES BN7 .....32 B4
Swanborough Hollow
 LEWES BN7 .....32 C3
Swanborough Pl ROTT BN2 .....47 F3
Swanbourne Cl
 LAN/SOMP BN15 .....39 H2
Swannee Cl PEAHV BN10 .....63 F4
Swillage La ANG/EP BN16 .....34 A1
Swiss Gdns SHOR BN43 .....41 E3
Sycamore Cl PTSD BN41 .....25 G4
 ROTT BN2 .....48 C2
 SEAF BN25 .....71 G5
The Sycamores PEAHV BN10 .....63 F4
Sydney St BRI BN1 .....3 G3
Sylvan Rd LAN/SOMP BN15 .....38 D4
Sylvester Wy HOVE BN3 .....25 G4
Symbister Rd PTSD BN41 .....43 G3

Talbot Crs BRI BN1 .....28 D1
Talbot Ter LEWES BN7 .....17 E3
Talland Pde SEAF * BN25 .....72 C1
Tamar Av SALV BN13 .....36 A2
Tamar Cl SALV BN13 .....36 A2
Tamarisk Wy FERR BN12 .....53 F5
Tamplin Ter ROTT BN2 .....3 J2
Tamworth Rd HOVE BN3 .....44 B3
Tandridge Rd HOVE BN3 .....44 A4
Tangmere Rd BRI BN1 .....28 A1
Tanners Brook LEWES BN7 .....17 F4
Tanyard La STEY/UB BN44 .....7 H3
Tarmount La SHOR BN43 .....41 F3
Tarner Rd BRI BN1 .....3 K4
Tarragon Wy SHOR BN43 .....42 A1
Tarring Cl NEWHV BN9 .....64 D3
Tarring Ga SALV * BN13 .....55 E1
Tarring Rd WTHG BN11 .....4 D2
Tasman Wy SALV BN13 .....36 A3

Taunton Rd ROTT BN2 .....47 F1
Taunton Wy ROTT BN2 .....47 G1
Tavistock Down BRI BN1 .....28 C5
Tavy Cl SALV BN13 .....36 A4
Tavy Rd SALV BN13 .....36 A4
Taw Cl SALV BN13 .....36 B3
Teg Cl PTSD BN41 .....25 G5
Telgarth Rd FERR BN12 .....53 E5
Telscombe Cliffs Wy
 PEAHV BN10 .....66 B1
Telscombe Pk PEAHV BN10 .....63 E3
Telscombe Rd PEAHV BN10 .....63 E3
The Templars HOVE BN3 .....38 A3
Temple Gdns HOVE BN3 .....2 C4
Temple St BRI BN1 .....2 C4
Ten Acres WTHG BN11 .....56 C2
Tenantry Down Rd ROTT BN2 .....47 E3
Tenantry Rd ROTT BN2 .....46 D2
Tennis Rd HOVE BN3 .....44 A4
Tennyson Rd WTHG BN11 .....4 D4
Terminus Pl BRI BN1 .....3 F1
Terminus Rd BRI BN1 .....3 F1
Terminus St BRI BN1 .....3 F2
The Terrace FERR * BN12 .....54 A3
 LAN/SOMP BN15 .....57 G1
Terringes Av SALV BN13 .....36 C5
Test Rd LAN/SOMP BN15 .....38 D4
Teville Ga SHOR BN43 .....4 F7
Teville Pl WTHG BN11 .....4 D2
Teville Rd WTHG BN11 .....4 D2
Thackeray Rd FIN/BW BN14 .....56 B1
Thakeham Cl ANG/EP BN16 .....52 B2
 FERR BN12 .....53 C3
Thakeham Dr FERR BN12 .....53 G3
Thalassa Rd WTHG BN11 .....56 D2
Thames Cl ROTT BN2 .....3 K4
Thames Wy SALV BN13 .....36 B3
The Thatch Ct
 LAN/SOMP * BN15 .....39 H2
Thesiger Cl WTHG BN11 .....56 C1
Thesiger Rd WTHG BN11 .....56 C1
Third Av FIN/BW BN14 .....37 H3
 HOVE BN3 .....44 D5
 LAN/SOMP BN15 .....39 G3
 NEWHV BN9 .....68 C2
Third Rd PEAHV BN10 .....66 C1
Thirlmere Crs FIN/BW BN14 .....38 D5
Thomas St LEWES BN7 .....17 G3
Thompson Rd BRI BN1 .....46 C1
 NEWHV BN9 .....65 F3
Thomson Cl SALV BN13 .....35 H4
Thornbush Crs PTSD BN41 .....25 F4
Thorndean Rd ROTT BN2 .....28 D4
Thornhill Av BRI BN1 .....14 A5
Thornhill Cl HOVE BN3 .....26 A5
Thornhill Ri PTSD BN41 .....25 E3
Thornhill Wy PTSD BN41 .....25 E3
Thorn Rd WTHG BN11 .....4 C6
Thurlow Rd WTHG BN11 .....5 H2
Thyme Cl SHOR BN43 .....42 A1
Ticehurst Rd ROTT BN2 .....47 F5
Tichborne St BRI BN1 .....3 G3
Tidy St BRI BN1 .....3 G3
Tilbury Pl ROTT BN2 .....3 J4
Tilbury Wy ROTT BN2 .....3 K3
Tilgate Cl ROTT BN2 .....28 D5
Tillstone Cl ROTT BN2 .....28 D5
Tillstone St ROTT BN2 .....3 K5
Timber Cl SALV BN13 .....36 A5
Timber Yard Cottages
 LEWES BN7 .....17 G3
Tintern Cl BRI BN1 .....46 B1
Tisbury Rd HOVE BN3 .....44 D4
Titch Hl LAN/SOMP BN15 .....20 D5
Titian Rd HOVE BN3 .....44 B3
Titnore La SALV BN13 .....35 E3
Titnore Wy FERR BN12 .....35 G5
Tivoli Crs BRI BN1 .....27 F5
Tivoli Crs North BRI BN1 .....27 F5
Tivoli Pl BRI BN1 .....27 F5
Tivoli Rd BRI BN1 .....27 F5
Tollgate PEAHV BN10 .....62 D4
Tongdean Av HOVE BN3 .....27 E4
Tongdean La BRI BN1 .....27 E3
Tongdean Ri BRI BN1 .....27 E3
Tongdean Rd HOVE BN3 .....26 D4
Torcross Cl ROTT BN2 .....47 E1
Toronto Cl SALV BN13 .....36 B4
Toronto Ter LEWES BN7 .....17 E3
 ROTT BN2 .....3 K3
Torrance Cl HOVE BN3 .....44 B3
Torridge Cl SALV BN13 .....36 A3
Tor Rd PEAHV BN10 .....63 F5
Tor Rd West PEAHV BN10 .....62 D3
Totland Rd ROTT BN2 .....46 D3
Tottington Wy SHOR BN43 .....41 H1
Towergate BRI BN1 .....27 G5
Tower Rd LAN/SOMP BN15 .....39 F5

 ROTT BN2 .....46 C4
 .....5 J3
Towers Rd STEY/UB BN44 .....8 B2
Trafalgar Cl PEAHV BN10 .....63 E4
Trafalgar Ct BRI BN1 .....3 H2
Trafalgar Ga ROTT BN2 .....59 F2
Trafalgar La BRI BN1 .....3 G3
Trafalgar Pl BRI BN1 .....3 G2
Trafalgar Rd PTSD BN41 .....43 F2
Trafalgar St BRI BN1 .....3 G2
Trafalgar Ter BRI * BN1 .....3 G2
Transit Rd NEWHV BN9 .....68 D1
Tredcroft Rd HOVE BN3 .....26 D5
Tree Tops Cl ROTT BN2 .....60 D3
Treharne Cl SALV BN13 .....36 B3
Tremola Av ROTT BN2 .....61 F5
Trent Cl LAN/SOMP BN15 .....39 E4
Trent Rd WTHG BN11 .....54 C3
Treveor Cl WTHG BN11 .....4 D4
Treyford Cl FIN/BW BN14 .....18 C1
Trinity St ROTT BN2 .....46 B3
Tristram Cl LAN/SOMP BN15 .....38 C3
Troon Cl SEAF BN25 .....69 G2
Truleigh Dr PTSD BN41 .....25 E3
Truleigh Rd STEY/UB BN44 .....8 B2
Truleigh Wy SHOR BN43 .....41 G3
Truro Ct WTHG * RN11 .....55 F4
Tudor Cl FIN/BW BN14 .....18 C1
 HOVE BN3 .....26 B5
 ROTT * BN2 .....60 D3
 SEAF BN25 .....70 B4
Tudor Dr STEY/UB BN44 .....8 A1
Tumulus Rd ROTT BN2 .....61 G3
Tunsgate STEY/UB BN44 .....7 F1
Turner Rd FIN/BW BN14 .....38 A4
Turnpike Cl PEAHV BN10 .....63 G5
Turton Cl ROTT BN2 .....46 D5
Tuscan Ct PEAHV * BN10 .....66 B1
Twineham Cl ROTT BN2 .....47 F3
The Twitten STHW BN42 .....42 C3
Twitten Cl STHW BN42 .....42 C3
Twittenside STEY/UB * BN44 .....8 B3
Twitten Wy SALV BN13 .....55 E1
Twyford Cl SALV BN13 .....36 C4
Twyford Gdns SALV BN13 .....36 C4
Twyford Rd BRI BN1 .....28 D1
 SALV BN13 .....36 C4
Tye Cl ROTT BN2 .....61 H5
Tyedean Rd PEAHV BN10 .....62 B5
Tye Vw PEAHV BN10 .....62 C4
Tyne Cl SALV BN13 .....36 A3
The Tynings LAN/SOMP BN15 .....39 C5

U

Uckfield Cl ROTT BN2 .....47 F4
Ullswater Rd LAN/SOMP BN15 .....38 D5
Underdown Rd STHW BN42 .....42 C2
Undermill Rd STEY/UB BN44 .....8 B2
Union Pl WTHG BN11 .....5 F4
Union Rd ROTT BN2 .....3 J1
Union St BRI BN1 .....3 G5
Uplands Av SALV BN13 .....36 D1
Uplands Rd BRI BN1 .....28 C5
Upper Abbey Rd ROTT BN2 .....58 D1
Upper Bannings Rd ROTT BN2 .....62 A2
Upper Bedford St ROTT BN2 .....58 C1
Upper Belgrave Rd SEAF BN25 .....70 D3
Upper Bevendean Av ROTT BN2 .....47 E1
Upper Boundstone La
 LAN/SOMP BN15 .....39 F3
Upper Brighton Rd
 FIN/BW BN14 .....37 C4
Upper Chalvington Pl
 ROTT BN2 .....47 E5
Upper Chyngton Gdns
 SEAF BN25 .....71 F4
The Upper Dr HOVE BN3 .....45 G2
Upper Dr ANG/EP BN16 .....52 B5
Upper Gardner St BRI BN1 .....3 G3
Upper Gloucester Rd BRI BN1 .....3 F2
Upper Hamilton Rd BRI BN1 .....45 G2
Upper High St WTHG BN11 .....5 G2
Upper Hollingdean Rd BRI BN1 .....46 B1
Upper Kingston La STHW BN42 .....42 B1
Upper Lewes Rd ROTT BN2 .....46 B3
Upper Market St HOVE BN3 .....2 B4
Upper North St BRI BN1 .....2 D4
Upper Park Pl ROTT BN2 .....3 K4
Upper Rock Gdns ROTT BN2 .....3 K5
Upper St James's St ROTT BN2 .....3 K5
Upper Sherwood Rd SEAF BN25 .....70 D4
Upper Shoreham Rd
 SHOR BN43 .....40 D2
Upper Sudeley St ROTT BN2 .....58 D1

Upper Valley Rd *NEWHV* BN9 ....**68** B2
Upper Wellington Rd *ROTT* BN2 ....**46** C3
Upper West Dr *FERR* BN12..............**53** E4
Upper West La *LAN/SOMP* BN15 ...**39** C3
Upper Winfield Av *BRI* BN1 ....**27** H1
Upton Av *STHW* BN42 ....**42** C1
Upton Gdns *SALV* BN13 ....**54** D1
Upton Rd *SALV* BN13 ....**54** D1

V

Vale Av *BRI* BN1 ....**13** G5
  FIN/BW BN14................................**18** D5
Vale Cl *SEAF* BN25 ....**71** E4
Vale Dr *FIN/BW* BN14 ....**18** D5
Vale Gdns *PTSD* BN41 ....**43** F3
Valence Rd *LEWES* BN7..................**16** D3
Valencia Rd *WTHG* BN11 ....**55** E2
Valentine Cl *FIN/BW* BN14 ....**37** F5
Valerie Cl *PTSD* BN41......................**25** F5
The Vale *ROTT* BN2..........................**48** C5
Vale Rd *PTSD* BN41..........................**43** F3
  ROTT BN2..**61** H2
  SEAF BN25......................................**70** D4
Vale Wk *FIN/BW* BN14....................**18** D5
Vallance Gdns *HOVE* BN3..............**44** C4
Vallance Rd *HOVE* BN3 ....**44** C4
Valley Cl *BRI* BN1 ....**27** E3
  NEWHV BN9..................................**64** B5
Valley Dene *NEWHV* BN9 ....**68** B1
Valley Dr *BRI* BN1 ....**27** E3
  SEAF BN25......................................**71** E3
Valley Ri *SEAF* BN25 ....**70** D4
Valley Rd *LAN/SOMP* BN15..........**39** E2
  LEWES BN7......................................**16** C4
  NEWHV BN9....................................**68** B1
  PEAHV BN10 ....**63** E3
  PTSD BN41 ....**25** E5
Vancouver Cl *SALV* BN13..............**36** B4
Vancouver Rd *SALV* BN13..............**36** A4
Vanguard Wy *SEAF* BN25 ....**73** E2
Varey Rd *SALV* BN13 ....**35** H4
Varndean Cl *BRI* BN1 ....**27** G4
Varndean Dr *BRI* BN1 ....**27** G4
Varndean Gdns *BRI* BN1 ....**27** G4
Varndean Holt *BRI* BN1 ....**27** H4
Varndean Rd *BRI* BN1 ....**27** G4
Ventnor Vls *HOVE* BN3 ....**44** D4
Vere Rd *BRI* BN1 ....**46** A2
Vermont Dr *ANG/EP* BN16 ....**52** A4
Vermont Wy *ANG/EP* BN16 ....**52** A4
Vernon Av *PEAHV* BN10 ....**67** F2
  ROTT BN2..**48** A1
Vernon Gdns *BRI* BN1 ....**2** D2
Vernon Ter *BRI* BN1........................**2** D2
Veronica Cl *ANG/EP* BN16 ....**52** A5
Veronica Wy *ROTT* BN2..................**3** K6
Verralls Wk *LEWES* BN7 ....**17** E4
Viaduct Rd *BRI* BN1 ....**46** A3
Vicarage Cl *NEWHV* BN9 ....**65** E3
  SEAF BN25......................................**70** D5
Vicarage Dr *SALV* BN13 ....**36** B3
Vicarage La *ROTT* BN2 ....**60** D4
  STEY/UB BN44................................**7** F1
Vicarage Ter *ROTT* BN2 ....**60** D4
Victor Cl *SEAF* BN25 ....**70** B3
Victoria Av *PEAHV* BN10 ....**67** E2
Victoria Gv *HOVE* BN3 ....**45** E4
Victoria Ms *ROTT* * BN2................**60** D4
Victoria Park Gdns *WTHG* BN11 ..**4** C3
Victoria Pl *BRI* BN1..........................**2** D3
Victoria Rd *BRI* BN1........................**2** D3
  PTSD BN41......................................**43** F2
  SHOR BN43....................................**41** E3
  STHW BN42 ....**42** B3
  WTHG BN11 ....**4** D3
Victoria St *BRI* BN1 ....**2** D3
Victory Ms *ROTT* BN2....................**59** G2
View Rd *PEAHV* BN10 ....**63** E5
Viking Cl *SEAF* BN25 ....**69** G2
The Village Barn *BRI* BN1 ....**13** G5
Village Wy *BRI* BN1 ....**30** A1
Villiers Cl *ROTT* BN2 ....**48** C2
Vincent Cl *LAN/SOMP* BN15 ....**39** F4
Vine Pl *BRI* BN1 ....**2** E3
Vineries Cl *SALV* BN13 ....**37** E4
Vines Cross Rd *ROTT* BN2............**47** F3
Vine St *BRI* BN1................................**3** H3

W

Wadhurst Dr *FERR* BN12 ....**53** H3
Wadhurst Ri *ROTT* BN2 ....**47** F5
Waite Cl *LEWES* BN7 ....**17** F2

Wakefield Rd *ROTT* BN2................**46** B2
Waldegrave Rd *BRI* BN1................**27** H5
Waldron Av *BRI* BN1 ....**28** D1
Waldron Pl *BRI* * BN1 ....**28** D1
Waldshut Rd *LEWES* BN7 ....**16** C1
Walesbeech Rd *ROTT* BN2............**61** H5
Wallace Av *WTHG* BN11 ....**54** D3
Wallace Ms *WTHG* * BN11............**54** D4
Wallace Pde *WTHG* * BN11..........**54** D3
Wallands Crs *LEWES* BN7 ....**17** E2
Walmer Crs *ROTT* BN2..................**47** G1
Walmer Rd *SEAF* BN25..................**71** G4
Walnut Cl *BRI* BN1..........................**27** G4
Walnut Ldg *FIN/BW* * BN14 ....**4** C1
Walnut Tree Wy *SALV* BN13 ....**35** H5
Walpole Av *FERR* BN12..................**54** B3
Walpole Rd *ROTT* BN2 ....**58** C1
Walpole Ter *ROTT* BN2 ....**46** D5
Walsingham Rd *HOVE* BN3 ....**44** B4
Walton Bank *BRI* BN1 ....**29** E2
Walton Cl *SALV* BN13 ....**36** D3
Walton Ldg *SALV* BN13 ....**36** D4
Wanderdown Cl *ROTT* BN2..........**60** C1
Wanderdown Dr *ROTT* BN2..........**60** C1
Wanderdown Rd *ROTT* BN2..........**60** B1
Wanderdown Wy *ROTT* BN2 ....**60** C1
Wantley Rd *FIN/BW* BN14 ....**37** E1
Warbleton Cl *ROTT* BN2 ....**47** E5
Warenne Rd *HOVE* BN3 ....**25** G5
Warleigh Rd *BRI* BN1 ....**46** A2
Warmdene Av *BRI* BN1 ....**27** H1
Warmdene Rd *BRI* BN1 ....**27** H1
Warmdene Wy *BRI* BN1 ....**27** H1
Warner Rd *FIN/BW* BN14 ....**56** B1
Warnham Cl *FERR* BN12................**54** B4
Warnham Ms *FERR* * BN12............**54** C4
Warnham Ri *BRI* BN1 ....**28** A2
Warnham Rd *FERR* BN12 ....**54** B3
The Warren *FERR* BN12 ....**53** F5
Warren Av *ROTT* BN2 ....**48** A1
Warren Cl *LEWES* BN7 ....**16** D4
  ROTT BN2..**47** H2
Warren Dr *LEWES* BN7..................**16** C4
Warren Gdns *FIN/BW* BN14 ....**37** F3
Warren Ri *ROTT* BN2 ....**47** H2
Warren Rd *FIN/BW* BN14 ....**37** F3
  ROTT BN2..**47** E3
  ROTT BN2..**48** A2
Warren Wy *PEAHV* BN10 ....**62** C4
  ROTT BN2..**48** B2
Warr Gn *LEWES* BN7 ....**16** D1
Warrior Cl *PTSD* BN41 ....**25** F5
Warwick Gdns *WTHG* BN11 ....**5** G5
Warwick La *WTHG* * BN11 ....**5** G5
Warwick Mt *ROTT* * BN2 ....**58** C1
Warwick Pl *WTHG* BN11 ....**5** H4
Warwick Rd *SEAF* * BN25 ....**70** C5
  WTHG BN11 ....**5** H5
Warwick St *WTHG* BN11 ....**5** H5
Washington St *ROTT* BN2 ....**3** K2
Waterdyke Av *STHW* BN42 ....**42** C3
Waterford Cl *PEAHV* BN10............**63** E3
Watergate La *LEWES* BN7 ....**17** E3
Waterhall Rd *BRI* BN1....................**27** E1
Waterloo Pl *LEWES* BN7 ....**17** F3
Waterloo St *HOVE* BN3 ....**2** B5
Watersfield Rd *FIN/BW* BN14 ......**37** F5
Watling St *STHW* BN42..................**42** C3
Waverley Crs *BRI* BN1 ....**46** B1
Wavertree Rd *FERR* BN12 ....**54** B2
The Way *ANG/EP* BN16 ....**52** A5
Wayfield Av *HOVE* BN3 ....**44** A1
Wayfield Cl *HOVE* BN3 ....**44** A1
Wayland Av *BRI* BN1 ....**27** E3
Wayland Hts *BRI* BN1 ....**27** E3
Wayside *BRI* BN1 ....**27** F1
  LAN/SOMP * BN15........................**39** E3
Wayside Av *SALV* BN13 ....**36** B3
Weald Av *HOVE* BN3 ....**44** B1
Weald Cl *LEWES* * BN7..................**17** E2
Weald Dyke *SHOR* BN43 ....**41** F4
Wear Cl *SALV* BN13 ....**36** A3
Wear Rd *SALV* BN13 ....**36** A3
Weavers Hl *ANG/EP* BN16 ....**34** A4
Weavers Ring *ANG/EP* BN16 ......**34** A5
Welbeck Av *HOVE* BN3 ....**44** A4
Welesmere Rd *ROTT* BN2 ....**61** E2
Welland Cl *SALV* BN13 ....**36** B2
Welland Rd *SALV* BN13 ....**36** B2
Wellesley Av *FERR* BN12..............**54** B3
Wellgreen La *LEWES* BN7 ....**32** B2
Well House Pl *LEWES* * BN7 ....**17** E4
Wellingham La *SALV* BN13 ....**36** C1
Wellington Pk *SEAF* BN25 ....**71** E5
Wellington Rd *NEWHV* BN9 ....**65** E3
  PEAHV BN10 ....**67** G2
  PTSD BN41......................................**43** F4

Wellington St *LEWES* BN7 ....**17** F3
  ROTT BN2..**46** C3
Wells Ct *WTHG* * BN11 ....**55** E4
Wembley Av *LAN/SOMP* BN15 ....**39** F4
Wembley Gdns
  LAN/SOMP BN15..........................**39** F4
Wenban Rd *WTHG* BN11 ....**4** E3
Wenceling Cottages
  LAN/SOMP BN15..........................**40** C5
Wendale Dr *PEAHV* BN10 ....**63** F3
Went Hill Pk *SEAF* BN25 ....**71** E5
Wentworth Cl *SALV* BN13 ....**36** D2
Wentworth Ct *ANG/EP* * BN16 ....**52** A4
Wentworth St *ROTT* BN2 ....**3** J6
West Av *LAN/SOMP* BN15 ....**40** A5
  WTHG BN11 ....**55** E3
West Beach Rd
  LAN/SOMP BN15..........................**40** C5
Westbourne Av *FIN/BW* BN14 ......**4** E1
Westbourne Gdns *HOVE* BN3 ......**44** C4
Westbourne Pl *HOVE* BN3 ....**44** C4
Westbourne St *HOVE* BN3 ....**44** C4
Westbourne Vls *HOVE* BN3 ....**44** B4
Westbrook *ROTT* * BN2..................**61** G3
Westbrooke *WTHG* BN11 ....**4** E4
Westbrook Wy *STHW* BN42 ....**42** D3
West Buildings *WTHG* BN11..........**4** D6
Westcourt Pl *FIN/BW* BN14 ....**4** D1
Westcourt Rd *FIN/BW* BN14 ....**4** D2
Westdean Av *NEWHV* BN9 ....**68** A3
West Dean Ri *SEAF* BN25..............**71** E4
Westdean Rd *FIN/BW* BN14 ....**37** F5
Westdene Dr *BRI* BN1 ....**27** E2
Westdown Rd *SEAF* BN25 ....**70** B4
West Dr *FERR* BN12........................**53** E5
  ROTT BN2..**3** K4
West End Wy *LAN/SOMP* BN15 ..**57** F1
Westergate Cl *FERR* BN12 ....**53** F3
Westergate Rd *ROTT* BN2 ....**29** E3
Western Cl *LAN/SOMP* BN15........**57** E1
Western Esp *PTSD* BN41................**43** H4
Western Ldg *LAN/SOMP* * BN15 ..**39** E3
Western Pl *WTHG* BN11 ....**4** D6
Western Rd *HOVE* BN3 ....**2** A3
  LAN/SOMP BN15..........................**57** E1
  LEWES BN7....................................**16** D3
  NEWHV BN9..................................**68** C2
  SHOR BN43....................................**41** E3
Western Rd North
  LAN/SOMP BN15..........................**39** E4
Western Rw *WTHG* BN11 ....**4** D6
Western St *BRI* BN1 ....**2** B5
Western Ter *BRI* BN1 ....**2** C4
  FIN/BW * BN14 ....**18** C5
Westfield Av *ANG/EP* BN16 ....**52** A5
  ROTT BN2..**61** H2
Westfield Av North *ROTT* BN2......**61** H2
Westfield Av South *ROTT* BN2......**61** H2
Westfield Cl *BRI* BN1 ....**28** A3
Westfield Crs *BRI* BN1 ....**28** A2
Westfield Ri *ROTT* BN2..................**61** H2
West Hl *SALV* BN13........................**18** C5
West Hill Cl *SALV* * BN13..............**18** C5
West Hill Pl *BRI* BN1 ....**2** E1
West Hill Rd *BRI* BN1 ....**2** E2
West Hill St *BRI* BN1 ....**2** E2
Westlake Cl *SALV* BN13 ....**36** D5
Westland Av *FIN/BW* BN14 ....**55** E1
Westlands *FERR* BN12....................**53** E4
West La *LAN/SOMP* BN15 ....**39** G4
Westmeston Av *ROTT* BN2............**61** F3
Westmount Cl *SHOR* BN43 ....**42** B2
West Onslow Cl *FERR* * BN12 ......**53** E2
West Pde *WTHG* BN11 ....**54** D5
Westpark La *FERR* BN12 ....**54** C3
West Quay *NEWHV* BN9 ....**68** D1
West Rd *PTSD* BN41 ....**43** F3
West St *BRI* BN1 ....**3** F5
  LAN/SOMP BN15..........................**38** D3
  PTSD BN41 ....**43** G3
  ROTT BN2..**60** D4
  SEAF BN25 ....**72** C1
  SHOR BN43....................................**41** E3
  WTHG BN11 ....**4** D6
West Tyne *SALV* BN13....................**36** B5
West Vw *HOVE* * BN3 ....**45** E2
  SEAF BN25 ....**72** C1
West View Ct *SEAF* * BN25 ....**72** C1
Westview Ter *FIN/BW* BN14..........**18** C1
West Wy *HOVE* BN3........................**25** H5
  LAN/SOMP BN15..........................**40** A5
  SALV BN13......................................**36** B1
Westway Cl *PTSD* BN41 ....**24** C3
Westway Gdns *PTSD* BN41 ....**24** C3
Wharf Rd *HOVE* BN3 ....**43** H4
Wheatfield Wy *ROTT* BN2 ....**29** F4
Wheatland Cl *PEAHV* BN10 ....**62** D3

Wheatsheaf Gdns *LEWES* BN7......**17**
Whichelo Pl *ROTT* BN2..................**46**
Whippingham Rd *ROTT* BN2........**46**
Whippingham St *ROTT* BN2..........**46**
Whitebeam Rd *SALV* BN13 ....**36**
Whitehawk Cl *ROTT* BN2 ....**47**
Whitehawk Crs *ROTT* BN2 ....**47**
Whitehawk Hill Rd *ROTT* BN2 ....**46**
Whitehawk Rd *ROTT* BN2............**47**
Whitehawk Wy *ROTT* BN2............**47**
Whitelot Cl *STHW* BN42................**42**
Whitelot Wy *STHW* BN42..............**24**
Whiterock Pl *STHW* BN42 ....**42**
White St *ROTT* BN2........................**47**
White Styles Rd
  LAN/SOMP BN15..........................**38**
Whitethorn Dr *BRI* BN1 ....**26**
White Wy *LEWES* BN7 ....**50**
Whiteway Cl *SEAF* BN25................**70**
Whiteway La *ROTT* BN2................**60**
Whittingehame Gdns *BRI* BN1......**27**
Whylands Av *SALV* BN13 ....**36**
Whylands Cl *SALV* BN13................**36**
Whylands Crs *SALV* BN13 ....**36**
Wickhurst Cl *PTSD* BN41 ....**24**
Wickhurst Ri *PTSD* BN41 ....**24**
Wickhurst Rd *PTSD* BN41 ....**24**
Wicklands Av *ROTT* BN2................**61**
Widdicombe Wy *ROTT* BN2 ....**29**
Widewater Cl *LAN/SOMP* BN15 ..**40**
Widewater Ct *SHOR* * BN43..........**40**
Wigmore Cl *BRI* BN1 ....**46**
Wigmore Rd *FIN/BW* BN14............**37**
Wilbury Av *HOVE* BN3 ....**45**
Wilbury Crs *HOVE* BN3 ....**45**
Wilbury Gdns *HOVE* BN3..............**45**
Wilbury Gv *HOVE* BN3 ....**45**
Wilbury Rd *HOVE* BN3 ....**45**
Wilbury Vls *HOVE* BN3 ....**45**
Wilby Av *STHW* BN42....................**42**
Wild Park Cl *ROTT* BN2 ....**29**
Wilfrid Rd *HOVE* BN3....................**43**
Wilkinson Cl *ROTT* BN2 ....**60**
Wilkinson Wy *SEAF* BN25 ....**70**
Williams Rd *SHOR* BN43 ....**41**
William St *PTSD* BN41....................**43**
  ROTT BN2..**3**
Willingdon Rd *ROTT* BN2 ....**47**
Willowbrook Rd *FIN/BW* BN14 ....**56**
Willow Cl *LAN/SOMP* BN15 ....**40**
  ROTT BN2..**48**
  WTHG BN11 ....**55**
Willow Crs *SALV* BN13 ....**36**
Willow Dr *SEAF* BN25 ....**71**
The Willow Est *NEWHV* * BN9......**65**
Willowhayne Av *ANG/EP* BN16....**52**
Willowhayne Cl *ANG/EP* BN16......**52**
Willowhayne Crs *ANG/EP* BN16 ..**52**
The Willows *FIN/BW* * BN14 ....**18**
  LAN/SOMP * BN15 ....**39**
  ROTT * BN2....................................**46**
  SEAF * BN25..................................**70**
Willow Wk *NEWHV* BN9................**64**
Wilmington Cl *BRI* BN1 ....**28**
Wilmington Pde *BRI* BN1 ....**27**
Wilmington Rd *NEWHV* BN9 ....**68**
  SEAF BN25 ....**70**
Wilmington Wy *BRI* BN1 ....**27**
Wilmot Rd *SHOR* BN43 ....**42**
Wilson Av *ROTT* BN2 ....**59**
Winchelsea Cl *SEAF* BN25 ....**71**
Winchelsea Gdns *WTHG* BN11 ....**54**
Winchester Rd *WTHG* BN11 ....**4**
Winchester St *BRI* BN1 ....**46**
Wincombe Rd *BRI* BN1..................**45**
Windermere Ct *FERR* * BN12 ......**53**
Windermere Crs *FERR* BN12 ....**36**
Windlesham Av *HOVE* BN3 ....**2**
Windlesham Cl *PTSD* BN41............**43**
Windlesham Gdns
  ANG/EP BN16................................**52**
  BRI BN1 ....**2**
  SHOR BN43....................................**41**
Windlesham Rd *BRI* BN1 ....**2**
  SHOR BN43....................................**41**
Windmill Cl *HOVE* BN3..................**26**
  STEY/UB BN44................................**8**
Windmill Dr *BRI* BN1 ....**27**
Windmill Rd *STHW* BN42..............**42**
Windmill St *ROTT* BN2 ....**3**
Windmill Ter *ROTT* BN2 ....**3**
Windmill Vw *BRI* BN1 ....**28**
Windover Crs *LEWES* BN7 ....**16**
Windrush Cl *SALV* BN13................**36**
Windsor Cl *HOVE* BN3 ....**26**
  SEAF BN25 ....**69**
Windsor Rd *WTHG* BN11 ....**5**
Windsor St *BRI* BN1........................**3**

...dsor Wy *LAN/SOMP* BN15 ....**40** B4
...nfield Av *BRI* BN1 ....**27** H1
...nfield Cl *BRI* BN1 ....**27** H2
...PTSD BN41.............................**25** E4
...nston Rd *LAN/SOMP* BN15......**57** E2
...nterbourne Cl *LEWES* BN7.......**16** D4
...nterton Wy *SHOR* BN43...........**35** H5
...nterbourne Hollow
   LEWES BN7 ....**16** D4
...nterbourne La *LEWES* BN7 .....**16** C4
...nterbourne Ms *LEWES* BN7.....**16** D4
...nterbourne Wy *SALV* BN13 .....**35** H5
...nterton Wy *SHOR* BN43...........**41** H4
...nton Av *ROTT* BN2.................**61** G3
...nton Pl *WTHG* BN11 ....**4** E4
...sh Rd *HOVE* BN3 ....**44** A4
...ston Av *FIN/BW* BN14...........**37** F5
...ston Cl *FIN/BW* BN14 ....**37** F5
...ston Rd *ROTT* BN2.................**47** F3
...ston Wy *ROTT* BN2.................**47** F3
...chdean Av *BRI* BN1 ....**27** F5
...ERR BN12.............................**53** H5
...chdean Cl *BRI* BN1.................**27** F4
...chdean Court Av *BRI* BN1 ....**27** F4

Withdean Crs *BRI* BN1 ....**27** G4
Withdean Ri *BRI* BN1 ....**27** F4
Withdean Rd *BRI* BN1 ....**27** F5
Withyham Av *ROTT* BN2.............**61** G5
Wivelsfield Rd *ROTT* BN2 ....**61** G2
Woburn Pl *BRI* BN1 ....**29** F2
Wolseley Rd *BRI* BN1 ....**28** D1
   PTSD BN41............................**43** E2
Wolstonbury Rd *HOVE* BN3 ....**45** G3
Wolverstone Dr *BRI* BN1 ....**28** C5
Woodard Rd *LAN/SOMP* BN15.....**39** H3
Woodards Vw *SHOR* BN43..........**40** D5
Woodbourne Av *BRI* BN1 ....**27** H3
Woodbridge Pk *ANG/EP* BN16 ....**52** A4
Woodhouse Rd *HOVE* BN3 ....**44** A3
Woodland Av *HOVE* BN3.............**26** D3
   SALV BN13 ....**36** C1
Woodland Cl *HOVE* BN3.............**26** D5
Woodland Dr *HOVE* BN3.............**26** D5
The Woodlands *BRI* BN1 ....**27** G2
Woodlands *HOVE* BN3 ....**27** E5
Woodlands Cl *ANG/EP* BN16 ......**34** A3
   PEAHV BN10 ....**62** D4
   SALV BN13 ....**35** F1

Woodland Wk *ROTT* BN2............**60** B1
Woodland Wy *BRI* BN1 ....**27** H3
Woodlea Rd *SALV* BN13.............**55** E1
Woodmancote Rd
   FIN/BW BN14 ....**55** F1
Woodpecker Wy *SALV* BN13 ....**36** A5
Woodruff Av *HOVE* BN3 ....**27** E5
Woodside Av *BRI* BN1................**27** F5
Woodside Rd *FIN/BW* BN14 ....**4** B1
Woods Wy *FERR* BN12...............**54** A2
Woodview *SHOR* BN43 ....**41** F1
Woodview Cl *BRI* BN1................**28** D1
Woodview Ct *SHOR* * BN43.........**41** F1
Worcester Ct *WTHG* * BN11 ....**55** E4
Worcester Vls *HOVE* BN3 ....**43** G3
Wordsworth Rd *WTHG* BN11 ....**4** B5
Wordsworth St *HOVE* BN3 ....**44** C3
Wychwood Gdns *WTHG* BN11 .....**56** D2
Wyke Av *WTHG* BN11 ....**5** G5
Wykeham Cl *STEY/UB* BN44.........**7** F1
Wykeham Rd *WTHG* BN11 ....**4** C4
Wykeham Ter *BRI* * BN1 ....**2** E4
Wyndham St *ROTT* BN2 ....**3** K6
Wynnes Ms *HOVE* BN3 ....**44** C3

Y

Yardley St *BRI* BN1 ....**46** A2
Yarrow Rd *LEWES* * BN7............**16** D2
Yeoman Rd *SALV* BN13 ....**35** H5
Yeoman Wy *SALV* BN13.............**53** H1
York Av *HOVE* BN3 ....**2** C2
York Gv *BRI* BN1.......................**45** H3
York Hl *BRI* BN1 ....**3** G1
York Pl *BRI* BN1 ....**3** H2
York Rd *HOVE* BN3......................**2** C2
   PEAHV BN10 ....**67** G2
   WTHG BN11 ....**5** C5
York Vls *BRI* BN1......................**45** H3
Youngsmere Cl *BRI* BN1............**28** B1

Z

Zion Gdns *BRI* BN1.....................**3** F4

Index - featured places

...E School
   BRI BN1 .... **28** C4
...rrington House Hospital
   HOVE BN3 .... **44** B4
...F Bowling
   WTHG BN11 .... **4** E6
...necy RC Primary School
   SEAF BN25 .... **71** E4
...ne of Cleves House Museum
   LEWES BN7 .... **17** E4
...uarena Swimming Pool
   WTHG BN11 .... **5** J5
...e Arden Foot & Health Clinic
   ROTT BN2 .... **3** H5
...dmore School
   WTHG BN11 .... **4** E4
...sembly Hall
   WTHG BN11 .... **4** E4
...lfour J & I School
   BRI BN1 .... **28** A4
...rn Theatre
   SEAF BN25 .... **72** C1
...llerbys College
   HOVE BN3 .... **45** E3
...ll Tower Industrial Estate
   ROTT BN2 .... **59** F1
...nfield Golf Club
   HOVE BN3 .... **25** G5
...nfield Junior School
   PTSD BN41 .... **43** G2
...vendean Primary School
   ROTT BN2 .... **29** F5
...atchington Mill School &
   Sixth Form College
   HOVE BN3 .... **44** C1
...atchington Road
   Industrial Estate
   SEAF BN25 .... **70** C5
...ooth Museum of
   Natural History
   HOVE BN3 .... **45** F2
...owden House School
   SEAF BN25 .... **70** C4
...amber Castle
   STEY/UB BN44 .... **7** H2
...amber Road First School
   FIN/BW BN14 .... **38** A4
...idge Industrial Estate
   NEWHV BN9 .... **64** D5
...ighton Business Centre
   BRI BN1 .... **45** H2
...ighton Central Library
   BRI BN1 .... **45** H3
...e Brighton Centre
   BRI BN1 .... **2** E5
...ighton College
   HOVE BN3 .... **44** C4
...ighton College of Technology
   BRI BN1 .... **45** H2
   ROTT BN2 .... **3** J1
...ighton College of Technology
   & Tower Theatre
   BRI BN1 .... **3** H2
...ighton County Court
   ROTT BN2 .... **3** H4

Brighton Fishing Museum
   BRI BN1 .... **3** F6
Brighton General Hospital
   ROTT BN2 .... **46** D3
Brighton & Hove Albion FC
   (Withdean Stadium)
   BRI BN1 .... **27** F4
Brighton & Hove Golf Club
   PTSD BN41 .... **11** H5
Brighton & Hove High School
   HOVE BN3 .... **45** E2
Brighton & Hove High
   School Gpdst
   BRI BN1 .... **2** C3
Brighton Hove & Sussex
   Sixth Form College
   HOVE BN3 .... **45** G2
Brighton Media Centre
   BRI BN1 .... **3** F5
Brighton Municipal Market
   ROTT BN2 .... **3** H3
Brighton Pier
   ROTT BN2 .... **3** H7
Brighton Racecourse
   ROTT BN2 .... **47** E3
Brighton RFC
   BRI BN1 .... **26** D1
Brighton Steiner School
   ROTT BN2 .... **59** E1
Brighton Youth Centre
   ROTT BN2 .... **3** K5
Brightwell Industrial Estate
   NEWHV BN9 .... **69** E1
British Engineerium - Museum
   of Steam & Mechanical
   Antiquities
   HOVE BN3 .... **26** D5
Broadwater & Worthing
   Cemetery
   FIN/BW BN14 .... **37** G5
Broadwater CE F & M School
   FIN/BW BN14 .... **37** G5
Broadwater Industrial Estate
   FIN/BW BN14 .... **38** B4
Broadwater Manor School
   FIN/BW BN14 .... **37** H5
Brooklands Trading Estate
   FIN/BW BN14 .... **4** B2
Bross Estate
   NEWHV BN9 .... **65** E5
Buckingham Middle School
   SHOR BN43 .... **41** F2
Buckle Caravan &
   Camping Park
   SEAF BN25 .... **69** H4
Cardinal Newman School
   HOVE BN3 .... **45** F2
Carlton Hill Primary School
   ROTT BN2 .... **3** J4
Castledean School
   BRI BN1 .... **28** C5
Centenary Industrial Estate
   BRI BN1 .... **46** B1
Chapel Royal
   BRI BN1 .... **3** G5

Charter Medical Centre
   HOVE BN3 .... **2** B1
Chesswood Middle School
   WTHG BN11 .... **5** H1
Child Clinic
   ROTT BN2 .... **3** H4
Churchill Square Shopping Centre
   BRI BN1 .... **2** E5
Cissbury Ring
   FIN/BW BN14 .... **19** F2
Clapham & Patching CE Primary
   School
   SALV BN13 .... **35** E1
Clarks Industrial Estate
   HOVE BN3 .... **44** D2
Cliffe Business Centre
   LEWES BN7 .... **17** G3
Cliffe Industrial Estate
   LEWES BN7 .... **17** H4
Coldean Junior School
   BRI BN1 .... **28** D1
Connaught Theatre & Cinema
   WTHG BN11 .... **5** F4
Conway Court Clinic
   HOVE BN3 .... **44** D2
Coombe Road Primary School
   ROTT BN2 .... **46** D1
Cornerstones Independent School
   HOVE BN3 .... **2** B3
Corn Exchange Theatre
   BRI BN1 .... **3** G4
Corsica Hall Education
   Training Centre
   SEAF BN25 .... **72** D1
Cradle Hill CP School
   SEAF BN25 .... **71** E3
Cradle Hill Industrial Estate
   SEAF BN25 .... **71** F3
Cuckmere House
   Special School
   SEAF BN25 .... **71** G5
Cyril Richings Business Centre
   SHOR BN43 .... **41** H3
David Lloyd Health &
   Fitness Centre
   ROTT BN2 .... **59** F2
Davigdor Infant School
   HOVE BN3 .... **2** A2
Davison CE Secondary
   School for Girls
   WTHG BN11 .... **5** K2
D-Day Museum
   SHOR BN43 .... **40** D3
Deacon Trading Estate
   FIN/BW BN14 .... **38** B5
Denton County Primary School
   NEWHV BN9 .... **65** E4
Dharma School
   BRI BN1 .... **28** A1
Dolphin House Clinic for Adults
   BRI BN1 .... **3** G4
Dolphin Industrial Estate
   SHOR BN43 .... **42** A3
Dome Cinema
   WTHG BN11 .... **5** G6

Downlands Business Park
   FIN/BW BN14 .... **38** A2
Downsbrook CP School
   FIN/BW BN14 .... **38** A5
Downsbrook Middle School
   FIN/BW BN14 .... **38** A5
Downsbrook Trading Estate
   FIN/BW BN14 .... **38** A4
The Downs Crematorium
   ROTT BN2 .... **46** D2
Downs Infant School
   BRI BN1 .... **46** A2
Downs Junior School
   BRI BN1 .... **46** A1
Downs Leisure Centre
   SEAF BN25 .... **71** E4
Downs Park School
   PTSD BN41 .... **25** F5
The Dr Jan De Winter Clinic for
   Cancer Prevention Advice
   BRI BN1 .... **3** G5
Duke of York's Premier
   Picture House Cinema
   BRI BN1 .... **46** A3
Durrington Health Centre
   SALV BN13 .... **36** B4
Durrington High School
   SALV BN13 .... **36** C5
Durrington Primary School
   SALV BN13 .... **36** C3
Dyke Golf Club
   BRI BN1 .... **11** G2
East Brighton Golf Club
   ROTT BN2 .... **59** F1
East Preston CP School
   ANG/EP BN16 .... **52** A3
East Sussex County
   Music School
   LEWES BN7 .... **17** E4
East Worthing Industrial Estate
   FIN/BW BN14 .... **38** B5
Elm Grove County First School
   WTHG BN11 .... **54** D2
Elm Grove Primary School
   ROTT BN2 .... **46** C3
English Bowling Association
   WTHG BN11 .... **5** H4
English Martyrs RC
   Primary School
   FERR BN12 .... **36** B5
Environment Agency
   WTHG BN11 .... **5** F5
Euro Business Park
   NEWHV BN9 .... **64** D4
Evolution Health Centre
   BRI BN1 .... **2** D3
Fairlight Primary School
   ROTT BN2 .... **46** C2
Fairway Trading Estate
   ROTT BN2 .... **29** E3
Ferring CE Primary School
   FERR BN12 .... **53** F3
Ferring FC
   FERR BN12 .... **53** E3
Ferryfield Industrial Estate
   NEWHV BN9 .... **69** E1

Ferry Terminal
NEWHV BN9 .... 68 D1
Field Place First School
FERR BN12 .... 54 B1
Fishersgate First School
PTSD BN41 .... 43 E3
The Fold School
HOVE BN3 .... 43 H3
Fort
NEWHV BN9 .... 68 D3
Freshbrook County First School
LAN/SOMP BN15 .... 39 G4
Freshfield Industrial Estate
ROTT BN2 .... 46 C5
Garcia Trading Estate
SALV BN13 .... 54 D2
Gardner Arts Centre Cinema
BRI BN1 .... 15 G5
Gemini Business Centre
HOVE BN3 .... 44 C2
Georgian House Business Centre
ROTT BN2 .... 3 H5
Glebe Middle School
STHW BN42 .... 42 B2
Goldstone Junior School
HOVE BN3 .... 44 A1
Goldstone Retail Park
HOVE BN3 .... 26 C5
HOVE BN3 .... 44 D2
Goring by Sea CE First School
FERR BN12 .... 54 A3
FIN/BW BN14 .... 37 H3
Goring Cricket Club
FERR BN12 .... 53 G3
The Grange Industrial Estate
STHW BN42 .... 42 B3
Grange Road Industrial Estate
PTSD BN41 .... 42 B4
Grays School
NEWHV BN9 .... 68 D2
Guildbourne Shopping Centre
WTHG BN11 .... 5 G5
Ham Bridge Trading Estate
FIN/BW BN14 .... 56 C1
Ham Business Centre
SHOR BN43 .... 41 G3
Hangleton County J & I School
HOVE BN3 .... 26 A5
The Hawthorns First School
SALV BN13 .... 36 A5
Hazel Cottage Clinic
ROTT BN2 .... 48 A2
Hazelwood Trading Estate
FIN/BW BN14 .... 56 B1
Heene CE First School
WTHG BN11 .... 4 C3
Heene Community Centre
WTHG BN11 .... 4 B5
Herbert Hone Clinic
ROTT BN2 .... 46 B3
Herons Dale School
SHOR BN43 .... 42 B1
Highdown Hill
FERR BN12 .... 35 E5
Highdown Special School
SALV BN13 .... 36 C5
Hill Barn Municipal Golf Club
FIN/BW BN14 .... 37 G2
Hill Fort
SEAF BN25 .... 73 E2
Hillside Special School
PTSD BN41 .... 25 F5
Hippodrome Bingo
BRI BN1 .... 3 F5
Hoddern County Junior School
PEAHV BN10 .... 62 D5
Hollingbury Castle
BRI BN1 .... 28 C3
Hollingbury Industrial Estate
BRI BN1 .... 14 B5
Hollingbury Park Golf Club
BRI BN1 .... 28 B3
Holmbush First School
SHOR BN43 .... 42 B1
Homecare Business Centre
LEWES BN7 .... 17 G3
Home Farm Business Centre
BRI BN1 .... 28 D4
Hove Business Centre
HOVE BN3 .... 44 D2
Hove General Hospital
HOVE BN3 .... 44 C3
Hove Medical Centre
HOVE BN3 .... 26 A5
Hove Museum & Art Gallery
HOVE BN3 .... 44 C3
Hove Park Upper School
HOVE BN3 .... 44 C1

Hove Polyclinic
HOVE BN3 .... 44 B1
Hove RFC
HOVE BN3 .... 44 D1
The Hyde Business Park
ROTT BN2 .... 47 F1
Ilford & Kensington CE
Primary School
BRI BN1 .... 45 G2
LEWES BN7 .... 32 E2
The John Horniman School
WTHG BN11 .... 5 H4
King Alfred Leisure Centre
HOVE BN3 .... 44 C5
Kings Beach
BRI BN1 .... 3 F6
Kings Manor Community College
SHOR BN43 .... 42 A2
Kingston Buci First School
SHOR BN43 .... 41 H2
The Knoll Business Centre
HOVE BN3 .... 43 H2
Lady Bee Marina
Industrial Estate
PTSD BN41 .... 44 C4
Lancing Business Centre
LAN/SOMP BN15 .... 39 E5
Lancing College
LAN/SOMP BN15 .... 22 A5
Lancing College Chapel
LAN/SOMP BN15 .... 22 B5
Lancing Health Centre
LAN/SOMP BN15 .... 39 G4
The Lanes
BRI BN1 .... 3 G5
The Laurels County First School
SALV BN13 .... 35 H4
Lewes Athletics Track
LEWES BN7 .... 17 G4
Lewes Business Centre
LEWES BN7 .... 17 E2
Lewes Castle & Barbican House
Museum
LEWES BN7 .... 17 E3
Lewes Golf Club
LEWES BN7 .... 17 G3
Lewes Leisure Centre
LEWES BN7 .... 17 G4
Lewes Little Theatre
LEWES BN7 .... 17 E3
Lewes Magistrates Court
LEWES BN7 .... 17 F3
Lewes Old Grammar School
LEWES BN7 .... 17 E3
Lewes Sports Club
LEWES BN7 .... 16 D5
Lewes Victoria Hospital
LEWES BN7 .... 16 C5
Lewes Wallands CP School
LEWES BN7 .... 16 C2
Library, Museum & Art Gallery
BRI BN1 .... 3 G4
Little Theatre
SEAF BN25 .... 72 C1
Longhill School
ROTT BN2 .... 60 C1
Longley Industrial Estate
BRI BN1 .... 46 A3
Lyndhurst First School
WTHG BN11 .... 5 K2
Malling Industrial Estate
LEWES BN7 .... 17 G2
Malt House Trading Estate
SHOR BN43 .... 41 H3
Manor Hall County
Middle School
STHW BN42 .... 42 C2
Manor Hall First School
STHW BN42 .... 42 D3
Manor House Hospital
HOVE BN3 .... 44 C3
Manor Sports Ground Pavilion
FIN/BW BN14 .... 37 H5
Marine Clinic
ROTT BN2 .... 61 E4
Marlborough Business Centre
LAN/SOMP BN15 .... 57 E1
Marlipins Museum
SHOR BN43 .... 41 E3
Martello Tower &
Seaford Museum
SEAF BN25 .... 72 C2
Martlets Trading Estate
FERR BN12 .... 54 A2
Meadow Road Industrial Estate
WTHG BN11 .... 56 D1
Meeching Valley CP School
NEWHV BN9 .... 68 B1

Meridian CP School
PEAHV BN10 .... 63 E4
The Meridian Industrial Estate
PEAHV BN10 .... 67 E1
Meridian Leisure Centre
PEAHV BN10 .... 63 E5
Middle Street Primary School
BRI BN1 .... 3 F5
Mile Oak Clinic
PTSD BN41 .... 24 D4
Mile Oak Primary School
PTSD BN41 .... 24 D4
Mill Road Industrial Estate
PTSD BN41 .... 43 F3
Mill View Hospital
HOVE BN3 .... 44 A1
Modern Moulds
Business Centre
WTHG BN11 .... 57 E1
Montague Shopping Centre
WTHG BN11 .... 5 F5
Morley Street Health Centre
ROTT BN2 .... 3 J3
Moulsecoomb Clinic
ROTT BN2 .... 29 E4
Moulsecoomb Health Clinic
ROTT BN2 .... 29 E4
Moulsecoomb Primary School
ROTT BN2 .... 29 E4
Mowden School
HOVE BN3 .... 45 F1
The Museum
STEY/UB BN44 .... 7 F1
Newhaven Flea Market
NEWHV BN9 .... 68 D1
Newhaven Health Centre
NEWHV BN9 .... 68 D1
Newhaven Tideway School
NEWHV BN9 .... 68 B2
Newlands Manor School
SEAF BN25 .... 71 E4
Newlands Preparatory School
SEAF BN25 .... 71 F4
New Venture Theatre
BRI BN1 .... 2 C4
Nore Down
NEWHV BN9 .... 64 A4
Northbourne Medical Centre
SHOR BN43 .... 41 G2
Northbrook College
FIN/BW BN14 .... 37 G5
SALV BN13 .... 53 H1
WTHG BN11 .... 5 F4
Northbrook Trading Estate
FIN/BW BN14 .... 38 A4
Northease Manor School
LEWES BN7 .... 51 E1
North Lancing First &
Middle School
LAN/SOMP BN15 .... 39 G2
Oaklands Business Centre
WTHG BN11 .... 54 D2
Odeon Cinema
BRI BN1 .... 2 E5
Old Darlington Mushroom Farm
Industrial Estate
ANG/EP BN16 .... 34 A5
Old Grammar School
LEWES BN7 .... 16 D3
The Orchards Community
Middle School
FERR BN12 .... 54 B1
Our Lady of Sion Junior School
WTHG BN11 .... 4 E4
Our Lady of Sion School
WTHG BN11 .... 4 D5
Ovingdean Hall School
ROTT BN2 .... 60 B1
Palatine School
FERR BN12 .... 36 B5
Paradise Family Leisure Park
NEWHV BN9 .... 64 D4
Parkland Business Centre
LAN/SOMP BN15 .... 57 F1
Park View Leisure Centre
HOVE BN3 .... 44 A3
Patcham High School
BRI BN1 .... 27 H1
Patcham House Special School
BRI BN1 .... 27 G1
Patcham Infant School
BRI BN1 .... 27 G1
Patcham Junior School
BRI BN1 .... 27 H1
The Pavilion Clinic
BRI BN1 .... 2 D4
Pavilion Retail Park
ROTT BN2 .... 28 C5

Pavilion Theatre
BRI BN1 3
WTHG BN11 5
Paxton Business Centre
HOVE BN3 43
Peacehaven Community School
PEAHV BN10 63
Peacehaven Golf Club
NEWHV BN9 68
Peacehaven Infant School
PEAHV BN10 66
Peacehaven Sports Centre
PEAHV BN10 67
Peacock Industrial Estate
HOVE BN3 45
Pells CE Primary School
LEWES BN7 17
Pells Primary School
LEWES BN7 17
The Peter Gladwin
Primary School
PTSD BN41 25
Phoenix Industrial Estate
LEWES BN7 17
Piggott's Business Park
WTHG BN11 4
Pool Valley Coach Station
ROTT BN2 3
Portland Business Park
HOVE BN3 44
Portland Road Trading Estate
HOVE BN3 43
Portslade Community College
PTSD BN41 25
STHW BN42 24
Portslade Health Centre
PTSD BN41 43
Preston Manor
BRI BN1 45
Preston Park Clinic
BRI BN1 46
Preston Park Surgery
BRI BN1 46
Prince Regent
Swimming Complex
BRI BN1 3
Priory Ruins
LEWES BN7 17
Priory School
LEWES BN7 17
Queen Alexandra Hospital Home
WTHG BN11 4
Queen Victoria Statue
HOVE BN3 45
Ranalah Estate
NEWHV BN9 65
Rich Industrial Estate
NEWHV BN9 65
Riverbank Business Centre
SHOR BN43 41
Riverside Business Centre
SHOR BN43 41
Riverside Industrial Estate
LEWES BN7 17
RNIB
HOVE BN3 2
Rodmell CE Primary School
LEWES BN7 51
Roedean School
ROTT BN2 59
Rottingdean FC
ROTT BN2 60
Royal Alexandra Hospital
BRI BN1 2
Royal Pavilion
BRI BN1 3
Royal Sussex County Hospital
ROTT BN2 58
Rudyard Kipling CP School
ROTT BN2 48
Sackville Trading Estate
HOVE BN3 44
St Andrews CE Primary School
HOVE BN3 44
St Annes Special School
LEWES BN7 16
St Aubyns School
ROTT BN2 61
St Bartholemews
Tutorial College
BRI BN1 3
St Bartholomews CE
Primary School
BRI BN1 3
St Bernadettes RC Primary School
BRI BN1 27
St Christophers School
HOVE BN3 44

Faith Clinic
ROTT BN2 .... 59 E1
John Baptist Primary School
FIN/BW BN14 .... 18 B1
Johns School
SEAF BN25 .... 70 C3
Josephs Business Park
HOVE BN3 .... 44 C2
Josephs RC Primary School
BRI BN1 .... 46 B1
Josephs Trading Estate
HOVE BN3 .... 44 B2
Lukes Swimming Pool
ROTT BN2 .... 46 C4
Marks CE Primary School
ROTT BN2 .... 47 E5
Martins CE Primary School
ROTT BN2 .... 46 C2
Mary Magdalen
Primary School
BRI BN1 .... 2 D3
Marys Hall School
ROTT BN2 .... 58 D1
Marys RC Primary School
HOVE BN3 .... 45 F2
PTSD BN41 .... 43 F3
WTHG RN11 .... 4 C4
Nicholas & St Mary CE
Primary School
SHOR BN43 .... 41 G2
Pancras Catholic
Primary School
LEWES BN7 .... 16 D3
Pauls CE Primary School
BRI BN1 .... 2 E3
Peters Infant School
PTSD BN41 .... 43 F3
Peters Medical Centre
BRI BN1 .... 3 H1
Peters RC Primary School
SHOR BN43 .... 41 G2
Itdean Primary School
ROTT BN2 .... 61 G3
ndhurst School
WTHG BN11 .... 5 J4
e Seaford Business Centre
SEAF BN25 .... 70 C5
aford Day Hospital
SEAF BN25 .... 70 D5
aford Golf Club
SEAF BN25 .... 70 D2
aford Head
Community College
SEAF BN25 .... 72 D1
aford Head Golf Club
SEAF BN25 .... 73 E2
aford Head Lower School
SEAF BN25 .... 72 D1
aford Health Centre
SEAF BN25 .... 70 C5
aford Primary School
SEAF BN25 .... 70 C4

Seaford RFC
SEAF BN25 .... 70 B5
Seaford Sports & Leisure Centre
SEAF BN25 .... 70 C5
Sea Life Centre
ROTT BN2 .... 3 H6
The Seven Dials Medical Centre
BRI BN1 .... 2 E2
Shoreham Airport
SHOR BN43 .... 40 C3
Shoreham Beach First School
SHOR BN43 .... 41 G4
Shoreham College
SHOR BN43 .... 42 B3
Shoreham FC
PTSD BN41 .... 43 F3
Shoreham First School
SHOR BN43 .... 41 E2
Shoreham Health Centre
SHOR BN43 .... 41 F3
Somerhill Junior School
HOVE BN3 .... 2 A2
Southdown Junior School
NEWHV BN9 .... 68 C1
South Downs Business Park
LEWES BN7 .... 17 G2
South Downs Health Clinic
BRI BN1 .... 5 F2
South Malling CE
Primary School
LEWES BN7 .... 17 F1
Southwick Business Centre
STHW BN42 .... 42 C3
Springfield First School
FIN/BW BN14 .... 56 A1
Stanford Road Junior School
BRI BN1 .... 45 H2
Stanley Deason Leisure Centre
ROTT BN2 .... 47 F5
Steyning Athletic Club
STEY/UB BN44 .... 7 E1
Steyning Grammar School
STEY/UB BN44 .... 7 F1
Steyning Health Centre
STEY/UB BN44 .... 7 F1
Stonelands School
HOVE BN3 .... 44 D4
Sussex Clinic
WTHG BN11 .... 4 C5
Sussex County Cricket Club
HOVE BN3 .... 45 E3
Sussex Downs College (Lewes)
LEWES BN7 .... 17 F4
Sussex Eye Hospital
ROTT BN2 .... 58 D1
Sussex House Business Park
HOVE BN3 .... 44 B2
Sussex Ice Rink
BRI BN1 .... 3 F4
Sussex Nuffield Hospital
HOVE BN3 .... 44 B4
ROTT BN2 .... 48 A2

The Sussex Toy & Model Museum
BRI BN1 .... 3 F2
Sussex University
LEWES BN7 .... 17 G2
Swandean Hospital
SALV BN13 .... 36 B2
Telscombe Cliffs Primary School
PEAHV BN10 .... 62 C5
Templars County Infants School
LAN/SOMP BN15 .... 38 D4
Theatre Royal
BRI BN1 .... 3 G4
Thomas A Becket First School
SALV BN13 .... 37 E5
Thomas A Becket Middle School
FIN/BW BN14 .... 37 F5
Thornberry Middle School
LAN/SOMP BN15 .... 39 H5
Ticehurst Clinic
HOVE BN3 .... 44 C4
Timberlaine Trading Estate
FIN/BW BN14 .... 38 B5
Town Hall Museum & Art Gallery
WTHG BN11 .... 5 F4
UGC Cinemas
ROTT BN2 .... 59 F2
University of Brighton
BRI BN1 .... 20 D2
ROTT BN2 .... 3 H4
ROTT BN2 .... 28 C5
University of Sussex
BRI BN1 .... 15 H5
University of Sussex
Sports Centre
BRI BN1 .... 29 G1
Uplands Special School
BRI BN1 .... 28 C5
Upper Beeding Primary School
STEY/UB BN44 .... 8 A2
Vale CP School
SALV BN13 .... 18 D5
Varndean College
BRI BN1 .... 27 H4
Varndean School
BRI BN1 .... 28 A4
Victoria Road Trading Estate
PTSD BN41 .... 43 G2
Volks Electric Railway
ROTT BN2 .... 3 K7
Waterhall Golf Club
BRI BN1 .... 26 C1
Waterworks Cottages
HOVE BN3 .... 26 C5
Waytefield Clinic
BRI BN1 .... 27 H5
Welfare Clinic
HOVE BN3 .... 26 A5
Westdene Primary School
BRI BN1 .... 27 E2
Western Road
Community School
LEWES BN7 .... 17 E4

Western Road Primary School
LEWES BN7 .... 16 C3
West Hill Community Hall
BRI BN1 .... 3 F1
Westholme Clinic
FERR BN12 .... 54 B3
WTHG BN11 .... 4 C5
West Hove Golf Club
HOVE BN3 .... 25 G2
West Hove Junior School
HOVE BN3 .... 44 B3
West Park CE Controlled School
FERR BN12 .... 54 B3
West Pier (Under Repair)
BRI BN1 .... 2 D6
West Sussex School of English
STEY/UB BN44 .... 7 F1
Whitehawk Clinic
ROTT BN2 .... 47 F5
Whitehawk Primary School
ROTT BN2 .... 47 E4
Whitestyles Middle School
LAN/SOMP BN15 .... 38 D4
Whytemead First School
FIN/BW BN14 .... 38 A5
Wigmore AFC
FIN/BW BN14 .... 37 H3
Wigmore Trading Estate
FIN/BW BN14 .... 38 B5
Wildfowl Reserve
LEWES BN7 .... 31 F4
Winston Business Centre
LAN/SOMP BN15 .... 39 E5
Woodingdean Primary School
ROTT BN2 .... 48 A2
Woodvale Brighton Crematorium
ROTT BN2 .... 46 D2
Worthing Athletics Track
WTHG BN11 .... 54 C2
Worthing & District
Magistrates Court
WTHG BN11 .... 4 D4
Worthing FC
FIN/BW BN14 .... 4 B1
Worthing Golf Club
FIN/BW BN14 .... 37 F1
Worthing High School
FIN/BW BN14 .... 55 G1
Worthing Hospital
WTHG BN11 .... 5 G2
Worthing Pier
WTHG BN11 .... 5 G6
Worthing RFC
ANG/EP BN16 .... 52 B1
Worthing Sixth Form College
SALV BN13 .... 54 C2
Worthing & Southlands Hospital
SHOR BN43 .... 41 H2